God and Goodness

'In emphasising how a version of the argument from design can lead to a religiously attractive view of God, Mark Wynn has contributed significantly to the literature of the subject. *God and Goodness* is a very worthwhile book.'

Richard Swinburne, University of Oxford

'Mark Wynn's *God and Goodness* presents the case for God's existence in a refreshingly original way. This book needs to be taken seriously by both friends and opponents of theism.'

William Hasker, Huntingdon College

God and Goodness presents a fresh approach to the argument from design, arguing that the goodness of the world echoes the goodness of its source. The book makes a case for supposing that the world exists because it is good that it should exist.

Mark Wynn argues that the goodness of the world provides an insight into what we should mean by 'God'. Here, he seeks to recover the mediaeval sense that the goodness of the world offers an image of the goodness of God, not simply in relation to the world, but in itself.

God and Goodness is distinctive in taking the discernment of value in the world as the starting point for natural theology. Wynn argues that the goodness of the world is the most basic fact about it, which accounts for its very existence.

Anyone interested in a re-examination of the existence of God, in relation to the argument from design, should read this book.

Mark Wynn is a lecturer in the Philosophy of Religion at the Australian Catholic University.

Routledge Studies in the Philosophy of Religion
Series Editor Peter Byrne

1 God and Goodness
A natural theological perspective
Mark Wynn

God and Goodness

A natural theological perspective

Mark Wynn

London and New York

First published 1999
by Routledge
11 New Fetter Lane, London EC4P 4EE

Simultaneously published in the USA and Canada
by Routledge
29 West 35th Street, New York, NY 10001

Routledge is an imprint of the Taylor & Francis Group

Typeset in Baskerville
by Curran Publishing Services Ltd
Printed and bound in Great Britain
by St Edmundsbury Press, Bury St Edmunds, Suffolk.

British Library Cataloguing in Publication Data
A catalogue record for this book is available
from the British Library.

Library of Congress Cataloguing in Publication Data
Wynn, Mark, 1963–
God and goodness : a natural theological perspective / Mark Wynn.
240 pp. 216 x 138 mm.
Includes bibliographical references and index.
1. God – Proof, Teleological. 2. Theodicy. 3. Faith. I. Title.
BT102.W86 1999
212—dc21 99–24145
CIP

ISBN 0–415–19915–8

To my parents, Robert and Alison, who first taught me to see the goodness of the world

Let us therefore state the reason why the framer of this universe of change framed it at all. He was good, and what is good has no particle of envy in it; being therefore without envy he wished all things to be as like himself as possible. This is as valid a principle for the origin of the world of change as we shall discover from the wisdom of men, and we should accept it.

Plato, *Timaeus,* tr. D. Lee, p. 42.

Contents

Preface

I would like to thank Brian Davies and Richard Swinburne who first introduced me to the philosophy of religion as an academic discipline. This work combines an interest in modern formulations of the argument from design with a desire to accommodate certain mediaeval intuitions concerning the divine nature. My debt to them (my Demea and my Cleanthes) in these respects will be evident to anyone who knows their work.

I am also profoundly indebted to Peter Byrne for his extraordinary generosity. Without his encouragement this book would never have been written. And without his patient and insightful readings of numberless drafts, it would not be half the book it is. I would also like to thank William Hasker, the Routledge reader, whose penetrating comments on an earlier draft persuaded me of the need to make the significant changes which have resulted in the current Chapter 2. Lastly, I am greatly indebted to the Gifford Committee of the University of Glasgow, and to Lord Gifford himself, since this work was largely written in 1997 during my time as the Gifford Research Fellow in Natural Theology and Philosophy at the University of Glasgow. My thanks in particular to Alexander Broadie, Joe Houston, Joel Marcus and Edmund Cusick for their keen interest in my work during my year in Glasgow.

On a personal note, I am very grateful to my colleagues at Australian Catholic University, who have provided a most supportive, and caffeine-rich, working environment. And above all, I would like to thank my family, especially my wife, Kate, whose love and friendship have helped me to feel at home in Australia, and my family of origin, Mum and Dad, Robert and Gerard, together with Sarah and Vanya, whose nurture first conveyed to me a sense of the goodness of the world.

Mark Wynn

Acknowledgements

The author gratefully acknowledges that the following have kindly given permission to use material from the following articles:

Cassell plc: 'Design arguments', in B. Davies (ed.) *Philosophy of Religion. A Guide to the Subject* (London, Cassell, 1998, pp. 59–64)

Faith and Philosophy: 'Natural theology in an ecological mode (1999, vol. 16, pp. 27–42).

Heythrop Journal: 'Evil and opportunity cost' (1996, vol. xxxvii, pp. 139–54) and 'Beauty, providence and the biophilia hypothesis' (1997, vol. xxxviii, pp. 283–99).

International Philosophical Quarterly: 'Trust-relationships and the moral case for religious belief' (1997, vol. 37, pp. 179–88) and 'Emergent phenomena and theistic explanation' (1999, vol. 39, pp. 141–55).

Kluwer Academic Publishers: 'Simplicity, personhood and divinity', (*International Journal for Philosophy of Religion* 1997, vol. 41, pp. 91–103).

Religious Studies: 'From world to God: resemblance and complementarity' (1996, vol. 32, pp. 379–94).

Sophia: 'Primal religions and the sacred significance of nature' (1997, vol. 36, pp. 88–110).

Introduction

The goodness of the world as its reason for existence

The central thesis of this work is easily stated: the world exists because it is good that it should exist. It is not to be expected that a thesis of this generality will admit of conclusive proof, and accordingly I shall represent this claim as a tenable hypothesis; that is, as a view which is rationally permissible for some, and not rationally obligatory for all. I shall also argue that understanding religious belief as a hypothesis in no way implies that it must be held tentatively or merely speculatively, as some have proposed. The first two parts of the book set out to defend the thesis from an epistemic point of view. In Part I, I argue that the goodness of the world has explanatory force: its goodness in various respects offers an understanding of why it should exist. Then in Part II, I take note of a range of disvalues, and consider how far they undermine the thesis that the world's goodness is its reason for existence.

The epistemic case presented in these first two sections will of course be appraised in different ways by different people, depending upon their life experiences and their epistemic commitments in other fields. Some may find the case is rationally compelling, but not all will do so. In Part III, I argue that even if this epistemic case falls well short of providing a coercive proof, we may still have good reason to subscribe to the hypothesis that the world exists because it is good it should exist. Here I argue that there are moral reasons for adopting this view. This section of the book reflects a larger concern which will be evident, I hope, in the discussion as a whole, namely, a determination to understand religious belief not simply as a commitment of the disengaged intellect, but in relation to its evaluative, practical, and social dimensions.

Historically, the thesis of this book has been defended by a family of arguments known collectively as the argument from design.

According to these arguments, the world owes its character to benevolent design: God (or a transcendent intelligence characterised in other terms) has made a world of this character on account of his or her goodness. (I take it that no deep truth hangs on any distinction of gender in this context; I shall use both masculine and feminine pronouns in the forlorn hope of accommodating different viewpoints on this question.) So this book could be read as a defence of the argument from design. But at the same time it aims to broaden traditional formulations of the design argument, in two ways above all. First of all, I shall seek to ground the argument more clearly in evaluative responses to the world. In recent times, design arguments have often taken as their starting point evaluatively neutral features of the world. For instance, in the eighteenth century, the apparent mechanical regularity of the world was commonly used as a premise in the argument. By contrast, the arguments of this book will be rooted in features of the world which are more clearly of valuational significance, notably its beauty and its tendency to produce richer and more complex forms of material organisation. Secondly, the argument of this book will try to break the traditional association between the argument from design and an anthropomorphic conception of God. The reasons for this association are evident enough: if we lay claim to understand God's purposes in making the world, and accordingly think of the world by analogy with the products of human agency, then it is tempting to suppose that God is as it were a human being writ large. The arguments I develop in Part IV offer another, less individualistic account of God's reality and religious significance. As well as broadening or re-focussing the design argument in these ways, I shall also seek to embed it within a wider context, by examining the problem of evil and the relevance of non-epistemic considerations to the reasonableness of religious belief.

Allowing that the book has these broader interests, it is worthwhile at the beginning of this discussion to note some of the differences and affinities between the argument from design and other strategies of theistic argument. I turn to this topic next. Then in concluding these introductory remarks, I shall set out some objections to the whole project of natural theology, before developing my response in detail in the main body of the book.

Some approaches to the rationality of religious belief

Of course, the design argument is just one of a family of natural theological arguments. These other arguments are not without merit, but there are reasons, I think, for resting any contemporary religious apologetic, of a natural theological kind, above all (though not exclusively) on the design argument. First of all, the design argument seems to represent more faithfully than the other traditional proofs the reasoning of the 'ordinary believer': Kant was surely right when he observed that this argument is 'the oldest, the clearest, and the most accordant with the common reason of mankind'.[1] Of course, the popularity of an argument need be no measure of its logical force; but the currency of an argument is important if a natural theology is aiming not merely to identify possible reasons for belief, but to throw some light on the rationality of belief as it is practised. So here is one reason for taking a particular interest in the design argument, and according it a certain priority in relation to the other traditional arguments: the design argument is distinguished by its closeness to the kinds of argument which believers typically cite in support of their belief; and if the rationality of a person's belief that a certain proposition is true depends not only on the strength of the reasons which might in principle be adduced in its favour, but on the considerations which she would cite, or on the considerations which would be cited by the people to whom she defers on this question, then we have good reason to study the argument from design as a measure of the rationality of religious belief in fact, rather than merely in principle.

Moreover, in our time, natural theology has particularly good reason to ground itself in evaluative responses to the world. Contemporary alienation from religion reflects, I suggest, not so much the sense that it lacks evidential support, but rather the belief that it is of no real consequence existentially. And any natural theology which appeals merely to the abstract intellect rather than drawing upon a range of affective and evaluative responses to the world is likely to contribute to this sense that religious belief lacks existential depth. Now of the traditional natural theological arguments, it is the design argument which is most naturally associated with an evaluatively engaged response to the world. The ontological argument is after all purely a priori, making no reference to the quality of our experience. And the cosmological argument turns upon notions such as dependence and contingency, which are not in themselves of any valuational significance. By contrast, as I hope to demonstrate at some length, the design argument can take as its starting point an appreciation of the goodness of the world in various respects.

Over the centuries, natural theologies have traded upon a variety of paradigms in natural science. The cosmological argument, as expressed by Aristotle and his many successors, is naturally wedded to a certain conception, drawn from physics of the time, of change and its preconditions. More recently, the design argument has found inspiration in the mathematical physics of Newton and others, substituting this mechanistic understanding of nature for the organic conception which was predominant in the ancient world. In our own time, if there is a science which bids fair to become the central theoretical framework in terms of which we make sense of our place in the world, that science is surely ecology. Significantly, ecologists do not merely theorise about the natural world, but are generally committed to its intrinsic value. A similar trend is evident in popular consciousness, with the rise of the green movement for example. The argument from design, when developed in an evaluative key, can take up these developments. In this way, like every effective form of natural theology, it shows some promise of being able to engage the intellectual culture of its day.[2]

In recent philosophy of religion, the traditional arguments, especially the a posteriori arguments, have been somewhat neglected. This constitutes a further, more superficial reason for a re-examination of the design argument.[3] In place of the traditional arguments, many modern commentators have turned to religious experience as a foundation for religious belief, or to the related idea that religious beliefs do not depend for their rationality upon the provision of arguments, because like perceptual beliefs, they are 'properly basic'.[4] The phenomena of religious experience must surely contribute something to the rationality of religious belief, although some scholars have doubted whether even this much may be said.[5] However, the argument from religious experience it seems to me calls for a broader theological framework of the kind that the design argument aims to provide. Above all this is because anyone who maintains that various experiences are properly taken as experiences of God, or experiences of God's presence, love and so on, must address this question: why are such experiences not more widely current? (Of course, behind this question lies the suspicion that religious experience may be merely subjective, or merely a cultural artefact, because of its lack of generality.)

In answering this question, it seems likely that some reference will be made to God's purposes. For instance, it is often proposed that God prefers not to be revealed by means of pervasive and overwhelming religious experiences so as to preserve our epistemic freedom in relation to himself or herself.[6] Whatever the merits of this reply, it seems to understand religious experience, at least in part, within the terms of the argument from design, by citing various divine purposes as a good explanation of the fact that religious experiences occur in such and such forms and with such and such generality. I shall not seek to develop a design argument of this kind myself. I note only that the current emphasis on the argument from religious experience is far from removing any role for the argument from design, and if anything demands further consideration of this same argument.

Of course, some have argued that the grounds provided by religious experience are not to be interpreted evidentially. Religious belief is, rather, properly basic (that is, such beliefs may be held, quite legitimately, without being inferred from any other belief). But this approach also seems to point to an enduring role for natural theology in the traditional style. After all, even if we accept the basic belief proposal on its own terms, there will still be many who cannot avail themselves of this route to theistic belief: as Plantinga and other advocates of the basic belief proposal readily concede, this approach is only open to those who find that the belief that God exists (or more plausibly beliefs like the belief *God is addressing me now*) belong within their set of basic beliefs; and just about everyone outside the theistic community, as well as many within it, will fall outside this category.[7] Moreover, as Plantinga again acknowledges, there is a need to cite evidence in order to rebut alleged defeaters of religious beliefs.[8]

There is also some reason to think that while some individuals within a particular epistemic community may hold religious beliefs basically on the strength of testimony, where this testimony is treated non-evidentially, the community as a whole cannot properly do so. Analogously, although I believe basically (on the strength of testimony) that there are electrons, my belief will ultimately be unwarranted unless some individuals in my community are capable of citing evidence in its support. If there are no such people, then my belief may remain rational to the extent that my trust in others was not in breach of any of my epistemic duties. But the belief will nonetheless be lacking in epistemic merit, in so far as my trust is in fact misplaced, even if through no fault of mine.[9] Here again, there appears to be a role for evidential considerations; and for the reasons I have suggested, the argument from design seems to have a particular importance in this regard.[10]

Two objections to natural theology

Of course, it has been urged that the whole enterprise of natural theology is misconceived in principle. My full answer to this objection is provided by the text which follows, but something may be said in more general terms at this juncture.

For instance, it may be contended that human sinfulness, or equally the sovereignty and majesty of God, require us to suppose that there is no affinity between the nature of the world (as understood by cognitively and morally deficient individuals such as ourselves) and the nature of God, and therefore no route from one to the other. There are many ways in which this general protest might be developed. Sometimes indeed it is combined with a belief that while some forms of natural theology are admissible the argument from design in particular is not, because it rests upon the claim to discern the divine purposes in creation, or because it is implicated in an anthropomorphic conception of God. This sort of challenge, it seems to me, impales itself upon a dilemma: either it will postulate a truly radical form of divine otherness, or it will acknowledge some sort of relation between the attractiveness of mundane things and the attractiveness of God. The first of these approaches will surely guarantee the emergence in unanswerable form of the existential challenge to theistic belief: if there is indeed no affinity between the goodness we recognise in the world and the goodness of God, then the divine goodness can have no real purchase on our imagination as a possible object of attraction. On the other hand, if we follow the second approach, and grant that there is some sort of analogy between the world and the divine nature, then we have admitted the possibility in principle of an argument from design, though establishing the viability of the argument in fact is of course a further matter.

A further general objection to the possibility of natural theology has to do with the problem of divine hiddenness. It may be asked: if there is a God, why should there not be some direct and unambiguous revelation of God's reality? This line of questioning threatens to develop into a *reductio ad absurdum* of the natural theological enterprise. If there is a God, as the natural theologian purports to demonstrate, then surely natural theology itself should not be necessary? This problem seems to arise in a particularly acute form when God is said to desire the fellowship of human beings and to love them. Surely such a God would not leave anyone in the position of having to resort to the somewhat hazardous process of inferring his or her reality?[11]

It seems to me that this challenge is not adequately met by supposing that lack of belief (be it disbelief or agnosticism) reflects in every case a failure of intellect or of will. It is surely possible that someone might study the best available natural theological proofs, and a suitable range of revealed texts, with a clear mind, and in good conscience, and yet fail to be convinced. In place of this sort of approach, which attributes nonbelief to deficiencies, cognitive or conative, of the atheist and agnostic, I shall argue that the condition of divine hiddenness is predictable in some degree on natural theological grounds, quite apart from human failing. If that is so, then hiddenness cannot after all establish the absurdity of natural theological arguments, since it is implied by them. The details of this case must wait for Chapter 3. However, I mention this objection here to provide some indication of the spirit in which the following enquiry will be conducted. I am not presupposing that everyone will be convinced by my arguments, nor even that everyone ought to be convinced if only they apply themselves thoughtfully and conscientiously to what I say. Again, my object is to show how the design hypothesis, and various supplementary ideas, constitute a legitimate intellectual possibility not necessarily for all but at any rate for some. Establishing this much is, I think, a large enough ambition for the natural theologian, and one which accords with the fact that divine hiddenness is apparently a deeply rooted facet of the human condition, and not merely a consequence of intellectual perversity or the vagaries of individual choice.

Part I

The goodness of the world as its reason for existence

1 Providence and beauty

The argument from design

The central thesis of this book is that the world exists because it is good that it should exist. In this first part of the book I shall argue that various phenomena, including natural beauty, life and consciousness, are well explained in terms of this thesis, and not well explained otherwise. This discussion will constitute a defence of the argument from design in relation to these phenomena. In Chapters 1 and 2, I shall defend three versions of the argument from design. But before proceeding to set out these arguments I shall offer a brief overview of the history of the design argument, in order to locate the sort of approach I am defending within a larger intellectual context.

The point I wish to emphasise here is that some forms of the design argument may have proved self-subverting: to the extent that it has concentrated on quasi-mathematical, evaluatively neutral features of the world (for example, its apparently mechanical regularity over space and time), the design argument may paradoxically have contributed to the demise of religious belief, by undermining our appreciation of the world, and thereby encouraging a secular, merely utilitarian interpretation of its significance.[1] By contrast the arguments I develop in this section will be clearly grounded in an evaluative engagement with the world. This approach will also aim to meet the charge that the argument from design (and other forms of natural theology) are religiously irrelevant because they can be understood, and even endorsed, by someone who professes to find their conclusions a matter of indifference. In the case of the arguments I discuss, there will be an internal connection between seeing the soundness of the argument and holding a set of evaluations which are congenial to religious belief in the fullest sense.

Design arguments are as old as western philosophy.[2] They are found in the works of the Presocratics, and defended in the writings of Plato.[3] For instance, in *The Laws*, Plato suggests that the existence and beneficence of the gods may be inferred from the regular movement of the heavenly bodies. Aristotle has also been taken as a source for the argument from design. Of course, the God of the *Metaphysics* is not a providential deity. But Aristotle does maintain that nature is ordered teleologically, and that God provides the ultimate explanation of this fact; and his thinking on this point was to exercise a profound influence on the writings of later, Christian authors. In Aquinas for example we find a clear association between the thought that individual things, including inanimate things, act for a purpose and the thought that these things are guided by an intelligence. Thus he writes that:

> Goal-directed behaviour is observed in all bodies obeying natural laws, even when they lack awareness. Their behaviour hardly ever varies and practically always turns out well, showing that they truly tend to their goals and do not merely hit them by accident. But nothing lacking awareness can tend to a goal except it be directed by someone with awareness and understanding.[4]

This is of course Aquinas's 'Fifth Way'. Interestingly, the passage cites two sorts of consideration in support of the idea of design: the fact that things act regularly and the fact that their behaviour is for the best. These same considerations are evident in *The Laws*, where Plato proposes that the regularity of the world, and especially the movements of the heavenly bodies, are a mark of the gods' benevolence.

In the seventeenth century in the wake of the new, mechanistic physics of Newton and others, the design argument entered a new phase. Whereas the ancients had tended to consider the universe by analogy with an organism, it now became common to think of it as machine-like, so providing the argument with a new analogical foundation.[5] After all, in the case of our own activity, it seems clear enough that mechanisms result not by chance but from the purposeful exercise of intelligence; and by extension, we might suppose that the mechanically ordered universe derives from a transcendent, non-mundane intelligence. Thus in Hume's *Dialogues,* Cleanthes urges his interlocutors to compare the universe to 'one great machine' and to marvel at the 'curious adapting of means to ends, throughout all nature'.[6] The same sort of appeal to a mechanical analogy is evident famously in William Paley's proposal that the world resembles a watch.[7] It is important to note that despite this change in its scientific basis, the argument retains its basic structure. Thus in these remarks of Hume there is an appeal once more to regularity and teleology. And in Paley's writings, too, we find reference both to the regular movement of the heavenly bodies, and to the intricate structure, apparently teleological, of individual organisms.

In the view of many commentators, Hume's arguments in the first *Enquiry* and above all in the *Dialogues* have decisively refuted this form of the design argument.[8] Through the character of Philo, Hume argues variously that the analogy between the universe and the products of human agency is weak (like any comparison between the parts of a thing and the thing as a whole, where the parts comprise an insignificant portion of the whole); that even if this analogy should work, there are other, competing analogies which are at least as persuasive (perhaps the universe is more akin to an animal or vegetable?); that this sort of argument is misconceived in principle (above all because we have no experience of the origins of worlds, and therefore no experiential basis for the idea that worlds like ours are more likely than not to derive from design); that the analogy is anyway of no use to theology, since it invites an anthropomorphic conception of the deity (indeed, Hume suggests, if we persist with the analogy we ought to postulate a number of such deities, since human artefacts are generally made in collaboration); and that the argument lacks any explanatory force because it postulates a further set of facts as much in need of explanation as those which it purports to explain (since the order of the divine mind must be isomorphic with the order of the world, in so far as the first involves a representation or design plan of the second).[9] Hume also explores the thought that a merely random exploration of possibilities will hit upon an orderly outcome given sufficient time, so removing any need for the design hypothesis.[10] And he suggests that while the world with all its imperfections may be compatible with belief in beneficent design, it can hardly provide a secure basis for that conviction.[11]

Later commentators have argued that even if the design argument is able to resist Hume's criticisms, the work of Darwin and his successors has definitively put an end to whatever plausibility it may have had. Darwin's theory, together with subsequent elaborations, threatens the argument at a number of levels. By proposing that a number of species have become extinct, it appears to undermine decisively the idea that in general creatures have been contrived so they can flourish in their respective environments. Moreover, the theory maintains, of course, that new species emerge over time, and that maladapted variations on existing types are eliminated, on account of their inability to compete effectively for scarce resources. Such a view implies that the neat fit between creatures and their environments which we observe in the present may reflect not the working out of a beneficent purpose, but the extermination of weaker, less competitive forms of life, and the survival of their fitter counterparts. Moreover, given the development of genetic theory, it now seems that the generation of new creaturely types is in large part a random process.

So from the perspective of evolutionary theory, we may wish to say that the adaptedness of creatures to their environments, which so impressed Paley and others, is best understood not as a matter of contrivance, but in terms of a random exploration of possibilities, coupled with a selection mechanism which ensures the elimination of any emergent heritable characteristic which damages the survival prospects of the individual.[12] Of course, this picture of the world as a scene of strife, where various creatures are pitted against one another in a struggle for survival, has posed a further challenge by suggesting not only that we do not need the notion of divine agency to account for the phenomena of adaptation, but also that the world itself is not a fitting product of design.

Not surprisingly, modern discussion of the argument from design has concentrated on the question of whether it can be plausibly reconstructed in a post-Humean, post-Darwinian form. Some scholars point towards alleged lacunae in the Darwinian account, but more commonly it is argued that there are certain general facts about the world which are suggestive of design, but necessarily elude Darwinian kinds of explanation, since they are presupposed in the processes described by Darwin. Thus it has been said that Darwinian kinds of mechanism cannot account for the overarching framework of natural law which undergirds the process of evolution. This broadening of the design argument's focus is evident in the writings of, for instance, Tennant, Hambourger, Swinburne and Walker.[13] As we have seen, this interest in the regularity of the world has clear antecedents in earlier versions of the argument.

As Kant anticipated, developments in science have continued to prompt new formulations of the argument.[14] Most notably, a range of new design arguments have been formulated in response to the proposal of cosmologists that there is a delicate relationship between the character of the cosmos as a whole and its suitability for the development of life.[15] It seems for instance that life would not have emerged in a universe with a rather different expansion rate or rather different ratio of hydrogen to helium in its early moments, to name just two examples from many. There are two widely canvassed explanations of this 'fine tuning' of the universe to the possibility of life. Some commentators suggest that we should postulate many universes. In that case, even if the conditions required for life are unlikely to be found in any one universe, it may be that they are likely to obtain at some point within such an ensemble of universes. Our presence in this special, life-permitting kind of universe should not call for further explanation, of course: it is unsurprising if *our* universe proves to be consistent with human life.[16] On the other side, it is said that this sort of 'explanation' is unacceptable, above all because it violates, in spectacular fashion, Ockham's Razor, and that we should therefore seek to explain the phenomena of fine tuning in terms of design.[17]This is an issue to which I shall return in Chapter 2, where I offer a defence of the fine-tuning version of the design argument.

These are some of the issues which have arisen over the course of some two and a half millennia of debate concerning the claim that the existence of the world is best explained in terms of the goodness of its existing. In the course of my discussion, I shall offer responses to a number of these criticisms of the design argument. But fundamentally, my object is to develop earlier versions of the argument, and especially the tendency of a great deal of recent discussion, by setting out a form of the argument which is clearly grounded in an evaluatively rich appreciation of the world. Hence it is not regularity understood abstractly or a quasi-mechanical conception of the world which will provide the basis of the arguments I consider, but rather the sense that the world is a locus of value.[18] Again, the reasons for preferring this perspective are not so much philosophical as religious: if the design argument is to be religiously relevant, it should not appeal simply to the disengaged intellect, and only as an afterthought, once the argument has run its course, seek to give its conclusions some evaluative or religious significance. Rather, the argument should have an evaluative commitment built into its premises. If we do not begin from a perception of the goodness of the world, then in corresponding degree we are likely to be left with an impoverished conception of the God who is said to be its source.

So following this rule of giving primacy to arguments which rest upon an evaluatively charged appreciation of the world, I shall now present an argument which takes as its premise our tendency to regard the world as an object of aesthetic appreciation. Most believers, it seems to me, are more likely to be impressed by the beauty of nature, when considering whether the world answers to a providential purpose, than by mere regularity or order. If philosophers have as a rule eschewed arguments of this kind, it is perhaps because they suspect that any such argument is bound to collapse into sentimentality or vagueness, in so far as beauty cannot be specified with the same quantitative exactitude as regularity. I leave the reader to judge whether the following argument does indeed fall into difficulties of this kind.

More exactly, I shall set out and at certain points refine an argument from the beauty of the world which is presented by F. R. Tennant in his *Philosophical Theology* (published in 1930).[19] A re-consideration of Tennant's argument is timely, I believe, in view of recent developments in sociobiology, which appear to offer both support and criticism of his approach, and in view of the growing tendency in our own times to suppose that nature (understood in an evaluatively rich sense) bears some sort of sacred significance. This latter development is evident for instance in certain strands of the environmental movement and in the growing interest in the religions of indigenous peoples.

Tennant's argument

Before moving to the details of Tennant's argument, we should note what he has to say about the ontological status of natural beauty. Tennant maintains that his approach does not require any commitment to the 'objectivity' of beauty. Thus he writes:

> If we minimise phenomenal Nature's gift by denying that her beauty is intrinsic, as is form or colour, we must allow to ontal Nature an intrinsic contribution such that minds can make beauty as well as nomic order out of it.[20]

Here Tennant grants that aesthetic properties may be of the mind's making (and may be so even if we suppose that colours, for example, are intrinsic to nature). But his argument is undisturbed by this idea, he thinks, for we can still ask: why should nature be so constituted that it is receptive to an aesthetic interpretation? I am inclined to agree with Tennant on this question in part. As we shall see, his case for explaining natural beauty depends on an empirical observation concerning the abundance of beauty in nature and its relative paucity in the world of human construction. In other words, he is interested in why beauty should be found frequently in one sphere and not in the other; and this question loses none of its force if we are told that beauty is mind-dependent, assuming that its mind-dependence holds equally in both spheres. However, if beauty does turn out to be a mental projection of some sort (albeit one to which nature is receptive), then Tennant's argument will be vulnerable to other kinds of criticism, which grant that beauty is to be explained, but doubt whether Tennant's explanation is the right one. Let us look at these criticisms briefly.

Perhaps it will be objected: if beauty is understood as a mental projection of some kind, then the designer who features in Tennant's argument need not have very extensive powers; after all, even we human beings have the power to shape the affective tone of our responses to the world in quite profound ways (by means of drugs and neurosurgery, for example). But here Tennant may reasonably reply that if the world is uniformly regular in the way we commonly suppose, then the activity of any designer will not be localised in the way that our activity is; rather, it must be woven seamlessly into the natural order of which brains form a part. Accordingly, there is no reason to suppose that the designer 'merely' affects the workings of the mind.[21]

However, there are other ways of developing the projectivist challenge which are more damaging to Tennant's case, and may call into question the need to postulate a designer in the first place. For example, we might introduce an 'error theory' to explain away our aesthetic responses to nature. Similarly, John Mackie has argued that our moral experience is to be explained away, in so far as it purports to disclose a realm of objective values. On Mackie's proposal, the apparent objectivity of moral values is merely a convenient myth, one to which we subscribe for the sake of social order. He writes:

> We need morality to regulate interpersonal relations, to control some of the ways in which people behave towards one another, often in opposition to contrary inclinations. We therefore want our moral judgements to be authoritative for other agents as well as for ourselves: objective validity would give them the authority required.[22]

On this account, moral experience is a kind of collective projection which is to be explained in terms of its social usefulness. Now if it could be argued similarly that our aesthetic experience, and specifically our aesthetic experience of the natural world, has a similar origin, then Tennant's argument would surely be damaged. Tennant himself allows that our aesthetic experience of nature may result from the normal functioning of natural processes. So he thinks that in at least some cases, naturalistic explanations pose no difficulty for his argument. However, the particular explanation which Mackie advances does not seem so benign. If it could be shown that our aesthetic appreciation of the natural world has its origins in pressures of social conformity, or something of that kind, then there would surely be little reason to invoke the design hypothesis in order to supplement this account. There is perhaps nothing amiss in the supposition that a designer might exploit our susceptibility to pressures of social conformity so as to induce an aesthetic appreciation of the natural world. But this sort of susceptibility does not seem puzzling in itself, granted the wider context of human evolution in a world such as ours; and accordingly while a connection between this susceptibility and our appreciation of the natural world may be compatible with the hypothesis of design, it does not obviously invite explanation in terms of design.

So Tennant's case does seem to require the rejection of at least some projectivist theories of value. Fortunately for Tennant, there are powerful considerations which count against such theories. Notably, they seem to be inconsistent with the phenomenology of a great deal of evaluative experience. For instance, moral values do not present themselves in our experience as socially constructed, or as instruments of social control. This is not to say that moral and other values cannot be understood in these terms, but it does suggest that the onus of proof here rests upon the projectivist. In fact, the motivation for projectivist theories seems to lie not with the phenomenology of moral and other kinds of value experience, but with a 'scientistic' conception of what can reasonably count as real (in other words, a sense that only those entities and relationships which feature in natural or social scientific descriptions of the world have a claim to be fully real). But this 'scientistic' mentality is controversial. Charles Taylor offers this larger understanding of what we should reckon as real:

> What is real is what you have to deal with, what won't go away just because it doesn't fit with your prejudices. By this token, what you can't help having recourse to in life is real, or as near to reality as you can get a grasp of at present.

And Taylor adds, commonsensically, that in order to understand people and everyday situations, we inevitably have recourse to a value-laden conception of the world which cannot be captured in the conceptual framework of the natural and social sciences.[23] In the absence of countervailing considerations, Taylor is claiming, these value experiences are to be taken at face value, that is, as relating us to an order of reality which is not merely of human making.

So there are general reasons for doubting whether a projectivist account of our value experience, at least in certain core areas, is going to work. It seems reasonable to include aesthetic experiences of nature within the scope of this claim, since these experiences, like moral experiences, have a 'transcendent' quality which it will be difficult to preserve within any naturalistic account of their significance. Peter Forrest puts the matter this way: 'Beautiful things and people suggest to us that there is something infinitely more beautiful'.[24] Allowing that experiences of beauty appear to refer beyond themselves in some such fashion, any naturalistic understanding of such experiences seems bound to be deflationary in tone. Again, this is not to say that such an account cannot work; but the onus of proof rests here, as always, on the one who doubts the appearances of things. Moreover, the projectivist may find it particularly hard to explain away aesthetic experiences of the natural world, since the social pressures which may play a role in our moral experience are less evident here.[25]

I suggest then that Tennant's claim that his argument does not depend on treating beauty as a mind-independent property is perhaps a little quick, since some projectivist accounts of value do seem to threaten his argument. However, these accounts appear to face difficulties of their own. Despite these difficulties, one such projectivist theory of our aesthetic experience of the natural world, expressed in sociobiological terms, has proved to be quite popular in recent years. For the reasons we have been considering, any contemporary defence of Tennant's case will need to engage with this account in some detail. This is what I shall do in the closing sections of this chapter. But first we must examine Tennant's case more fully.

On Tennant's account the beauty of nature is basically sensuous, and is to be distinguished therefore from, for instance, the beauty which physicists detect in the elegance of mathematically formulated natural laws.[26] Moreover, it is clear that, despite his tendency to refer simply to beauty, Tennant is also interested in what philosophers conventionally call 'the sublime'.[27] Two claims in particular provide the *explanandum* of Tennant's argument. First of all, he speaks of 'the saturation of Nature with beauty' and remarks that:

> On the telescopic and on the microscopic scale, from the starry heaven to the siliceous skeleton of the diatom, in her inward parts (if scientific imagination be veridical) as well as on the

surface, in flowers that 'blush unseen' and gems that 'unfathomed caves of ocean bear', Nature is sublime or beautiful, and the exceptions do but prove the rule. However various be the taste for beauty, and however diverse the levels of its education or degrees of its refinement, Nature elicits aesthetic sentiment from men severally and collectively; and the more fastidious becomes this taste, the more poignantly and lavishly does she gratify it.[28]

Here Tennant maintains that the natural world is uniformly or at least very largely beautiful. As a very broad generalisation about the experience of people in our (modern, western) culture, this seems to me to be true. His argument depends in addition on a further claim: in the absence of aesthetic or artistic intent, the products of human agency are rarely beautiful.[29] This notion also has something to be said for it. The very existence of art as a distinct category in human life suggests that the production of objects of beauty (or more generally of aesthetic value) will depend upon the application of a variety of carefully honed skills.[30] Drawing upon these ideas, Tennant's argument takes the form of a sort of *reductio*:

1 If nature has its origins in forces which are indifferent to aesthetic values, then it is no more likely to exhibit beauty *in general* than are the works of human beings, whenever these works are made without artistic intent.
2 But nature is uniformly beautiful, whereas the products of human beings are rarely beautiful in the absence of artistic intent.
3 So the premise must be denied: we should suppose that most probably nature does not derive from forces which are indifferent to aesthetic values.
4 In turn this suggests that nature is the work of a mind, and more particularly of a mind attuned to aesthetic kinds of fulfilment.

The basic proposal advanced by this argument, though simple, has a certain prima facie plausibility. Surely there is a widespread tendency to think of nature as beautiful, and surely we do find in our own experience that the production of things of beauty calls for a certain skill in conception and execution. Granted these familiar ideas, what could be more obvious than to think of the world as the product of an aesthetic design?

Humean responses to Tennant

But before we may give our assent to Tennant's argument, we must first consider various objections to it. Here we may recall two of the criticisms of Hume we noted above:

1 Arguments from design claim that a world like ours is *unlikely* to have arisen except by design. But such a judgement of likelihood surely lacks any empirical support. Since we have no experience of the origins of worlds, we have no experiential basis for supposing that a world like ours will derive from design in such and such a proportion of cases. But if the argument from design makes use of a judgement of probability which is not of this relative frequency type, of what type is it, and what reason have we for subscribing to it?[31]

2 Even if we find that there is a strong analogy between the character of the world and the character of human artefacts of various kinds, there are other analogies which are just as apt and carry no implication of purposeful agency.[32]

Let us consider these objections in turn. In reply to the first point, Tennant would surely contend that he is using, as Hume requires, an empirically grounded measure of probability. The belief that beauty is relatively unlikely to obtain in the absence of artistic intent is very well evidenced empirically, Tennant might say, since we have (in relation to human agency) many examples of activity which lack artistic intent and many examples of activity where artistic intent is present, and we can show that, proportionately, things of beauty arise more frequently in the latter case. Of course, this reply does not engage directly with Hume's complaint about our lacking experience of the origin of worlds. But it does enough, I think, to shift the burden of proof on to the sceptic. Given our experience in the human context of the conditions which should obtain for the production of an aesthetic object, there is a presumption that similar conditions will apply in other spheres, unless some reason can be given for thinking otherwise.[33]

The other Humean objection I noted just now (unlike the first) grants that in principle we may be able to move from an analogy between the character of the world and the products of human agency to the conclusion that the world derives from a source with certain human-like properties, in particular, intelligence. While allowing the admissibility in principle of this sort of argument, this objection proposes that it is in practice of no use to the proponent of design because the analogy with the products of *human* agency is only one of several. Thus Hume notes for instance that human beings are not alone in being able to produce order reliably: animals and vegetables also do so, notably when they reproduce themselves. An argument of this form therefore gives us no more reason to think of the world as the product of design than to suppose that it derives from some process of generation or vegetation. By extension, it might be said that Tennant's argument is vulnerable to this same difficulty in so far as animals and (less certainly) vegetables reliably produce beauty when they reproduce themselves. Here, Tennant might reasonably reply that this is to beg the question against the design argument. For the argument claims that natural beauty in general, including animal beauty, is ultimately the product of design. Thus to take animal reproduction (or some other process in nature which seems reliably to give rise to beauty) as evidence of what may result in the absence of design is merely to presuppose the falsity of the design argument. If we are not to beg the question in this way, Tennant might urge, we must take examples where indisputably aesthetic intent is either absent or present, and this suggests turning to the case of human agency. Again, this reply seems to me effective, to the extent that it shifts the burden of proof back to the sceptic.

It is worth noting that design arguments which take the regularity of the world as their premise (and it is these arguments which were the primary target of Hume's strictures) may not be able to address these objections so straightforwardly. For we may wish to say that most states of the world can be considered as ordered in relation to one or other classificatory scheme, including states produced by human beings where they have no intention of producing order. So if the argument from order is to be defended in this same kind of way, it will be necessary first of all to discriminate between different kinds of order, and to show that some kinds are reliably produced by human beings only when they intend to do so.

There is one other Humean objection which is worth recalling here, though I shall not venture an answer in any detail until later. As we have seen, Hume suggests that the argument from design, when it takes the world's regularity as its premise, is bound to be circular, because there must be an order in the designer's mind which is exactly isomorphic with the order of the world (assuming that there is in the divine mind some kind of 'blueprint' corresponding to the structure of the world). Similarly, we might suppose, the argument from beauty will face the same sort of problem, in so far as the designer is said to be beautiful, and in so far as worldly beauty is said to echo divine beauty. Of course, the simplest response to this challenge would be simply to deny that there is any affinity between mundane beauty (of the kind that Tennant discusses) and divine beauty. For instance, it might be said that the first but not the second is material. However, for reasons I have touched on in the Introduction, and will develop more fully in Part IV, I wish to suppose that mundane beauty does offer an intimation of divine beauty; so I shall not pursue this response to Hume's challenge.[34] Here I note simply that when I come to discuss the concept of God, and its relation to the concept of worship, I shall seek to meet Hume's charge by supposing that God's beauty is to be explained by reference to God's own activity, so that it is after all explained, and not merely posited as a 'brute fact'.

I pass to a further objection. To my mind, this objection points, if anything, to a strength in Tennant's case. It may be said that Tennant's argument simply exaggerates the extent of the natural world's beauty, and the fulfilment which human beings can derive from their contemplation of it. In response to this criticism, we could embark upon a discussion of the kind familiar from other areas of aesthetic disagreement, where each party tries to bring the other to share their own perspective, by the citing of examples, and so on.[35] I am not going to offer such an argument here. I note simply that Tennant should welcome an objection of this kind in so far as it seems to locate the disagreement between believers (or at any rate, some believers) and non-believers in the right sort of place, namely in a difference of evaluative response to the world. By contrast, as I have noted, some forms of the design argument appear to imply that the question of whether there is a God might be resolved merely by reference to generally acknowledged empirical facts, for instance the fact that the world is temporally or spatially regular. Such arguments seem bound to understate the extent to which religious belief involves strong and distinctive evaluative commitments. Again I suggest that while arguments of this empirically based variety may have a role to play as part of a cumulative-case natural theological argument, they should surely be supplemented by other arguments which are more clearly rooted in evaluative responses to the world.

When philosophers consider the viability of arguments from design, they concentrate invariably upon two kinds of objection: first, objections of the Humean variety, and secondly, of course, the sort of objection which draws its inspiration from Darwinian accounts of the order of the natural world. We have touched on some of the ways in which Tennant's case may seek to meet the first sort of objection, but there is also ample scope for a critique of his approach in the style of Darwin. Clearly, the Darwinian kind of explanation most obviously applies in relation to those versions of the design argument which take the adaptedness of creatures to their environments as evidence of a benign direction of the course of nature. In recent discussion in sociobiology, it has been urged that our aesthetic appreciation of the natural world is to be understood as precisely such an adaptation. This development throws an interesting new light on Tennant's argument, by suggesting a novel way of developing a projectivist challenge to his case.

The sociobiological critique

Sociobiological attempts to explain aesthetic responses to the natural world are, as I say, of relatively recent provenance (more recent than the application of sociobiological theories to the phenomena of ethics and religion, for example). They have been prompted, I suggest, not so much by the internal logic of Darwin's argument, but more by recent social scientific research which concludes that aesthetic responses to nature are in certain important respects culturally invariant. As we have seen, Tennant's argument depends upon a contrast between our responses to natural and man-made features of the environment. There are a number of cross-cultural studies which have a particular relevance in this regard, since they set out to compare responses to urban and natural landscapes. The findings of these studies seem dramatically to endorse Tennant's claim that there is a difference in response to landscapes of these kinds, and that this difference is not culturally relative. Thus Ulrich reports that:

> A clear-cut finding in this research is a strong tendency for diverse European, North American, and Asian groups to prefer natural landscape scenes over urban or built views, especially when the latter lack natural content such as vegetation and water . . . Even mediocre natural scenes consistently receive higher ratings than do all but a very small percentage of built settings lacking nature.[36]

Notice that these studies do not maintain that human beings' responses to the natural world are the same in the sense of finding expression in similar cultural forms (similar traditions of landscape painting, for instance). The suggestion is simply that natural landscapes are consistently preferred to environments of human construction. Notice too that Ulrich's summary does not make explicit reference to an *aesthetic* preference for natural environments. Nonetheless, it seems clear that fundamentally, this is what the subjects were commenting upon, whether or not their rankings were explicitly tied to aesthetic criteria of evaluation.

One caution should be entered here. In Tennant's usage 'natural' seems to connote 'free from human influence'. (Think again of what he chooses to list when giving examples of nature's beauty.) However, in these studies, rural scenes, clearly bearing the mark of human activity, are also strongly preferred to urban scenes. Tennant's argument can accommodate this finding easily enough with a little elaboration. We might say that rural scenes, while they have been shaped by human activity, retain a significant presence of natural objects, in the form of trees, grass, and so on, and to this extent are reasonably distinguished from built-up urban environments. On this understanding, we can still press the difference-of-response question in relation to 'natural' and man-made environments, while recognising that there is a distinction between what we might call the rural and the wilderness components of 'Nature'. In fact, Tennant's argument, bearing in mind his location in England, was presumably governed from the start, at least implicitly, by a contrast between urban and rural as much as by a contrast between urban and wilderness.[37] I suggest that in general Tennant's argument is strongest when framed in terms of this sort of distinction between landscapes, rather than descending to the details of whether we find individual organisms (earthworms?) of aesthetic interest.[38]

So far then, modern empirical research seems to lend strong confirmation to Tennant's basic proposal. Prior to this research, many would have dismissed his argument, I suggest, on the grounds that the tendency to value natural landscapes (and natural objects more generally) and to prefer them to environments of human construction is a cultural artefact, apparent in certain cultures but not in others. To this extent then, Tennant's argument has been strengthened. However, these same findings have also helped to foster a naturalistic account of our tendency to find aesthetic significance in the natural world. Some of this work has been motivated by environmental concerns, and the thought that if we can show that an appreciation of nature is part of our biological inheritance, and a prerequisite therefore of a fully human life, then we will have powerful reasons for resisting further human encroachment upon the natural world. However, the search for a naturalistic framework in terms of which these empirical findings can be understood is also an acknowledgement of the force of Tennant's case. As Tennant argued, if there is a difference in our response to natural and urban environments, which is not merely a function of culture, then we have good reason to ask what accounts for it.

From the naturalistic point of view, the obvious explanatory resource in this context is the theory of evolution. In his book *Biophilia*, E. O. Wilson has argued that if we human beings evolved in a world of diverse life forms, then in all likelihood we will have retained a genetically encoded preference for biodiversity.[39] And by extension, it has been argued that our felt affinity for natural environments is explicable in terms of the role such environments played in our evolution. Since the publication of Wilson's book, various studies have offered empirical support for this claim.[40] For instance, a number of empirical studies have suggested that human beings are biologically predisposed to respond defensively to stimuli such as snakes and spiders.[41] If this should be so, we might suppose, then we should expect to find that biophilic responses are also conditioned by evolutionary considerations. (Incidentally, this research points to a feature of human responses to the natural world which Tennant overlooks, despite its relevance to his argument, namely our tendency to respond with aversion to certain aspects of the natural world. At the same time, these examples offer Tennant a way out of this apparent difficulty: such responses, it may be said, have an obvious rationale in terms of protecting human well-being, and are therefore quite consistent with the hypothesis of design.)

There are also data which bear directly on the claim that favourable responses to the natural world have their origins in our evolutionary history. For instance, it has been argued that our preference for natural over urban environments is more exactly a preference for those kinds of natural environment which would have proved advantageous in our evolutionary history, notably settings marked by water and spatial openness.[42] These features, it is observed, are precisely those which obtain in savannah, the preferred habitat of early human communities. One commentator, Jay Appleton, summarises the state of debate in this area as follows:

> In the opinion of most authorities, if there is a type of environment which we as a species can recognise as our natural habitat, it has to be the savannah, that type of plant association which takes a variety of forms in different parts of the world but consists essentially of trees spaced widely enough to permit the growth of grasses between and underneath them. This is now

generally agreed by the anthropologists to be the kind of environment in which the first recognizable hominids made their home.

Appleton supposes in addition that this pattern of preference will have persisted beyond the conditions of its initial appropriateness. Thus he continues:

> The power of attraction, whatever its *modus operandi*, which drew [the first hominids] towards this favorable kind of landscape, has not been eliminated from our genetic make-up but has survived – in Jungian terminology – as an archetype, whose influence is still to be seen in many ways, not least in the widespread attraction which people feel towards 'parkland', an idealized contrived arrangement of well-spaced trees within a tidily groomed grassland.[43]

(So when you walk in a suburban park, paper under arm, you are recalling some ancestral experience on the African savannah!)

As well as arguments of this kind, to the effect that the types of natural environment which human beings prefer are those which would have had greatest survival value for early members of the species, in terms of providing security and an abundant source of food, it is also suggested that experiences of nature have a measurable effect on stress levels. For example, patterns of electrical activity in the brain apparently point to the restorative effect of exposure to natural scenes.[44] (Of course, a great deal of anecdotal evidence could be cited in support of this same idea.) This suggests a further way in which we could connect human beings' preference for natural environments and the thought that such environments confer an evolutionary advantage, assuming that relief from long-term stress will enhance the survival prospects of an organism. Again, studies in this field lend some support to the idea that these stress-relieving effects are greatest in relation to landscapes of the savannah type. (Of course, the tendency of certain kinds of natural setting to offer relief from stress may in turn point to their evolutionary significance as a source of food and security, in which case this consideration would not play a distinct explanatory role.)[45]

In summary, these recent developments in comparative sociology and sociobiology seem to bear on Tennant's argument at two points. First of all, such research offers empirical support for the central premise of Tennant's argument, namely the thesis that there is a differential response to natural and urban environments which is not merely a product of cultural conditioning. On this point then, Tennant's argument looks today perhaps more robust than it did when first proposed. Secondly, such research points towards an understanding of the difference-of-response thesis which appeals not to design, but to the advantage conferred upon human societies in pre-historic times by certain kinds of natural environment. To this extent, the sociobiologists' proposal apparently poses a challenge to Tennant's argument, by furnishing an explanation of its central empirical claim which requires only the normal functioning of Darwinian kinds of selection mechanism. Our next task must be to reach some sort of assessment of the overall plausibility of Tennant's argument given these developments.

Naturally, in trying to reach a verdict on these matters, we should turn first of all to Tennant's text, to see whether he anticipates this sort of evolutionary explanation of our appreciation of natural beauty. He was of course familiar with Darwinian-inspired attempts to overturn other forms of the design argument, such as Paley's. Suggestively, Tennant objects to attempts to treat 'the beauty of Nature as Paley treated organic adaptations'. But the weakness of such arguments, he goes on to say, lies in their supposition that 'since in human art a beautiful or sublime production is the outcome of human design, similar effects must everywhere be due to design'.[46] His own argument meets this difficulty, he notes, by recognising that it cannot purport to be a 'proof'.[47] Later, he turns explicitly to the issue of evolutionary explanations, and responds dismissively to the thought that our valuing of the natural world in aesthetic terms might have some adaptive value. Thus he writes:

> In the organic world aesthetic pleasingness of colour, etc., seems to possess survival-value on but a limited scale, and then it is not to be identified with the complex and intellectualised sentiments of humanity, which apparently have no survival-value.[48]

A recent study of the idea that natural beauty affords evidence for design is similarly sceptical of the power of evolutionary explanations to account for the phenomena. With the exception of our propensity to find other human beings beautiful, Peter Forrest suggests, our tendency to find beauty in the world resists explanation in terms of Darwinian considerations. Thus he writes:

> I suspect that naturalists will have to say that the appreciation of

> beauty is a by-product of something else for which there is a more direct naturalistic explanation such as the ability to see something as a whole and not just as a collection of parts. But such an explanation cannot begin to explain the special quality of appreciating beauty or why there is such an abundance of both sensuous and nonsensuous beauty.[49]

Clearly, Forrest and Tennant alike fail to address the specific proposals of the sociobiologists. However, I shall argue that their suggestions can be incorporated constructively within an approach which takes explicit account of the biophilia hypothesis.

In general, the contemporary advocate of Tennant's kind of argument has two options. First, she can dismiss, or downplay, the sociobiological hypothesis in relation to the particular range of aesthetic phenomena it is intended to explain. Second, she can argue that regardless of whether the hypothesis has application in this context, it fails to account for other aesthetic phenomena which invite explanation in terms of design. I shall consider these responses in turn.

The first of these responses has found advocates in the field of art criticism, where attempts to introduce evolutionary theory to explain canons of aesthetic judgement have encountered determined resistance. For instance, one commentator has offered this assessment:

> I do not doubt that as part of nature we intuit strong links between its processes and forms and those of our own bodies... But such intuitions are so transformed, overlain and mediated by social, cultural and economic as well as personal meanings historically, that to trace the biophysiological bases of environmental . . . response seems largely futile at best, and at worst pandering to the most dangerously ideological interpretation of 'human nature'.[50]

Evidently, human beings' aesthetic responses to nature are indeed informed to a significant degree by their cultural setting and by their personal histories, and careful exponents of the biophilia hypothesis as applied to the aesthetic appreciation of nature must surely grant this.[51] Speaking of such matters as alcoholism and mathematical aptitude, as well as responses to nature, one proponent of the biophilia approach sums up the scholarly consensus in these terms:

> The debate has shifted from bipolar nature/nurture distinctions to discussion of eclectic perspectives that recognize the crucial

> roles of both learning and genetics. In several key areas, the main question is no longer whether genetic factors play a role. Rather the mainstream theoretical and research debate increasingly accepts the role of genetics but asks: is the genetic contribution 20 per cent or 50 per cent?[52]

It is important to note that an evolutionary explanation of aesthetic responses to nature could in principle operate at the level of culture (or nurture), and not simply at the genetic level. (The biophilia hypothesis confines itself to the latter possibility.) So we could envisage an overarching evolutionary explanation, which includes genetic and cultural evolution. But such an explanation, as applied to our aesthetic appreciation of the natural world, is unlikely, I suggest, to be significantly stronger than one which appeals to genetic factors alone. Even if cultural forms helped to reinforce an initial, genetically encoded preference for savannah types of environment, there is surely no evidence of an ongoing cultural tradition, dating back to early hominid times, which has sought to inculcate these same values; nor is there evidence that the adoption of such values by societies in more recent times has conferred any significant adaptive advantage. For ease of exposition therefore, I shall concentrate on the case of genetic evolution.

I suggest then that this assessment of the strength of biophilic or evolutionary kinds of explanation leaves ample room for the operation of other factors in our valuation of the natural world. Following this line, an advocate of Tennant's view could grant that evolutionary considerations account in some measure for our positive, affirming response to certain kinds of landscape, but argue that these factors are not enough to explain the sheer 'abundance' of beauty which we find in such environments. This sort of response is implicit in Tennant's claim that it is the 'saturation' of nature with beauty which provides his case with its impetus. More exactly, we can recognise the role of personal and (local) cultural factors but maintain, first, that there remains even so a universal predisposition to find nature attractive. (This seems to be the implication of the social scientific data I have cited.) We may then claim, second, that this universal predisposition (even granting that it relates most clearly to environments of the savannah type) cannot be fully explained by reference to evolutionary kinds of argument. (This seems to be the implication of standard assessments of the explanatory power of evolutionary kinds of explanation in this sort of context.) This is a logically consistent set of proposals, and one which seems consonant with the basic structure of Tennant's argument. We may reasonably conjecture that were Tennant writing today, his response to the sociobiological approach would, in part, take this form.

That leaves a second kind of response, which does not seek to question the explanatory power of the biophilia hypothesis within its own sphere of application, but to identify other phenomena which lie beyond its scope. Here too, Tennant's argument provides some indication of how we might proceed. We have seen how the sociobiological approach may be developed in relation to our appreciation of natural landscapes of certain kinds. But even granting its effectiveness in this domain, there are further phenomena which fall within the purview of Tennant's argument and remain to be examined. For instance, Tennant includes in his list of objects of natural beauty the 'starry heaven', and we might suppose that evolutionary considerations can have little role to play in explaining our appreciation of the world in this respect, however successful they may be in explaining our regard for savannah types of landscape. However, before endorsing this thought, we should consider this attempt to provide an evolutionary context for our response to modulations of light and dark:

> Alertness to the sunset and the shadows that signal the coming of darkness, and the need to change patterns of behaviour in order to ensure warmth and safety, has clear advantage over disinterest. Reaction to the appearance of the Sun when it is far from rising and setting, by contrast, offers far less of vital importance to organisms. You don't need to know that the Sun is overhead in order to tell that you are getting too hot. With the darkness comes the importance of fire; flickering flames still fascinate us. The fire was the focus of life after dark, offering warmth and safety, fellowship and light. It inflames strong emotions – positive and negative – by its paradoxical offerings of comfort and danger.[53]

Analogously, it might be said that an interest in the stars 'has clear advantage over disinterest', in so far as attention to the movements of the stars is useful for purposes of, for instance, gauging the approach of dawn. Or again, it may be said that our appreciation of starlight is simply a by-product of our appreciation of light in darkness in the contexts distinguished in this passage. And perhaps it could be argued that starlight offers some sort of consolation, from an evolutionary perspective, in so far as it signifies that the night sky is clear of cloud, which in turn could contribute towards visibility. An account of this kind, it seems to me, is not entirely devoid of explanatory power, but it seems at any rate weaker than the kind of explanation which may be offered in relation to our enjoyment of savannah types of landscape, since it does not identify so clearly a vital connection between some feature of the world and our prospects of survival.

Some of Tennant's other examples suggest a similar conclusion. The beauty of things which have only been disclosed since the invention of the microscope cannot be explained as the direct consequence of some evolutionary selection mechanism. At most, as Forrest suggests, the naturalist will need to appeal to the thought that our appreciation of such things is a by-product of some straightforwardly useful capacity. But again, it is not clear that the aesthetic appreciation in question is fully reducible to order recognition, or to some other form of awareness whose evolutionary rationale can be made evident.

This sort of response to the biophilia proposal, considered as an explanation of our appreciation of natural beauty, could be pushed further if it could be argued that we have a tendency to value aesthetically landscapes which are basically hostile to human well-being, or at any rate far removed qualitatively from the savannah type of natural environment. The obvious candidates in this connection are desert and ice landscapes. Here again, we must acknowledge the contribution of culture in shaping our reactions to our surroundings. Think for example of the way in which the response of the desert fathers to their environment was conditioned by what the desert represented to them socially and theologically.[54] However, the descriptions given by explorers of such places provide some basis for the thought that we are predisposed to respond to them favourably. One commentator, drawing upon the experiences of Fridtjof Nansen, Richard Byrd and others, writes that 'explorers of desert and ice may be said to be half in love with piercing beauty and half in love with death'.[55] This quotation neatly records both the aesthetic qualities of such places, and the sense that our appreciation of them is not easily related to any drive for self-preservation. Moreover, the responses of explorers are not merely quirky, I suggest, but reflect evaluations which have a place in human life more generally. Consider for instance the oddity of the expression 'How *ugly* the desert (or the snowfield) was!' The certainty of our sense about which kinds of aesthetic response are admissible in this sort of context is evident from the fact that we are likely to find such expressions not merely odd but unintelligible. By contrast, the expression 'How beautiful the desert was!', while hardly required from a visitor to desert regions, has an obvious meaning and appropriateness.[56]

So in these various ways, Tennant's argument can make appeal to the aesthetic value of phenomena which are not easily subsumed within the biophilia framework. Here again, it is the 'saturation' of nature with beauty which drives the argument. In this case, the richness of our aesthetic experience is all the more significant, from the point of view of Tennant's hypothesis, in so far as evolutionary kinds of consideration seem to have little if any role to play in explaining the phenomena. It is worth noting that this line of reflection calls into question the force of the many-universes objection as a response to this particular version of the design argument. That objection maintains that it is unsurprising that we should find ourselves in, say, an ordered world, because we can only exist in such a world. But if Darwinian explanations of our aesthetic responses to the natural world are only partially successful, then it is not so clear that we can only exist in a pervasively beautiful world.

To summarise, I suggest that Tennant's argument remains, in large part, cogent, even when the perspectives represented in modern sociobiological theories have been given due recognition. This is first of all because evolutionary mechanisms seem to offer at most a partial explanation of those aspects of our aesthetic appreciation of the natural world which fall most obviously within their scope.[57] Moreover, Tennant's argument retains its persuasiveness because there are further facets of our aesthetic responses which are not addressed by the biophilia hypothesis, and which extend no clear evolutionary benefit. The empirical data, in so far as they establish a preference for savannah types of natural environment over other forms of natural environment, suggest that this second sort of case is less compelling than the first. On the other hand, biophilic considerations apply less clearly in this second case, so leaving a larger role for design.

In view of the dramatic collapse of arguments from design in the style of Paley, following the development of evolutionary biology, proponents of the design argument have learnt to ask whether the phenomena they are seeking to explain are explicable even in principle in scientific terms. Putting this question to Tennant's argument, we might understand the kind of explanation which he is offering in either of two ways. He might be supposing that there are certain gaps within the framework of natural law, which have to be filled by divine agency, in order to ensure that the natural world can be an object of aesthetic appreciation. Or he might be supposing that divine agency is to be introduced in order to explain the capacity of the natural order to give rise to natural beauty through the working out of its own processes. It seems clear that Tennant favours the second approach, and to this extent, his account is not vulnerable to a scientific counter-argument. In other words, he grants that our aesthetic appreciation of nature is explicable in principle in terms of the normal operation of natural laws. (Indeed, this is the very feature of the world he wants to explain.) So his argument will not be disturbed by scientific developments which provide a fuller picture of how the normal operation of natural laws has this consequence.

However, Tennant is committed, I have suggested, to the insufficiency of evolutionary kinds of explanation of our aesthetic responses to the natural world. A scientific explanation of this kind would threaten his argument, he seems to feel (despite his nonchalance about the possibility of projectivist accounts of aesthetic experience). I think he is right about this. In particular, the law which maintains that less competitive forms of life will be eliminated in conditions of scarcity seems to be tautological (once sufficient definitional precision has been supplied). If it could be shown that our tendency to value the natural world aesthetically can be explained by reference to this law, then there would be little pressure to consider why this law, and not some other, should obtain. But subject to this qualification, Tennant's view implies that developments in the sciences can take what form they may without undermining his argument.

Of course, Tennant's argument would be vulnerable to any naturalistic explanation which was able to show that any set of natural laws consistent with human life must result in a world which is beautiful. Such an explanation seems possible in principle. For instance, it may be that an appreciation of savannah types of landscapes, of the kind that was required for our survival, demands (not merely in terms of actual physical laws, but logically or metaphysically) a brain structure of the kind that will promote aesthetic appreciation of all manner of landscapes. But in the absence of positive reason for thinking that such an explanation can in fact be developed, these considerations seem to pose no threat to Tennant's case.

It may be thought that Tennant's argument, and my reformulation of it by reference to recent sociobiological studies, overlooks one crucial historical fact: the appreciation of certain features of the natural landscape is actually quite a recent phenomenon, at any rate in the context of European civilisation. As John Haldane has remarked, even in recent times, 'sensitive and thoughtful authors have dismissed what are now canonised landscapes in terms which are at least striking and which some will regard as blasphemous'.[58] In illustration Haldane cites this passage from Dr Johnson, who observed that the Scottish hills:

> exhibit very little variety; being almost wholly covered with dark heath, and even that seems to be checked in its growth. What is not heath is nakedness, a little diversified by now and then a stream rushing down the steep. An eye accustomed to flowery pastures and waving harvests is astonished and repelled by this wide extent of hopeless sterility.[59]

This suggests that the sociological data I have cited may reflect a cross-cultural consensus concerning the aesthetic value of natural landscapes which has been achieved only relatively recently. Any such shift in attitudes towards the natural world would have an obvious socioeconomic dimension: where natural landscapes are felt to be threatening, or where such landscapes signify economic marginalisation, it is only to be expected that they will evoke suspicion and even hostility. As Kate Soper remarks:

> Where the nature at your doorstep is not a pastoral green, but rude, rugged and tempestuous, and you are still in the midst of the 'struggle against' its encroachment on *your* space, it is the aesthetic of the cultivated landscape that tends to prevail - as was the case in the North American preference well into the nineteenth century for a Concordian rather than a sublime aesthetic. It is only, by contrast, where there is rather less wilderness left 'unfanged' that a landscape designer could promote the virtues of the 'sublime' garden .[60]

This variability over time in our appreciation of natural environments does not pose any fundamental difficulty for Tennant's argument, I suggest, but it does indicate a further respect in which his argument invites elaboration. So a modern reformulation of Tennant's case might give more weight to adverse responses to the natural world, while noting that a person's relationship to her natural environment can be conditioned by fears for her physical or socioeconomic well being. Allowing that all of this is so, Tennant is still free to press his central question: once such fears have been resolved, why should it be that human beings find the natural world in general a fitting object of aesthetic appreciation? After all, Tennant might note, while fear may account for a negative response to the natural world, mere lack of fear need not imply any tendency to value it positively. (Compare again his remarks on human artefacts.)

Conclusions

I do not claim that the argument I have just rehearsed can provide a persuasive case in isolation from other arguments. In practice, a cogent natural theology will have to appeal to a set of such arguments, each of which lends some plausibility to the hypothesis of theism (or at any rate of design). Of course, this is one reason why natural theological questions tend to prove so intractable: if a credible natural theology needs to draw on a profusion of different approaches, then its effectiveness overall will be correspondingly difficult to assess. However, I hope this examination of one strand of such a cumulative case throws some light on issues which are likely to be relevant more generally.

Suppose for the sake of argument that, setting aside its aesthetic qualities, the world is neutral in terms of its implications for the design hypothesis. And suppose furthermore that there is no reason to believe that the prior probability of the hypothesis (its probability independently of the evidence) is particularly low.[61] Under these conditions, how strong a case could be mounted in support of the hypothesis of design? Would such a case serve to show that the idea of design is overall more probable than not? I am inclined to say that it would. But, clearly, at this point we have abstracted rather dramatically from the abundance of factors which are in fact relevant to our question, given the actual constitution of the world. Prominent among these factors are of course the facts of suffering and frustration in their myriad forms. If the design argument is to have any plausibility, even in its cumulative-case form, something must be said on this topic. This issue will form the subject matter of Part Two. But before moving to that discussion, I want to bring into view another range of evaluatively rich phenomena, and to see what corroboration of the design hypothesis they may provide.

The burden of the argument in this chapter has been that in aesthetically charged encounters with nature, of the kind that all of us know, we are offered an intimation of the world's meaning. It is important to see the commonsensical character of this case. The beauty of the natural world is for most people an overwhelmingly obvious fact; and we are surely bound to give some sort of account of the power of natural beauty, in so many cases, to evoke the profoundest of human responses. One obvious account is that proposed by the design hypothesis: the world's beauty speaks to us of the ultimate meaning of our existence, which is one of consolation rather than despair. In this chapter, I have been arguing that this interpretation is not overturned either by Humean kinds of objection or by the modern, sociobiological understanding of our relationship to nature.

2 The world as a source of value

Introduction

Like the argument of Chapter 1, the argument of this chapter will take as its premise a feature of the world which is charged with religious and evaluative significance. The evolutionary history of the world, and of the cosmos itself, reveals a development towards richer and more complex material structures, as we move from the phenomena which form the subject matter of physics to those which are studied in chemistry, biology and psychology. On first inspection, this staggering truth about our cosmological and planetary history seems to sit comfortably with the thought that the world's goodness is its raison d'être. The purpose of this chapter is to see how far this commonsensical thought stands up to examination. I shall begin by surveying two design arguments of this general type, presented by Richard Swinburne and John Haldane. I shall argue that the questions which provide the focus of these discussions may not offer the most promising starting point for a natural theological understanding of the world's tendency towards greater complexity. I shall then expound and defend two further arguments, which pose rather different questions, one drawing upon the work of Holmes Rolston, and the other building upon the claim that the world is 'fine-tuned' to the possibility of life. The reader who wishes may move directly to this later discussion, where I develop my own case.[1]

Swinburne's argument from consciousness

In recent years, a number of philosophers have argued that at crucial points the evolutionary history of the world is inexplicable in naturalistic terms, or at any rate more readily explicable in terms of the framework of theism. The examples which are standardly cited in this connection include the phenomena of life, sentience, and concept use. These features of the world are, plainly, emergent in a chronological sense; but according to these writers, they are also emergent in a logical sense, in so far as they are not adequately explained by reference to earlier phases of the evolutionary process.[2]

For example, Richard Swinburne has argued that phenomenal properties (properties such as blueness and tasting sugar) provide the basis for a good 'C-inductive' theistic argument (that is, an argument which raises the probability of the theistic hypothesis in significant degree, although not necessarily to the point where it is more probable than not).[3] The fundamental premise of this argument, that there are phenomenal properties or qualia, we may allow to stand without comment, although of course it has been contested by some philosophers.[4] Granted this premise, Swinburne puts this sort of question to the naturalist: assuming that a particular brain state B1 is correlated with a red after-image, another such state B2 with a blue after-image, B3 with a yellow after-image, and so on, why should it be that this particular set of correlations holds and not some other? Why for instance should B1 be correlated with a red after-image and B2 with a blue image rather than vice versa? (The term 'correlated' here is intended to be neutral between different theories of the ontological status of qualia.) According to Swinburne, any scientific account of such matters would need to explain, for example, 'why sodium chloride tastes salty rather than sweet in terms of the brain-event which tasting sodium chloride normally produces having a natural connection with saltiness'.[5] Notice that in this quotation, the *explanandum* of Swinburne's argument seems to be more exactly the fact that one set of regular, type–type correlations between brain states and qualia holds and not some other. Fundamentally, the problem appears to be not: why does sodium chloride have the same taste at different times, or: why are there any qualia, but: why does sodium chloride consistently taste salty and not (for example) sweet? I shall say more about the nature of the *explanandum* of Swinburne's argument below; but it is clear enough why Swinburne thinks that there is little prospect of a naturalistic explanation of facts of this kind. He writes that:

> Brain-states are such different things from experiences . . . that a *natural* connection between them seems almost impossible. For how could brain-states vary except in their chemical composition and the speed and direction of their electro-chemical interactions, and how could there be a natural connection between variations in these respects and variations in the kind of respects in which [experiences] differ . . . ?[6]

Of course, this argument has a definite intellectual ancestry. In substance, and even in phraseology, it recalls Locke's discussion of these issues. Thus Locke writes that:

> the production of Sensation in us of Colours and Sounds, etc. by impulse and motion . . . being such, wherein we can discover no natural connexion with any *Ideas* we have, we cannot but ascribe them to the Will and good Pleasure of the Wise Architect.[7]

Locke's view appears to be that matter alone could never give rise to thought, although God has the power to give to 'some Systems of Matter fitly disposed, a power to perceive and think'.[8] Swinburne's view seems to be, characteristically, that while there is some low probability that material structures will give rise of themselves to the regularities of our conscious lives, this account is much less likely than its theistic rival.[9]

Given the weight which Swinburne and Locke place on the failure of materialism to identify a 'natural connection' between brain states and phenomenal properties, we want to know why the theist should consider her own account of these same connections any more transparent. In response to this enquiry, Swinburne maintains that there is a natural connection between intentions and their fulfilments, and that accordingly, a divine intention to establish a particular set of correlations between brain states and qualia ensures that these correlations are after all natural, or intelligible. Thus he writes that:

> There is a very natural connection between an agent's intention to bring about X, and the occurrence of X; for the intention has written into it one thing with which it is naturally correlated: its fulfilment – whereas a brain-event does not have written into it a mental event with which it is naturally correlated.[10]

What are we to make of Swinburne's argument? Clearly, it depends on two claims: that theism offers an attractive account of the correlations between brain states and qualia, and that naturalism fails on this point. Suppose we consider these claims in turn.

The naturalist may well feel that Swinburne's own explanation of the connections between qualia and brain states falls short of the explanatory ideals which he propounds when finding fault with the naturalistic account. For instance, Swinburne remarks that an adequate scientific account of these matters should postulate 'laws which fit together with each other in a theory from which one can deduce new correlations hitherto unobserved'.[11] But of course his own theory hardly allows us to deduce further correlations between brain states and qualia. This objection need not trouble Swinburne too much, I think. He can reasonably reply that the criteria for adequacy of explanation in regard to scientific and theistic explanations are different, so that a theistic explanation is not shown to be defective merely because it lacks some of the desiderata of a good scientific explanation. However, this objection does draw attention to a further issue of some importance.

Our inability to use Swinburne's theory to predict further psycho-physical correlations (relating qualia and brain states) is not to be attributed merely to a failure to grasp God's reasoning in these matters. For on Swinburne's view it appears there is no reason why God should establish one set of regular psycho-physical correlations in preference to others.[12] So it seems that naturalism and Swinburnean theism alike fail to provide any deep explanation of why certain correlations hold and not others; on Swinburne's account, the theist can say only that these correlations take the form they do because God wills it, and not because God wills it for this reason or that. If theism shares with naturalism a failure to provide any deep explanation of these matters, then we might wonder why we should grant that it provides a more satisfactory stopping point for explanation. On this issue, Swinburne urges that reference to personal choice offers a natural terminus for enquiry even where that choice is (to borrow Locke's term) 'arbitrary'. Thus he writes that:

> personal choice among equally good alternatives is a mechanism which we see intuitively to be a simple and natural mechanism for selecting alternatives; for it is a mechanism, indeed the only mechanism, of which we have inside experience and whose operation is thus comprehensible.[13]

This account seems to tie the simplicity of theistic explanation to the fact that we have direct experience of the sort of agency to which it appeals. But in view of comments he has made in an exchange with John Mackie, Swinburne is also committed to the thought that the simplicity of a hypothesis can be judged independently of whether or not it is familiar to us from our own experience. Thus he rejects Mackie's charge that the hypothesis of unmediated fulfilments of intention (Swinburne makes use of this notion in expounding the character of divine agency) is antecedently improbable, because we have no experience of this sort of intention fulfilment. In reply to this charge, Swinburne maintains that judgements of simplicity may be entirely a priori, and that, where the hypothesis of theism is concerned, the relevant judgements of simplicity are indeed altogether a priori.[14] So there is perhaps an internal strain here which Swinburne's argument needs to address. But again, I do not find that this consideration deprives the argument of all its force. For instance, we could interpret the passage I have just cited as holding that while the simplicity of the personal choice model is revealed in our immediate experience, its simplicity is not reducible to the fact that we have this sort of acquaintance with it.

So the first of the two claims on which Swinburne's argument depends – the claim that the theistic account of psycho–physical correlations is adequate – may call for further exploration. In particular, we may wonder whether Swinburne's theistic explanation offers a sufficiently informative response to the question which is said to defeat the naturalist, and whether its commitment to the simplicity of the model of personal choice is inadmissibly reliant on the character of our own experience. However, the issue which I want to concentrate on is rather the second claim which underpins Swinburne's argument, namely the claim that the naturalistic account of psychophysical correlations is deficient.[15]

In this connection, it is important to bear in mind the place of the argument from consciousness within the overarching cumulative case for theism which Swinburne assembles in his book *The Existence of God*. It is worth noting in particular that this argument is introduced after Swinburne has taken account of the evidential force of the world's regularity (both spatial and temporal), in Chapter 4 of this work. So in the terms of Swinburne's Bayesian framework, the argument from consciousness has as background knowledge the fact that 'there is an orderly (and beautiful) world'.[16] I suggest that, implicitly, Swinburne's argument also includes within our background knowledge the fact that there are qualia, and that qualia are correlated with brain states, since he is asking why the correlations between qualia and brain states should assume a particular regular form, not why there should be any such correlations. Now granted a world in which the regularities recorded in the physical sciences obtain, and granted that there are qualia, and that qualia are correlated with brain states, and granted the truth of naturalism, how likely is it that there will be regular correlations between brain states and qualia? Some may feel that there is nothing much we can sensibly say on such questions. But supposing that we are required to reach a view one way or other, we may feel that given such background knowledge, it would be unsurprising if the correlations between brain states and qualia should prove to be regular, because it is only to be expected that a world which is pervasively regular in the ways recorded in the physical sciences will prove to be broadly regular in any further respect in which it admits of being regular or irregular. Of course, a world in which there are psycho–physical regularities is, other things being equal, more profoundly regular than one which lacks phenomenal properties. And to this extent, given a Swinburnean approach to regularity, there is more about such a world that stands in need of explanation. But if naturalism is able to accommodate the vast regularities which are recorded in physics, then we may feel that it is somewhat unlikely that its epistemic standing will be altered significantly by the fact that these psycho–physical correlations are also regular rather than irregular, even allowing that the laws which arise in this case lack the simplicity and breadth of application of the fundamental laws of physics.

When trying to establish that psycho–physical correlations call for explanation, Swinburne actually notes the parallel between the *explanandum* of the argument from consciousness and the *explanandum* of the argument from design which he has presented earlier in the book. Thus he writes: 'As we saw in Chapter 4 . . . [where he develops an argument from the regularity of the physical world], regularity in the midst of complexity cries out for explanation.'[17] Allowing that this is so, and that the evidential force of the regularity evident in physics has already been taken into consideration, we might wonder whether the further regularity evident in psycho–physical correlations will make a significant additional contribution to the evidential case for theism.

Now Swinburne might reply that this line of reflection has not identified closely enough the particular *explanandum* of his argument. What the argument seeks to explain, he might say, is not the fact that there are regular correlations between brain states and qualia, but the fact that these regular correlations take the particular form they do. That this is the *explanandum* of the argument is suggested by the question Swinburne poses in relation to the sodium chloride example I cited earlier. The same concern seems to be evident in passages such as this:

> I do not wish to deny that there is a satisfactory scientific explanation given by the biological theory of evolution of the evolution of more and more complex beings which interact in

> increasingly complex ways. But there is not, I have argued, a scientific explanation of their increasing complexity of physiological organization and behavioural response giving rise to the *particular* conscious life to which it does give rise [my emphasis].[18]

But allowing that it is the particular character of the regular correlations between brain states and qualia which needs explaining, Swinburne's argument may still be vulnerable to the kind of consideration we have just noted. In a similar vein, we might suppose that if naturalism is able to accommodate not only the fact that the physical world is pervasively regular, but also the fact that it is regular in this way rather than that, then the fact that there are certain psycho–physical regularities rather than others will make little additional difference to the evidential standing of theism.[19]

To this it might be replied that there is a natural connection of some sort between the intrinsic character of the basic particles of physics and their effects, but no such connection between brain states and qualia. So the second sort of connection does after all pose more of a problem, or at any rate a different sort of problem, for naturalism. However, so far as I can see, this is not the issue Swinburne is seeking to press. Moreover, if the ultimate constituents of matter lack any internal complexity, then we may wonder whether there could be a natural connection between their intrinsic character and their behaviour.[20] But putting these concerns to one side, we may still doubt whether the argument from qualia can proceed effectively on this basis. Again, granted that there are qualia and that they are correlated with brain states, and granted that the physical universe is in other respects regular, and granted the truth of naturalism, would it not be, if anything, more surprising if brain states of a given type were correlated with qualia of varying types than if there were regular type–type correlations between these two sets of phenomena?[21] And if we agree that on this background knowledge, naturalism predicts with reasonable probability the existence of psycho–physical regularity of some sort, why suppose that the occurrence of one set of psycho–physical correlations rather than another poses a difficulty? After all, if there is to be regularity, it has to take some form or other. I do not think these considerations simply overturn Swinburne's argument. But they do put in question, I think, his sense that naturalism is obviously in need of a theory of these matters, given background knowledge of the kind he postulates.

Whatever our verdict on these issues, it is clear that any assessment of an argument in this general style will need to give careful attention to precisely which causal question we are proposing to answer, and precisely which features of the world are already contained within our background knowledge. The first of these issues is helpfully clarified by Robert Adams, who has defended an argument from consciousness of the same general type as those of Swinburne and Locke. In the course of his article, Adams poses various questions, among them the following:

i Why do brains with such and such physical qualities give rise to phenomenal qualia at all?
ii Why do red things look the way they looked yesterday?
iii Why do red things look the way they look and not the way yellow things look?
iv Why do these type–type relationships between brain states and phenomenal qualia obtain rather than others?[22]

Putting the matter in terms of brain states and qualia, we might suppose that the theist may raise any of the following issues, in order of increasing particularity:

(a) Why are there any qualia at all?
(b) Why are there type–type correlations between brain states and qualia?
(c) Why is this token brain state correlated with a red rather than a blue after-image?
(d) Why do the type–type correlations between brain states and qualia take the particular form they do?

The focus of Swinburne's argument seems to be the last question, (d). This question also seems to be the fundamental concern of Adams' enquiry, though he also gives some attention to (a). For instance he writes that:

> it is hard to conceive of any reason why a pattern of electrical activity would be naturally connected with the peculiar kind of experience that I call the appearance of red, rather than with that which I call the appearance of yellow. Indeed, it is hard to conceive of any reason why a pattern of electrical activity would be naturally connected with either of these appearances, rather than with no phenomenal qualia at all.[23]

Here Adams seems to pose respectively questions (d) and (a). But it is noteworthy that when he gets to develop his case in detail, in Section V of his paper (entitled 'The impossibility of any scientific explanation'), he is interested in showing that science is necessarily unable to account for the *particular character* of the regular correlations between brain states and qualia, for instance because: 'There is no plausible, non-ad-hoc way of associating phenomenal qualia in general (let alone conscious or mental states in general) with a range of mathematical values, independently of their empirically discovered correlations with physical states'.[24]

So Adams' case, I suggest, like Swinburne's, does not have the first question – the question of why there should be any qualia at all – as its primary focus. But it seems that the theist does have good reason to press this question. Indeed she may have reason to give more weight to this question than to questions relating to the particular character of the correlations between qualia and brain states. After all, if there is no 'natural connection' between any state characterised in purely physical terms (including brain states) and the existence of phenomenal properties, and if we take as background knowledge the existence of a complex and regular physical universe, then it may be doubted whether we have any basis, on a naturalistic worldview, for anticipating the existence of such properties.

By contrast, if the naturalist is granted as background knowledge the existence of qualia (and a pervasively regular physical universe), then she may not be too perturbed by the issues raised by questions (b), (c) and (d). Given such background knowledge, it may seem unsurprising that there are regular type–type correlations between brain states and qualia, so depriving question (b) of its force. That leaves the question of why certain correlations of this regular kind should arise rather than others. But here we might urge again, for example, that if naturalism is not defeated by the question of why the regularities in physics should take the particular form they do, then it is unlikely to be defeated by the question of why psycho–physical regularities should take the particular form they do. If that is so, then the question (d) has also been disarmed. And if it is allowed that the naturalist can accommodate this question, then it should also be allowed that she can accommodate question (c); for once we have admitted that the existence of one set of psycho–physical regularities rather than another is not a problem for naturalism, then the naturalist can treat as unproblematic the fact that, for example, a particular brain state is correlated with a red rather than a blue after-image.

The upshot of this discussion is therefore that the question which

Swinburne poses in his argument from consciousness may not after all embarrass the naturalist, if we follow his approach in relation to background knowledge. There is however another question which is worth considering in this connection, one which is implicit in Swinburne's discussion, and brought out more clearly in Adams' paper, namely the question of why there should be any qualia at all. This question, it seems to me, offers the theist a more promising starting point.[25] I shall return to this proposal shortly, but first I want to examine briefly a further attempt in the recent literature to treat emergent phenomena as evidence for theism.

Haldane's argument from concept use

In a fascinating debate with Jack Smart, John Haldane has argued that our powers of concept use are in principle inexplicable in naturalistic terms, and that we should seek to explain them by reference to theism.[26] In this section, I shall outline this argument, and ask what further light it throws on our general topic.

Haldane notes that in the history of philosophy, there have been two accounts of how human beings acquire their concepts: *innatism* maintains that we are simply born with them, or a significant number of them, while *abstractionism* holds that we acquire concepts by selective attention to what is revealed in our experience of the world. Neither of these accounts will do, Haldane suggests. Innatism proves unattractive since it generates questions such as these: 'Are we born with the concept *square* and the concept *rectangle* or just the one and, if so, which one? Are our innate geometrical concepts Euclidean or non-Euclidean? How could we be born with concepts of things that didn't exist at the time?' And so on.[27] Abstractionism fails because it gets things back to front: attending to the squareness of relevant objects, in isolation from their other properties, just is an exercise of the concept *square*, and it is no use therefore invoking this sort of activity to explain our possession of the concept in the first place.[28] Haldane goes on to offer an alternative, broadly Wittgensteinian account of concept acquisition. On this view, I acquire the concept *cat*, for example, when my prior disposition (or potentiality) to acquire the concept is actualised by virtue of the agency of someone who already has the concept. Thus Haldane writes that:

> Alice will not pick up the meaning of the term 'cat' unless she has a relevant potentiality, unless the structure of her receptivity is of the right sort. By the same token that potentiality will not be

actualized except by an intellect that is already active in using the concept, her older brother, James, for example.[29]

Of course, this further account sets up a regress: Alice's acquisition of a given concept depends upon the agency of James, whose acquisition of the concept in turn depends upon the agency of Peter, and so on. Haldane notes that this sort of regress instantiates the basic structure of Aquinas's First Way (in so far as it invokes the same sort of potentiality–actuality framework), though it represents a more specific instance of this structure, in so far as coming to be a thinker depends upon the agency of someone who is already a thinker, whereas other sorts of change need not conform to the principle: [$\forall x \exists y$ (if x comes to be F, then y is F and y makes x to be F)].[30] Haldane supposes, of course, that this regress, explaining one person's conceptual powers in terms of the prior conceptual powers of a further person, must reach a terminus; and he infers that we need to postulate 'an actualizing source whose own conceptual power is intrinsic'. In conclusion he notes that such a source is 'precisely what God is traditionally taken to be'.[31] I turn now to an assessment of this argument.

Although Haldane assimilates his approach to that of the First Way, it seems clear that there is an important difference between the two (in addition to their different renderings of the potentiality–actuality framework in the respect we have just noted). In claiming that the regress of changing things bringing about change in other things must have a stopping-point, Aquinas does not seem to have been thinking about a temporal regress. (After all, in his view, there is no philosophical proof of the beginning of the world.) By contrast, Haldane's regress is clearly temporally extended: James instructs Alice, having been instructed at some earlier time by Peter, and so on. This difference between the two arguments results in rather different understandings of the relationship between divine and creaturely agency, as I shall now argue.

Of course, we have sound empirical reasons for thinking that the regress which features in Haldane's argument does not extend into the past *ad infinitum*. Suppose we also grant Haldane's suggestion that the first term in this regress, from the point of view of the natural order, is clearly defined in principle. (Haldane rejects the idea of a 'fading conceptuality': on his view, concept use cannot be represented as the end point of a smooth continuum of possibilities, stretching back into prototypical forms of concept use.)[32] Suppose we call the first natural concept user 'Adam'. Now we might ask: how did Adam acquire the (first-order) power of conceptual thought?[33] It seems that he cannot have acquired this power as a result of the activity of any natural agent. For by hypothesis, there are no natural concept users who pre-exist Adam; and we have been told that the only way in which a (second-order) power to acquire the power of conceptual thought may be actualised is through the agency of an already existing concept user. This suggests that Haldane's First Thinker argument and Aquinas's First Mover argument invoke the idea of divine agency in rather different ways. The First Way does not depend on the idea that at any point in time, God's activity bypasses the framework of natural or secondary causality. By contrast, Haldane's argument seems to suggest that in evolutionary history, the first instance of concept acquisition (and perhaps others) cannot have been brought about through the agency of secondary causes: on Haldane's account, it seems that in this first instance, concept acquisition must be attributed to the miraculous intervention of God in the natural order of things.[34]

Of course, some theologians – deists and others – have expressed disquiet about this sort of understanding of divine agency. But setting aside these concerns, we may ask: how is divine agency supposed to explain Adam's first-order conceptual powers? Granted that in this case God does not work through the agency of created things, it seems that God must simply implant relevant concepts in the mind of Adam. But of course this understanding invites us to raise the very questions which Haldane posed for the innatist. (Thus we might ask: does God implant the concept of rectangle and that of square, or only one of these concepts? And so on.)[35] I suggest therefore that Haldane's First Thinker argument needs, ultimately, to rely upon a model of concept acquisition which is, by his own reckoning, dubious. This need not defeat the argument, of course. It may be that the naturalistic account of the beginnings of concept use is still more dubious. But it does suggest that explanation in terms of divine agency may not be as straightforward a matter as the theist had hoped.

These issues can be brought into clearer focus by noting the place of Haldane's First Thinker argument within the overarching case he presents in *Atheism and Theism.* On Haldane's account, there are other developments in evolutionary history which are also necessarily beyond the reach of any naturalistic explanation, notably the emergence of life and of self-replicating entities.[36] Predictably, Smart contests this claim. For instance, he professes to find Haldane's reasoning on the origin of replication question 'obscure' and asks flatly: 'Why could not a self-replicating molecule come about through the coming together of a number of non-replicating molecules?'[37]

In reply, Haldane reaffirms that there is no possibility of giving a naturalistic explanation of such an event.[38] His reasoning here is in part that natural selection operates across generations, and therefore presupposes the existence of powers of replication, rather than explaining them.[39] So the standard naturalistic explanation of adaptedness fails in this case. Moreover, he maintains, no such explanation will work. At least in part, this is because the power of self-replication is 'novel', that is to say: 'it is not just a linear combination of instances of the same property type . . .'[40] He concludes that on the naturalistic account 'contrary to its implausibility, the claim has to be that [the emergence of the first replicative powers] occurred in a single step; somehow non-replicating entities just turned into reproducing species'.[41]

It may be that we can identify a *via media* between these two viewpoints. With Smart, we may be inclined to suppose that on the naturalistic scheme, the transition from non-replicating to replicating entities need not have just happened. (In other words, we need not follow Haldane in attributing to the naturalist the view that non-replicating things 'just turned into' replicating things.) Why should we not suppose instead that, when combined in the right sort of way, certain non-replicating things will give rise to replicating things by virtue of the operation of their own powers?[42] But in the spirit of Haldane's argument, we may suppose (for reasons I shall develop below) that the fact that certain non-replicating things have this capacity is itself puzzling on the naturalistic scheme; and to this extent we may endorse his view that the emergence of replicators calls into question the explanatory adequacy of a naturalistic worldview.

This same sort of approach may be followed in relation to Haldane's argument from human beings' powers of concept use. If we find the idea that God directly implanted concepts in Adam's mind unacceptable, for the kinds of reasons which Haldane gives in his discussion of innatism, then we may prefer to say that Adam acquired his concepts through the operation of the natural order. But here again, there may be room for a theistic argument, if it can be shown that the fact that the natural order has such powers is itself puzzling on a naturalistic worldview.

So Haldane's discussion, I suggest, should encourage the theist to raise questions of this kind: why should the natural order give rise to replicators? Or again: why should it give rise to minds? These questions are of the same form as question (a) above, which asks: why should the natural order give rise to qualia? If all of this is so, then we may be interested in the possibility of an argument for theism which takes as its starting point the very existence of emergent phenomena, without supposing (as Haldane appears to) that the difficulties for naturalism in this regard have to do with a breakdown in secondary causation, and without supposing (as Swinburne appears to) that it is the particular order assumed by these phenomena, rather than their very existence, which is most significant in this context. I shall now sketch out an argument in this style.

The world as a generator of value

The argument I shall present in this section, like the argument from beauty, has its roots in a commonsensical response to the world. It is common knowledge that over time, the world has generated a succession of richer and more complex material forms. Yet there is no evident requirement that a material world which has the general character of our cosmos (beginning with a big bang, and initially comprised of hydrogen and helium) should go on to produce, for example, the rich and varied life forms that we observe around us today. Under these circumstances, it is common sense, and not a rationalist prejudice, to ask: why should the universe act as a value generator in this way? I shall consider this question from two related points of view. First of all, in the style of Swinburne and Haldane, I shall ask whether we have reason to advance a teleological explanation of the emergence of life, sentience, and conceptual thought. Secondly, I shall take note of the phenomena of 'fine-tuning' and consider whether they provide further reason for thinking of the world's goodness as its reason for existence.

A naturalistic account of the world's tendency to give rise to greater complexity over time is likely to have recourse in the first instance to the theory of evolution. After all, this theory purports to explain the origin of species; and sentience and powers of concept use would have developed in step with the evolution of species. However, while evolutionary theory may lay down a set of necessary conditions which any species must observe if it is to survive, it is not so clear that it actually predicts the emergence of sentience or powers of concept use. Indeed evolutionary theory would surely be unembarrassed by the failure of more complex life forms to emerge. All that the theory requires is that those creatures which do survive should be 'fit', not that they should be complex. As Holmes Rolston observes:

> Nothing in the theory [of evolution] makes probable a continual ascent, since, at every point in time, the probabilities of descent,

> stagnation, and ascent are equally great. Nothing says that the better adapted are more complex.[43]

Rolston concludes that while evolutionary theory has predictive power in relation to the details of evolution, it fails to account for the overarching trend towards increasing complexity. He comments:

> So we know why hair gets longer and whiter in cold climates. We know why horns evolve repeatedly. But we know nothing at all of the trend toward sentience, toward awareness, why humans come, why things grow more complex. We know all about the microevolution and nothing about the macroevolution. Natural selection reads the *subplots*, but is really powerless to explain the *big story*.[44]

Here Rolston sketches an argument which has a rather different character from those proposed by Haldane and Swinburne, though it concerns the same range of phenomena. For example, he is not of the view that the development of life is flatly inexplicable in terms of natural processes. 'Life,' he writes, 'is not an accident, whatever place dice-throwing plays in its appearance and maturation. It is something arranged in the *nature of things*. The dice are loaded.'[45] In other words, on Rolston's view, the web of secondary causation does not have to be breached to account for the emergence of life. The difficulty for naturalism lies rather in explaining why natural processes should take this form, when some other form would be equally consistent with the naturalistic hypothesis.[46]

In talking of the emergence of consciousness, Rolston shows rather more interest in the kinds of question which exercise Haldane, but again the focus of his attention lies with the inability of naturalism to account for the general shape of natural processes, not with the inability of natural processes, as they are actually constituted, to explain the phenomena. For instance he writes that:

> When consciousness arises, this will, of course, be said to have survival value. The animal can conduct trial-and-error thought experiments, and bad ideas can get eliminated without the death of the organism. But nothing in such an explanation gives insight into how subjective experience arises by the complication of mere objects, and where subjective experience has never yet arisen (as in plants), or if subjective experience had never arisen at all, natural selection would remain quite untroubled by its absence.[47]

Here Rolston poses a question which is reminiscent of Haldane's discussion, when he remarks that evolutionary explanations fail to illuminate how consciousness emerges in the first place, allowing that it has some survival value once it has. However, I think his sense of the insufficiency of naturalistic explanations again relates, fundamentally, not to any suggestion that there is no possibility of a material cause giving rise to consciousness, but rather to the sense that as a general theory, naturalism is indifferent to such developments. Hence he notes that naturalism would be 'untroubled' by the absence of consciousness.

In sum, there is good reason to think that the predictive power of evolutionary theory in relation to sentience and concept use is low. And in turn this provides initial reason for thinking that naturalism will have a low predictive power in relation to these same phenomena. Similarly, we might suppose that the predictive power of naturalism in relation to the emergence of life is low. (I take it that evolutionary theory presupposes the existence of life, and has nothing to say therefore about its origins.) For again, naturalism as such would be unembarrassed if a cosmos of the same general character as ours, that is, one which began with a big bang, and was initially comprised of a mix of hydrogen and helium, should fail to give rise to life. Of course, it is possible that given the initial state of our cosmos, the subsequent development of life, sentience and concept use according to natural processes was all more or less inevitable. Nonetheless, what naturalism fails to predict is that a cosmos will take this form.

One standard reply to this observation postulates the existence of an ensemble of universes, large enough to ensure there is a reasonable likelihood of at least one universe which will permit the development of life and sentience. On this view, although our own universe is marked by a tendency to favour the development of complex material forms, there is no such tendency overall (that is, across this ensemble of universes). Hence, overall, there is no apparently purposeful drive (towards life and sentience) which might embarrass the naturalist. The fact that we find ourselves in a universe of this special, life-permitting kind is of course unsurprising, since we could not exist in a universe of any other kind. So in this respect too, there is no lingering demand for explanation which might trouble naturalism.

The proponent of design need not be too dismayed by this argument, I suggest. First of all, the many-universes hypothesis grants that life and sentience are indeed in need of explanation, and that there is no adequate naturalistic explanation of their emergence given an ontology which extends no further than this cosmos. Anyone who grants this much is already working within the general framework of the design argument, in terms of their willingness to seek extra-mundane explanations, and their willingness to appeal to such an explanation in this case in particular.

Moreover, the many-universes hypothesis postulates a tendency to ontological plenitude. There are various ways of developing this approach, but they all imply that reality has an inherent drift towards multiplicity and diversity. This assumption too may invite a relatively sympathetic assessment of the argument from design. Critics of the idea of design sometimes maintain that while the hypothesis may have a reasonable predictive power, its prior probability is low, for instance because we have no experience of a transcendent mind. But if we adopt the assumption of ontological plenitude, then the supposition that there is a transcendent designer should no longer strain credulity. If reality has a tendency to admit lots of possibilities, then why not this one? Or to put the matter another way, the postulate of many universes is surely likely to invite the same kinds of objection, in terms of prior probability, as the hypothesis of design, in so far as both move well beyond the data of observation.

I suggest then that naturalism can after all predict the existence of a universe which is a value generator, without committing itself to the thought that reality as such is a value generator, by supposing that a value-generating universe will arise at some point given a sufficiently permissive ontology. But this reply to the design argument at the same time grants the validity of certain central assumptions of the argument, concerning the need to explain the general character of our cosmos, and the legitimacy of metaphysical forms of explanation. Moreover, the many-universes hypothesis also invites the thought that in this context we should allow the predictive power of a hypothesis to trump any initial concerns we may have about its prior probability. If all of this is so then the design hypothesis is, I suggest, at least a good explanation of the phenomena of life, sentience and concept use, albeit it that it is not the only possible explanation of these phenomena.

At this juncture, the cumulative-case character of the design argument assumes some importance. In particular, if there are other phenomena which invite explanation in terms of design, but which are not so clearly necessary for the existence of human life, then the many-universes hypothesis will begin to look less attractive as a competitor to the idea of design. The discussion of Chapter 1 has identified one such phenomenon, I suggest: while human beings cannot exist in a world which does not permit life, or sentience, or concept use, it is far from evident that they cannot exist in a world which lacks the pervasive beauty of our planet and cosmos.

I have been arguing that as long as its ontology is restricted to this universe, naturalism has a low predictive power in relation to the phenomena which are cited by Swinburne and Haldane. Given as background knowledge a cosmos which began with a big bang, and was initially comprised of hydrogen and helium, naturalism surely does not predict the emergence of qualia (here with Swinburne); and it surely does not predict the emergence of self-replicating entities, or concept use (here with Haldane). Notice however that the argument I am developing here does not depend on the particular assumptions made by Swinburne and Haldane. It is not seeking an explanation of the fact that qualia, allowing that there are qualia, are related in one regular way to brain states rather than another. And it does not depend on the claim that there is no process in nature which can explain the emergence of life or concept use. It suggests only that a universe in which there are such processes is not predictable given the truth of a this-worldly naturalism.

So Rolston offers I think an example of how the explanatory poverty of naturalism may be understood in terms rather different from those proposed by Haldane and Swinburne. His concern lies fundamentally, I suggest, not with gaps in the natural order, as in Haldane, nor with the details of how the phenomena of consciousness are related to the (wider) material order, as in Swinburne. What provokes his astonishment is instead the tendency of the world to generate, in an apparently reliable way, richer and more complex material forms over time.[48] Rolston's approach should not be scientifically controversial, I suggest. After all, unlike the arguments propounded by Swinburne and Haldane, it is not committed to the insufficiency of scientific explanations of these matters. On the contrary, it tends to think that there must be some naturalistic account of the tendency of the world to act as a value generator, since this tendency is deep-seated, and accordingly somehow written into the material order itself. Rolston's view invites us to suppose that scientific explanations of natural value generation can take what form they may, providing we recognise the insufficiency of Darwinian accounts. What matters is this very propensity of the natural order which science describes. In this respect, Rolston's approach offers a clear parallel with the general structure of Tennant's argument from beauty. A willingness to see the world's tendency towards complexity as in principle scientifically intelligible and as theologically significant also finds expression, famously, in the work of Pierre Teilhard de Chardin, and Rolston's work could be viewed as a contemporary reworking of Teilhardian themes.[49]

There are further objections which might be raised in response to this Rolstonian argument from value generation, but I suggest that we consider them in connection with a further version of the design argument, one which has excited much comment in recent years, namely, the argument from 'fine-tuning'. This argument depends on the findings of cosmologists, and is clearly consonant with Rolston's argument, since it invites us to think that the tendency of the cosmos to generate life is somehow embedded in its basic structure. The details of 'fine-tuning' have been documented in detail in many publications, of varying complexity, in recent years.[50] Here, it is enough to note a few examples. In general, the point made by these examples is that the emergence of life depends not simply on a process of evolution on this planet, but upon a larger, cosmic evolution, which gives rise to the heavier elements, which then make possible the development of life. This cosmic evolution in turn depends on the emergence of stars which will provide suitable conditions for the formation of these heavier, life-enabling elements.

It seems for example that electromagnetic and gravitational forces, together with the strong and weak nuclear forces, must all fall within a narrowly delimited range of values if this process of cosmic evolution is to be possible. Thus John Leslie observes that: 'Had the weak [nuclear] force been appreciably stronger then the Big Bang's burning would have proceeded past helium and all the way to iron. Fusion-powered stars would then be impossible.'[51] At the same time, if the weak force had been significantly weaker, then the universe would have been comprised entirely of helium. Similarly, if the *strong* nuclear force had been some 2 per cent stronger, then atoms would not have existed, and if some 5 per cent weaker, then the universe would have comprised nothing but hydrogen. Again, it appears that stars of the kind needed for life will only exist if electromagnetic forces fall within a restrictive range of values.[52] And gravity too is fine-tuned to the possibility of life: if it were ten times stronger, then a star such as our sun would only burn for a million years, and if ten times weaker, then there would be little prospect of any stars forming. Moreover, gravity must lie within a narrow range of values if the universe is to expand at just the right rate, neither too quickly nor too slowly for galaxies to form.[53] (Leslie suggests that the expansion rate may need fine-tuning to within one part in 10^{55}.)[54] Similarly, the neutron–proton mass difference is also sensitively related to the possibility of life. Were it slightly greater, no elements other than hydrogen would have formed; and if slightly smaller, then the universe would have been a collection of neutron stars and black holes.[55]

Many more examples of this kind could be given, but these are enough to suggest that the emergence of life, and in turn of sentience and powers of conceptual thought, is dependent upon a precise set of cosmological preconditions. And this might suggest that the emergence of life calls for some sort of explanation. It might be said: we surely cannot suppose that these precisely circumscribed conditions arose merely by chance. And if chance cannot account for the phenomena, then what could be more obvious than a teleological explanation: the universe takes this form *so that* life will emerge.

This interpretation of the significance of the data of fine-tuning has proved controversial, of course, and we should pause to note some of the standard objections. I shall deal summarily with two rather weak objections, before passing to some more challenging criticisms. It might be said: if there is a universe at all, it must take some form or other; but given the truth of naturalism, the actual universe is presumably no less likely than any other, so where is the problem? But this objection fails. Naturalism may indeed imply that our universe is no less likely than others (where universes are distinguished in terms of expansion rate, and so on). However, if only a relatively small range of expansion rates (or values of the various forces) are compatible with the development of life, then this suggests that naturalism (of the one-cosmos variety) fails to predict the existence of a life-generating universe. By contrast, on the hypothesis of design, where evaluatively rich outcomes are favoured, it is, at least, unsurprising if the universe has a life-supporting character. Thus it appears that the design hypothesis has a higher predictive power than naturalism, where the evidence to be explained is the universe's openness to the development of life.

Another objection might run: we can only exist in a universe consistent with life, so what can be surprising about the discovery that our universe is fine-tuned to the possibility of life? But this objection takes for granted the existence of life, and asks: assuming that there is life, how likely is it that the universe will have a life-supporting character? But in the present context, the pertinent question is: how likely is the existence of life *in the first place*, on the hypotheses of naturalism and design?

Peter Forrest has posed another, more interesting objection to the fine-tuning argument. He suggests that the argument's proposal that there is a relatively small proportion of universes which are friendly to life is difficult to sustain, because we cannot hope to survey all possible universes, and establish in what proportion they permit life. He writes:

> We have, then, no reason for saying that there is a high proportion of systems of laws that are life-friendly. But we have no reason for saying that there is a low proportion either. Rather we have no way of deciding whether there is a proportion at all, or if it is high or low.[56]

As Forrest notes, even if this is so, the design hypothesis is not thereby rendered impotent. It may still offer a superior understanding of the life-friendly character of the universe, when compared with naturalism. But he proposes that these facts imply the inadmissibility of a strictly probabilistic form of the argument from fine-tuning.

It seems to me that this understanding is perhaps too pessimistic. What the theist requires here is some sense not of the proportion of universes in general which are sympathetic to life, but the proportion of universes of our general type which are favourable to life, that is, universes which begin with a big bang, and are comprised initially of hydrogen and helium. The fine-tuning discoveries surely do suggest that only a small proportion of universes of this general character are receptive to life. So we can ask: granted that our universe is of this general type (beginning with a big bang, etc.), what is the likelihood that it will prove favourable to life, on the hypotheses of naturalism and design? Even if no precise probabilistic answer to this question is possible, the considerations we have been examining suggest that on the hypothesis of naturalism, it is highly unlikely that a universe of this type will be life-friendly. By contrast the design hypothesis surely leads to at least a weak presumption that a universe of this kind will be predisposed to generate valuable outcomes, including life, which is valuable in itself, and is a precondition of sentience and conceptual thought.[57]

Another objection, in the style of Hume, might maintain that the notion of probability has no application here since we lack any empirical frame of reference. On what basis can we say that universe *x* is as likely as universe *y* given the truth of naturalism, when we only have experience of one universe? The argument from fine-tuning suggests, I think, a novel line of response to this familiar objection.[58] The reply to this objection we canvassed in Chapter 1 turned on an appeal to our knowledge of relative frequencies in another context: in relation to human agency, we know that beautiful things are unlikely to result merely by chance; and this establishes an initial presumption that, in general, such things are unlikely to arise in the absence of appropriate skills of conception and execution. The fine-tuning argument suggests another line of reply to Hume's criticism of the appeal to probabilities in this context. This is because it deals in possibilities which are specified in quantitative terms.

To take an analogy, in the absence of any detailed background knowledge, we would surely suppose that the probability of a square having sides of 1.2 cm is no more or less than the probability of its having sides of 1.3 cm. Note, we are not merely unable to think of any consideration which might be relevant to the prior probability (under these conditions) of one possibility but not relevant in just the same degree to the prior probability of the other possibility; more profoundly, it seems there *cannot be* any such consideration. For the two possibilities are so closely alike that it is surely inconceivable that any factor which might figure in background knowledge of this indeterminate kind would favour one possibility over the other. Now analogously, we might suppose that in the absence of detailed background knowledge there is no reason to suppose that a universe with an expansion rate of *x* is either more or less likely than a universe with an expansion rate of *y*. If that is so, then it seems we have sound reason to say that on indeterminate background knowledge, the probability of a universe (of our general type) proving to have an expansion rate of a life-consistent kind is low. The same sort of argument may then be developed in relation to other examples of fine-tuning, which can also be specified in numerical terms, as we have seen.

This approach to relative prior probabilities appeals to something like the principle of indifference in probability theory. According to this principle, given *n* mutually exclusive and logically exhaustive outcomes, and in the absence of any reason for assigning a higher probability to any one of these outcomes, we should suppose that the probability of each outcome is $1/n$. However, it is well known that the principle of indifference easily generates paradoxical results. For example, suppose tests reveal that the mass per unit volume of a certain alloy lies between 1 and 2, and suppose we have no further information on this matter. Applying the principle of indifference, we might infer that there is a probability of 1/2 that the mass per unit volume will lie between 3/2 and 1. But then we might argue similarly in relation to the volume per unit mass of the alloy. We know that volume per unit mass will lie between 1/2 and 1; and accordingly, by reference to the principle of indifference, we might suppose that there is a probability of 1/2 that volume per unit mass will lie between 3/4 and 1. But that is to say that there is a probability of 1/2 that the mass per unit volume lies between 4/3 and 1, which disagrees with the result of our first application of the principle of indifference.[59]

This kind of example shows that the line of argument I have just developed in relation to the fine-tuning argument needs to be implemented rather cautiously. For instance, we might suppose not that in the absence of detailed background knowledge, a gravitational force of *x* is precisely as probable as a gravitational force of *y*, but only that these probabilities are roughly equivalent. The fine-tuning argument will still go through given this more cautious claim. But suppose it can be shown that even this response generates paradoxical conclusions. In that case, a further solution is available. We may review each of the ways of apportioning probabilities, according to the principle of indifference, and consider the probability of life in relation to each of these ways (looking in turn at expansion rate, and so on). We need not suppose that any one of these ways of allocating probabilities is privileged; it is enough to note that whichever approach we take, the probability of life on limited background knowledge will remain low. (I say this because whether we apply the principle of indifference in the first instance to differing gravitational forces, or expansion rates, or whatever, in each case it will appear that the probability of life is low.) In reply, it might be said: surely these paradoxes show that the whole framework proposed by the principle of indifference is at fault. But this reply, it seems to me, fails to engage with the strong theoretical basis of the principle: surely if two possibilities are closely alike (where this closeness is spelt out by means of examples like that of the square I gave just now), then there must be a strong presumption that their prior probabilities, on minimal background knowledge, cannot diverge too sharply.

I turn now to what is probably the most common naturalistic objection to the fine-tuning argument, an objection we have already reviewed in relation to Rolston's argument from complexity. It may be said: even if all of the above holds, at most it shows that *if* there is only one universe, then that universe is unlikely to be life-friendly on the hypothesis of naturalism. But why suppose there is only one universe? Nothing forbids us supposing that there are many universes, each with a different expansion rate, gravitational force, and so on. In that case, the existence of at least one life-friendly universe will even be likely, given a large enough set of universes. In other words, the hypothesis of many universes can have just as high a predictive power as the hypothesis of design; so if relative predictive power is the key measure of the relative overall probability of naturalism and the design hypothesis, then the design hypothesis has surely failed to make its case.

I have already noted a number of responses to this line of argument. Again, it is worth emphasising that this reply to the fine-tuning argument shares with the argument a willingness to shake off Humean reservations about probability judgements in relation to the universe as a whole, and accordingly a willingness to 'explain' the universe by introducing an ontology which reaches beyond this cosmos.[60] I also observed earlier that according to some commentators, this 'explanation' is really no explanation at all, because it fails to make our picture of reality any simpler. (On the contrary, it involves a vast multiplication of entities.) However, the notion of simplicity is of course slippery, and its relevance to theory construction holds not only in relation to the numbers of entities postulated, but also in regard to the elegance of the theory itself.[61]

In addition to these reservations, another is worth noting. The many-worlds hypothesis cannot be pushed too far, it seems, without calling into question inductive reasoning. After all, there is, we might suppose, a possible universe which resembles ours until the very moment when you read this sentence, but then degenerates into chaos. If we adopt the many-worlds hypothesis in a truly radical form by supposing that every possible universe is realised, then we will have no reason, it seems, for supposing that order will persist beyond the present moment. To avoid this difficulty, the many-worlds hypothesis could be framed more restrictively, so that it does not include universes of the kind that would threaten inductive reasoning. But then we might wonder, why is the hypothesis restricted in precisely this way? And hasn't the hypothesis come to seem rather ad hoc at this point?[62] In addition to these difficulties, we may recall again that the many-universes hypothesis, even in its restricted form, will lack the predictive power of the design hypothesis in relation to value-laden phenomena which are not reasonably regarded as necessary pre-conditions or concomitants of human life. And again, we might think of natural beauty as one such phenomenon.

So far, I have been considering a range of objections which bear specifically on the argument from fine-tuning and the argument from complexity. I shall now examine a number of more general objections to the design argument, objections which apply to the argument from beauty as surely as to the arguments we have examined in this chapter. A consideration of these objections will bring to a close our discussion of the argument from design.

For example, it may be said: often enough, presentations of the design argument concentrate on the relative predictive power of naturalism and the design hypothesis. But of course, this is not enough. For as Bayes' theorem indicates, the relative overall probability of two hypotheses on certain evidence concerns not only the relative predictive power of the hypotheses, but also their relative prior probability.[63] But how can we sensibly claim to know the prior probability of the hypothesis of design? We have already noted one line of response to this question. It may be said: the many-universes hypothesis (and other metaphysically adventurous versions of naturalism) also appear to proceed independently of any precise conception of the prior probability of the hypothesis being defended. But setting aside this *ad hominem* response, what else might be said on this question?

The claim that we cannot establish the relative prior probability of the hypotheses of naturalism and design is not obviously an embarrassment for the proponent of design. Indeed if we want to be thoroughly sceptical about these matters and say there is no such probability, then the consequence is surely that there is no way of overturning the greater predictive power of the design hypothesis by noting that it has a significantly lower prior probability, as compared with its naturalistic rival. Under these circumstances, the reasonable response is surely to be governed by the relative predictive power of the hypotheses. In general, if one hypothesis predicts the evidence much more readily than another, and if there is no reason to assign the first hypothesis a lower probability independently of the evidence, then we should consider the first hypothesis more likely overall. Indeed, reverting to the principle of indifference, in these circumstances, it is tempting to say that we should simply identify the prior probabilities of the two hypotheses, and accordingly suppose that their relative overall probability coincides with their relative predictive power.

Peter Forrest has raised another issue which is relevant here. It may be said: any attempt to estimate the relative overall probability of naturalism and the design hypothesis is forlorn, because there may be further ways of developing these hypotheses which we have not anticipated and which are crucial for a well-grounded understanding of their relative overall probability. Forrest takes this consideration to show that agnosticism remains a reasonable response to the debate between theist and naturalist: even if the theist can show that theism (or design) offers a better explanation of the phenomena, it is always open to an objector to suspend judgment on the issue, by drawing attention to the possibility (likelihood even) of an as yet unknown hypothesis. Thus Forrest writes: 'It is mere caution, not irrationality, to take seriously the possibility of as yet undiscovered explanations. Best explanation apologetics cannot, therefore, exclude agnosticism.'[64]

Of course, Forrest is not suggesting that it is *very likely* that there is some as yet unknown hypothesis which would *radically challenge* our present understanding of the relative explanatory force of theism and naturalism. In that case, agnosticism would presumably be the *only* rational response to these issues. (I am assuming that this new hypothesis might show that theism offers a significantly *better* understanding of the data than we had thought, perhaps for reasons that are quite different from those we have anticipated.) This cautionary note sits comfortably with the general drift of the argument in this book. As I noted in the Introduction, the aim of this work is to defend the rational permissibility, and not the rational obligatoriness, of the belief that the world's goodness is its reason for existence. Forrest's comments provide a further reason for thinking that the case I am developing will not imply that this belief is rationally obligatory. At the same time, since he is talking only of the possibility (and not the likelihood) of an as yet unknown hypothesis which will radically alter our understanding of these questions, Forrest's comments do not undermine our case, assuming that it is read simply as an argument for the rational *permissibility* of belief in design.

We have considered the objection that the prior probability of the design hypothesis is simply indeterminate, for example because the whole notion of a priori probabilities is confused. Another objection might accept the possibility of judgments of prior probability in this sort of context, but contend that the prior probability of design is low. For instance, an objector might reason as follows. We know that in general, the more specific a hypothesis, the lower its prior probability. For example, on minimal background knowledge, the probability that a figure is a square must be less than the probability that it is a rectangle (where being rectangular includes being square). Now the design hypothesis is surely a very specific hypothesis. Allowing the permissibility of postulating a transcendent intelligence of some sort, why suppose that this intelligence has, more exactly, the powers and disposition to produce a world such as ours? In other words, if the predictive power of the design hypothesis is to be reasonably high, we surely have to build into our description of the designer a whole set of assumptions, concerning the powers and intentions of the designer. And in this way we will make the hypothesis of design a highly specific hypothesis, and accordingly a hypothesis of low prior probability.

Richard Swinburne has offered a strikingly bold way of dealing with this question of the prior probability of design. He argues that while theism postulates an agent of a highly determinate character (omnipotent, perfectly good, and so on), nonetheless the theistic hypothesis remains of high prior probability on account of its simplicity. For example, the lack of any restriction on the designer's powers contributes to the simplicity of the supposition that there is a designer.[65] I suggest that powerful considerations can be adduced in support of Swinburne's approach on this point. However, I shall sketch out another line of reply to this objection, one which is consistent with Swinburne's argument, but does not depend upon it.[66]

The design hypothesis depends crucially on the assumption that there is no cause for surprise if a transcendent intelligence should seek to make a world which permits the development of life, sentience, and powers of conceptual thought. However, not all theories of the relationship between goodness and divinity will carry this implication. For instance, some accounts suggest that God's will arbitrarily defines the nature of goodness. On this view, a world devoid of life would have been better than one in which there are sentient agents (who live a life of reasonable contentment and perpetrate no moral evil), if only God had decreed as much. On this voluntarist hypothesis, there is no independent yardstick to fix the will of a designer. And therefore, whatever the designer (or at any rate, God) wills will be good, whether that be a lifeless world, or some other world. Accordingly, on the voluntarist hypothesis, while we may feel confident that a transcendent intelligence will make a 'good' world, we cannot predict that that world will be one which permits the emergence of life, sentience and so on. Thus, assuming the truth of voluntarism, the predictive power of the design hypothesis in relation to the existence of life, for example, will be low. So clearly, the design argument depends on some other, non-voluntaristic account of the relationship between the divine will and standards of goodness.

For the purposes of this discussion I shall simply assume that this radical version of divine voluntarism is mistaken. In this I am concurring with the majority report of the Christian tradition and recent commentary on these matters. It is worth noting in passing that in assuming that the divine will does not arbitrarily fix standards of goodness, we are not thereby committed to the view that God's will cannot define the nature of our obligations in various respects.[67] Granted the falsity of extreme versions of divine voluntarism, we can suppose that it is at least unsurprising if a transcendent intelligence (with the requisite powers) should be drawn to make a world which permits the development of life, sentience, and so on. This is above all true if we assume the truth of some version of moral or evaluative internalism (that is, assume that the recognition of a value is inherently motivating). However, even if we suppose that an agent can recognise what is good and yet fail to be moved by this recognition, there is surely no cause for surprise if an agent who recognises what is good should be motivated to act in accordance with this recognition, and should in fact act accordingly.

These considerations suggest that the design hypothesis does not have to be framed all that specifically (on a non-voluntarist view of goodness) in order to have a reasonable predictive power. What is crucial is that the designer should have the capacity to understand ideals of goodness, where these ideals are specified independently of its will. Granted that capacity, there is some reasonable prospect that such an agent will be drawn to bring about a world which permits the emergence of a succession of more complex material forms. To put the matter another way, the design hypothesis can treat the goodness of the world as an explanatory resource which is independent of any specification of the designer's will. By contrast naturalism will always struggle, I suggest, to accord the goodness of the world an independent explanatory role. For instance, the many-worlds hypothesis does not explain our world by reference to its goodness, but merely by reference to some larger tendency to ontological plenitude. Similarly, a single-cosmos version of the naturalistic hypothesis will not be able to understand the world's tendency to give rise to life in terms of the goodness of this outcome.

In turn, this suggests that the hypothesis of naturalism, in its various forms, cannot appeal to a consideration which places a check on our need to advance the design hypothesis in a thoroughly specific form. Again, the design hypothesis does not need to be proposed in a specific form to the extent that there is an inherent connection between the idea of a transcendent intelligence and the idea of an agent who will be motivated to bring about a good world. By contrast, whatever reality is metaphysically fundamental for naturalism, it will not be related to the existence of a value-generating world by means of such an inherent connection. Accordingly, naturalism must either suppose that reality in general is not characterised by a tendency towards value-generation (this is the approach of the many-worlds hypothesis, of course), or suppose that it is characterised by such a tendency where this fact is basically a mystery, rather than being explicable in terms of the goodness of various outcomes.

These remarks hardly constitute a full reply to the objection that the prior probability of design is low. But they suggest that the design hypothesis has one clear advantage over its naturalistic rivals in these matters. In general, we can trade off the predictive power of a hypothesis against its prior probability. By making the hypothesis more specific (by building more assumptions into it), we can raise its predictive power; but in doing this, we are liable to reduce its prior probability, as we have seen. The ability of the design hypothesis to treat the goodness of the world as an independent explanatory resource gives it an advantage over naturalism in relation to this trade-off. To be sure, a naturalistic hypothesis can have a high predictive power (in relation to the existence of a value-generating world) if we define it precisely enough, but only at the expense of significantly reducing its prior probability. By contrast, I have been suggesting, a relatively unspecific version of the design hypothesis can still have a reasonable predictive power, because of the inherent connection between the idea of a transcendent intelligence and the existence of a value-generating world.

Notwithstanding all this, suppose someone produces a good argument in support of the claim that the prior probability of the design hypothesis is low. Here, we might recall that in familiar situations in everyday life, we tend to place much more emphasis on predictive power than on prior probability. For instance, suppose I seem to see my brother across the street. Of course, this experience is readily predicted by the hypothesis that he is indeed across the street. Yet the prior probability of his being precisely there (rather than anywhere else) is surely very low. Even so, we take the predictive power in such a case as decisive. Perhaps this sort of example is not entirely apt, since it rests on perceptual experience, which is arguably governed by its own, distinctive epistemic considerations. Nonetheless, the example suggests that even if someone should show that the prior probability of the design hypothesis is low, its great predictive power might still render the hypothesis overall reasonable.[68]

I turn now to one final question of general relevance to the argument from design. I have been arguing that there is an inherent connection between the idea of a transcendent intelligence and the idea of design, and commending the hypothesis of design on this basis. But not all versions of the design argument appeal to the notion of a transcendent intelligence. For instance, John Leslie has argued that the world's goodness can be explained by supposing that evaluative ideals are of themselves (quite apart from any designer) causally efficacious. He identifies this approach with a longstanding philosophical tradition:

> Neoplatonism is today often expressed in such formulae as that God 'is not a being but the Power of Being'. On my interpretation, what such dark sayings say is that God *is the world's creative ethical requiredness* or, equivalently, that God *is the creatively effective ethical need that there should exist a (good) world.* The suggestion is that the ethical need for a universe or set of universes itself bears creative responsibility for that universe or set of universes.[69]

Clearly, this general approach shares the advantages of versions of the design argument which appeal to the notion of a transcendent intelligence. For on this approach too, the goodness of the world serves as an explanatory resource. I do not have any deep-seated objection to Leslie's rendition of the design argument. In fact, I think that in practice it will tend to converge with a personalistic theism. After all, if we grant that consciousness is a profound value, then we are likely to suppose that there is an ethical requirement that there be a supreme consciousness. So the question of whether Leslie's approach is right is perhaps more a matter of religious sensibility than a matter of ontology, since his ontology is likely to include both a set of causally efficacious ethical requirements and a transcendent intelligence.[70] In these circumstances, the question 'Is there a God?' becomes a question about which of these realities is appropriately considered divine. (Or it may even be that both have a claim to this title.) I shall discuss the rationale for ascriptions of divinity in Part IV, where I argue that we can rightly think of a personal God as Being Itself, and not merely as another individual existent. On this point too, the approach I am commending is closely aligned with the spirit of Leslie's account.

In this chapter I have been defending two versions of the design argument: a Rolstonian argument from complexity, and the argument from fine-tuning. The reader might be wondering how these arguments relate to each other. I have suggested that the fine-tuning argument sits comfortably with the argument from complexity in so far as both represent the world as a value generator, and both understand this tendency to value generation as written into the basic constitution of the material order. However, it might be thought that the fine-tuning argument renders the argument from complexity redundant. For instance, suppose we adopt a physicalist theory of the mind; and suppose we believe that once the cosmological conditions for life, as specified in the fine-tuning argument, are in place, then the broad direction of the evolutionary process thereafter is fixed. Given these assumptions, it seems that once we have accounted for the character of the cosmos at the time of the Big Bang, in the respects suggested by the fine-tuning argument, then we have accounted for the subsequent development of matter, and therefore the development of mind, which on this view is an entirely material phenomenon. And if that is so, then what remains for a Rolstonian kind of argument to explain?

I suggest that if we start from these assumptions, then the fine-tuning argument will indeed do all the work. However, the assumptions are not evidently true. For instance, if we are substance or property dualists, then establishing the requisite material conditions will not guarantee the mind's emergence. Moreover, it is by no means evident that a cosmos with the right expansion rate, the right forces, and so on, will inevitably generate life. Rolston himself inclines to the view that our universe will inevitably generate life (in so far as the dice are 'loaded'). But this may reflect other structural features of the universe, or facts about its initial state, in addition to those identified in the fine-tuning argument. So while the fine-tuning argument may be capable of doing all the work, I suggest that we are not in a position to know this. In these circumstances, Rolston's kind of argument retains an epistemic independence, and is therefore to be retained as a separate case within the armoury of the natural theologian.

Conclusions

The thought that there might be some sort of connection between emergent phenomena and the plausibility of theism is hardly novel. Indeed, a great deal of contemporary philosophy could be read as a sustained meditation on this general theme. In a reductionist vein, some philosophers have sought to refute the existence of such a connection by denying that there are any radically emergent phenomena; others have tried to break the connection by defending a non-reductionist account of the world which remains consistent with naturalism; and still others (a minority, including figures like Swinburne, Haldane, Rolston and Adams) have argued in support of the connection.[71] The discussion of this chapter is intended as a small contribution to this last school of thought.

Evidently, there are many ways of taking emergent phenomena as evidence for theism. In this discussion, I have considered two recent approaches, those of Swinburne and Haldane, and I have proposed that while their arguments are suggestive, they can perhaps be strengthened, either by addressing rather different questions, or by adopting a rather more generous (and, I think, more plausible) understanding of the causal powers of the physical universe. More exactly, I have suggested that Swinburne's approach may be strengthened by asking not so much why the regular correlations between brain states and qualia take the particular form they do, but rather: why are there qualia at all? And I have suggested that Haldane's approach may be stronger if we suppose that the difficulty for naturalism resides not in the fact that the natural order is punctuated by 'miracles' (events which cannot be explained in terms of the operation of secondary causes), but in the fact that the natural order proves to be so productive of evaluatively rich phenomena.

In short, I have argued that the predictive power of the design hypothesis is greater than that of naturalism in relation to the phenomena of life, sentience and concept use, because naturalism would be unembarrassed by the non-existence of all of these phenomena, whereas the design hypothesis seems to make their existence at least unsurprising. I have supplemented this Rolstonian case by drawing on recent work in cosmology, which suggests that the emergence of life, and in turn therefore of sentience and powers of conceptual thought, requires a precise set of cosmological conditions, which are unlikely therefore to have arisen on a one-off basis merely by chance.

In the course of these first two chapters, I have been arguing that some of the most striking features of the world, notably its beauty and its propensity to generate more complex material structures, leading eventually to sentience and conceptual thought, are readily understood in terms of the framework of design, and not readily understood otherwise. On this understanding, the goodness of the world is to be given an explanatory significance: the world is as it is because it is good that it should be so. But of course, this understanding of the world's character lends itself to the charge of partiality: surely we have only examined one half of the case so far. What about the many phenomena which seem indifferent to the generation or preservation of value? This question provides our subject matter in the next two chapters.

Part II

Disvalues and the goodness of the world

3 Providence and evil

Introduction

In Part I, I have argued that the goodness of the world in various respects should be seen as its *raison d'être.* The principal challenge to this line of argument rests, of course, with the evident fact that the world seems to be productive not only of values but of disvalues. This challenge forms the subject matter of the next two chapters. In Chapter 3, I shall offer a general discussion of the 'problem of evil' and note various standard approaches to the question. Among the issues I would like to highlight in this discussion are the delicate relationship between certain theodicies and the argument from design, and the charge that the very attempt to provide a theodicy is spiritually unwholesome. In Chapter 4, I shall consider the problem of 'natural' evil. Here I argue that the holism and non-anthropocentrism of recent work in environmental ethics and ecology throw new light on the values and disvalues in nature and the relationship between them.

According to some commentators, the following propositions cannot (logically cannot) be jointly true:

1 There is a God.
2 God is omnipotent and omniscient.
3 God is perfectly good.
4 There is evil.

Evil it is said must indicate either that God does not care about the fate of creatures, so contradicting point (3), or cares but is unable to offer them any relief, so contradicting point (2). Other scholars have argued more moderately that while the propositions 'there is a God' and 'there is evil' may not be flatly contradictory, even so evil disconfirms theism in significant degree. Accordingly, we may distinguish between the 'logical' and 'evidential' forms of the problem of evil: the first maintains that God and evil cannot coexist, the second that they are unlikely to coexist. In turn therefore, there are two kinds of response to the problem of evil. A 'defence' offers a response to the logical problem; a 'theodicy' aims, in addition, to reply to the evidential problem. The proponent of design has good reason to be interested in the possibility of developing a theodicy, and not merely a defence: for the argument from design maintains that overall the world provides good evidence for theism (or at any rate, good evidence for design). Such an argument seeks to establish rather more than the thought that the world's character is consistent in principle with the reality of God. So I shall consider the problem of evil with a view to seeing whether it is possible to provide a theodicy. I should note that on my understanding a theodicy is not necessarily an attempt to give the reasons which God might have for tolerating various evils; it is simply an attempt to rebut the evidential form of the problem of evil.

I shall consider three ways of developing a theodicy. These approaches seem to me to constitute prima facie the most plausible lines of response available to the theodicist, and they have a particular interest for us because of their implications for the design argument. First of all, it may be said that a given evil, *E*, may be the logically necessary concomitant of a more than compensating good, or a logically necessary condition of the absence of an evil at least as great as *E*.[1] If that is so, then even an omnipotent God will have to tolerate *E*, if he or she is to achieve the good of which it is the logically necessary precondition, or avoid the evil whose non-existence is logically tied to the existence of *E*.[2] And, we might suppose, a good God would be justified in permitting *E*, in so far as the good which is thereby made possible is indeed more than compensating, or the evil which is thereby avoided is indeed at least as great.[3] (For ease of exposition, from here on, I shall omit the case where evils are said to be tolerated in order to ward off other evils, at least as great, and speak simply of the case where evils are said to be tolerated on account of the goods they make possible. It is this case which is of particular relevance for our discussion.) This is one way of trying to preserve the ideas of divine omnipotence and divine goodness in the face of evil. As I shall note, it is not without its difficulties.

A second line of reply might uphold the idea of divine goodness while maintaining that God's purposes (concerning, for example, the greater goods which various evils make possible) are in large part inscrutable to us. Of course, if this claim were merely asserted it might seem no more than an ad hoc manoeuvre to accommodate the existence of evil. But in fact, there are good reasons to suppose that the inscrutability of God's purposes is anyway a part of the theistic scheme, quite apart from what may need to be said in order to render theism consistent with evil. For if God is omniscient, or similarly if our relationship to God is modelled on the relationship of child to parent (the dominant image in the Christian tradition), then it is only to be expected that God's projects in creation will in many respects transcend human understanding.[4] We do not expect a small child to understand why her parents should sometimes expose her to trial and frustration; even so, the child is justified, we feel, in continuing to trust her parents. How much less should we expect human beings to grasp the purposes of God, the theodicist will urge. And how rash we would be, therefore, to take the afflictions of human life as a token of divine indifference. At any rate, so it might be, and has been, argued.

The first of the replies I have sketched amounts in a way to a questioning of the fourth premise in our initial statement of the problem of evil. Of course, advocates of this approach will not generally deny there is evil, but they maintain that evil when considered in a broader context contributes to good, and therefore has no tendency to impugn God's goodness. The second response in a way questions the third premise. It is said: yes, of course God is perfectly good, but we must recognise that, from our limited, finite vantage point, we cannot fully understand what perfect goodness in a creator would amount to, in part because there are some values we simply fail to recognise, and in part we cannot grasp all of the ways in which evils may serve as the logically necessary preconditions of the values which we do recognise. For this reason, it might be said, the existence in some degree of unintelligible evil (evil which cannot be understood – at least not by us – in terms of the compensating goods idea) has no tendency to disconfirm the theistic hypothesis. Indeed, on this view, the presence in some measure of unintelligible evil constitutes, paradoxically, a confirmation of theism; for a world without such evil would be comprehensible in moral terms to human beings, and we have reason to think that a world which derives from an omniscient creator God will lack this sort of transparency to human reason.

A third response might seek to question the second premise, and the idea that God is omnipotent. It might be said that what matters for religious purposes (what figures in the Christian creeds for example) is the idea that God is almighty, where almightiness implies holding sway over the destiny of all creatures, rather than being able to do absolutely any logically conceivable thing (consistent with being divine).[5] Almightiness, it may be said, is sufficient for salvation, and is therefore sufficient for the sort of trust that the faithful place in God. On this view, it may be that God is bound to tolerate certain evils as a precondition of realising various more than compensating goods where the precondition is not one of logical necessity, but reflects some contingent constraint on God's powers.

Each of these three responses clearly engages with the issue. However, they all face difficulties, and the natural theologian may have good reason to discard one or more of them altogether. The first response, according to which evils are the logically necessary concomitants of more than compensating goods, where the goods in question are identifiable by human beings from their current vantage point, suffers from a number of deficiencies. First of all, it offends against the thought, expressed in our second response, that human beings should not expect to achieve a God's-eye view of creation, from which the harmony between world and divine purpose is clearly apparent. If we think we have attained such a viewpoint, then something must have gone wrong. More fundamentally, such an approach may appear to contradict the religious perspective on the world which it is allegedly trying to uphold. Thus some believers have felt that the whole project of trying to identify the goods which various evils make possible is impious, for it implies that we should look to God for some sort of pay-off in exchange for evils undergone. Would not a properly religious attitude be one of acceptance, rather than one of 'bargaining' (epistemically) with God, or of testing the divine goodness? Any presentation of this first sort of theodicy will need at some point to address this issue. Moreover, while we might suppose that God would tolerate a given evil only on condition that it makes possible some more than compensating good, the mere fact that an evil does make possible such a good need not imply that permitting the evil (let alone bringing it about) is justified, assuming we adopt some non-consequentialist understanding of moral justification. Indeed, on such an understanding, some evils may be unacceptable no matter how much good they make possible. On this view, the thought that a given evil makes possible a more than compensating good may be a necessary condition of God's permitting the evil, but will not be a sufficient condition. And in that case, a theodicy of this first type will still have some work to do even if it should succeed in showing that a given evil makes possible a good which is more than compensating.

The second kind of response must also be pursued with caution.

Above all this is true for the natural theologian who wishes to propound an argument from design. For the design argument depends on the thought that, in certain fundamental respects, the divine purposes are indeed open to human view. Hence the proponent of design can hardly offer unqualified support for a doctrine of divine inscrutability. Moreover, while an uncompromising form of this second kind of response would put an end to the problem of evil at a stroke, it would also deny any affinity between our human conception of goodness and the divine conception, and at that point human experience itself must be judged of dubious worth, if indeed it is so bereft of any insight into the real value of things. So this response must be adopted only reservedly not only by advocates of the design argument, but by anyone who wishes to uphold (as theists surely must) the fundamental point of human life and human projects. The third kind of response must also be entertained with moderation. Of course, theists often maintain that God is essentially omnipotent. But even allowing the admissibility in principle of this third response, the theodicist must take care not to carry the qualification of divine power too far, or we shall be left with no God at all, but merely another individual confined like ourselves within an overarching order of events. Moreover, this third approach seems likely to undermine the second: if we limit God's powers (and knowledge), and thereby qualify the transcendence or otherness of God, then the inscrutability response will be weakened.

So it is evident that the task of constructing a theodicy is likely to be a rather complicated one, even supposing that the theodicist is not required to specify in every case the morally sufficient reasons which God might have for permitting various evils. Providing a theodicy will be a matter of picking out ideas from the various responses we have noted with careful attention to invoke each in due measure, and in such a way as to secure overall consistency. The responses which make appeal to divine inscrutability and limits on divine power seem to me to have a sort of residual role here. It seems natural to press our understanding as far as it will go, by seeing what sense we can make of the various evils we encounter (by reference to the goods which they make possible), and then to attribute whatever evils remain to be understood in this way either to a deficiency in our understanding or to a deficiency in divine power. Of course, such a project might fail: we might find that the residual evils are so large as to require radical human ignorance of the divine purposes, or radical deficiencies in divine power. In that case, we would need to conclude that so far as we can tell, evils of the kinds and on the scale that we find in the world undermine theism to a significant degree, and perhaps decisively.

How good is good enough?

If this is the right way to approach the task of constructing a theodicy, then we should begin our discussion with the first of the responses I have distinguished, and then proceed to the others. There is a large literature purporting to identify the connections between various evils and the goods which they allegedly make possible. Rather than rehearsing this sort of material, I want to pose a question which is of central importance if we are to understand the final significance of any such attempt to relate evils and goods. Granted that there are some integral wholes of this kind comprising good–and–evil, we need to ask: how good does such a whole have to be overall if it is to be consistent with the purposes of a beneficent God?[6]

The details of a theodicist's approach will usually disclose her stance on this matter, even if this view is not articulated explicitly. For instance, it is sometimes asked why God should have made human beings with a capacity to choose wrongly, and to inflict serious harms thereby. And in reply it is standardly said that if we compare these two states of affairs we can see that the second is better:

1 Human beings always choose what is good, because it is predetermined (by the God who made them) that they shall not choose evil.
2 Human beings have the freedom to do wrong, and sometimes exercise this capacity, at considerable cost to themselves and others.

Here we find two integral wholes being compared with each other, one consisting of limited or perhaps no human freedom and an absence of moral evil, and the other consisting of extended human freedom and various abuses of that freedom. (Moral evil here is evil which consists in or can ultimately be traced to wrong human choice.) In the development of such a theodicy (or defence), it will be stressed of course that even an omnipotent God cannot secure the good of significant human freedom (understood as a libertarian freedom to bring about serious evil) without running the risk of that freedom being abused: hence (2) here identifies an integral whole, where the evil is logically bound up with the good. What is striking about this sort of exchange, familiar from the literature on the problem of evil, is the apparent assumption that the second integral whole is consistent with God's goodness only if it can be shown to be *better than* its alternative.[7]

We might suspect that theodicists who argue in this fashion are trying to prove more than is really necessary. When arguing so, the theodicist does not merely claim that a world comprising significant freedom and moral evil is (other things being equal) good, but that it is better than alternative types of world, namely those containing no freedom at all (where all choices are good), or freedom that is limited to the making of good choices. This sort of approach to theodicy sits somewhat uneasily with the thought that there is (according to believers) a world radically better in kind than ours, namely heaven; and it leaves one wondering about the goodness of divine freedom, which as traditionally represented does not include the freedom to choose evil. However, these are only reasons for showing some initial scepticism towards this sort of account. What I want to do now is to argue at greater length that this approach does indeed try to prove more than is necessary. But before doing that, I shall cite some further examples of the sort of theodicy I have in mind, because I want to persuade you that I am not out to criticise a straw man.

We might begin by considering John Hick's now classic 'soul-making' theodicy. Hick proposes that 'natural evils' (evils which are not moral evils) have a part to play in promoting the moral and spiritual development of human beings. According to Hick, there is a problem here to do with the fact that God could have created human beings in a state of moral and spiritual perfection from the beginning. Thus he writes:

> But if God could, without logical contradiction, have created human beings as wholly good free beings, why did he not do so? Why was humanity not initially created in possession of all the virtues, instead of having to acquire them through the long hard struggle of life as we know it? The answer, I suggest, appeals to the principle that virtues which have been formed within the agent as a hard-won deposit of his own right decisions in situations of challenge and temptation, are intrinsically *more valuable* than virtues created within him ready made and without any effort on his own part.[8]

Here we find Hick wondering why human beings should have been made morally imperfect or morally immature. And he clearly feels it necessary to show not merely that existence in a state of moral immaturity (with the possibility of moral growth) is good, but that such a state is better ('more valuable') than its alternatives, and in particular better than a state of moral maturity which is not the result of some process of moral maturation. Again, one wonders about the consistency of this claim with standard representations of God, whose goodness presumably is not the result of some such process of development. But more importantly, here again we find a rather ambitious conception of what the theodicist needs to establish. On this view, it is not enough to show that our world in a given respect is overall good. It is also necessary to show that a world of this type is preferable to worlds of other types. I do not say that Hick wishes to show that our world is the best possible, since presumably on his view human beings might (conceivably) have matured morally without the many catastrophic choices which in fact litter human history. But he does seem concerned to show that this world is of the best possible type, in so far as it is an instance of the type of world which allows for spiritual growth from an initial state of moral immaturity.

Hick appears to argue in the same sort of way in other connections. For instance, he suggests that the epistemic distance of creatures from God (that is, their inability to know certainly that there is a God) is a condition of their free growth into spiritual maturity (a growth which is not coerced by an overwhelming sense of the divine presence); and free growth into spiritual maturity when it culminates in certain knowledge of God is *better than* having certain knowledge from the start.[9] Again, we might wonder whether it would be enough for the theodicist to show that epistemic distance is a good, when it includes the possibility of a growth in knowledge. Why think it necessary to establish in addition that a world which involves epistemic distance is better than other kinds of world?

Critics of theodicy also seem to share this assumption about what needs to be shown, though here too the assumption often remains tacit. For instance, David Hume notes 'the great frugality with which all powers and faculties are distributed to every particular being' in the world, and he suggests that 'an indulgent parent would have bestowed a large stock to guard against accidents'.[10] Here again the assumption seems to be that the superiority of the latter state (the having of a large stock of powers and faculties) is enough to establish that a good God would have brought it about in preference to the first. Admittedly, Hume does supply some justification for this thought (the idea that the Christian God would be an 'indulgent' parent). But in these remarks, he too appears to subscribe to the principle we have noted in Hick: if a given state of affairs is to be consistent with the goodness of God, it is not enough that it should be overall good; it is also necessary that, in terms of general type, it should be superior to its alternatives.

Before proceeding to my own critique of this principle, I note one other argument in the literature which purports to establish its mistakenness. George Schlesinger suggests that the notion of the best, or even *a* best, possible world is incoherent: there is nothing, he proposes, which could answer to this notion.[11] This seems plausible. We might suppose for example that any candidate for the title of best possible world could be improved by the addition of one further sentient being which enjoys a life of reasonable contentment without detracting from the well-being of its fellows.[12] Schlesinger goes on to argue that we may therefore reply to Hume's kind of argument along these lines. The mere fact that the world could be improved upon in the respect indicated (by substituting liberality for frugality) is not enough to show that it could not derive from a beneficent deity. For a charge of the same kind could be laid against any world, in so far as all worlds are open to improvement. And in that case, if the argument is enough to establish that a God ought not to create our world, it will also be enough to establish that a God ought not to create at all. But this seems unreasonable: surely there are some worlds which would be fitting objects of divine creation (which is not to say, of course, that God has an overriding reason to create)?

However, the atheologian need not frame the problem of evil in this way. She may well prefer to say: granted that any world can be improved (for there is no best possible world), none the less we would expect any world which has God as its creator to meet certain minimum standards; and our world fails to meet those standards. Clearly, this way of setting out the problem does not carry the implication that God ought not to create at all. This question of the minimum standards which must be satisfied by the world, if it is to be consistent with the goodness of God, is the issue I want to take up in the following discussion.

I suggest then that *in practice* the first of our three approaches to theodicy often involves more than an attempt to show that various evils are the logically necessary preconditions of more than compensating goods; it involves in addition an attempt to show that these evils and the integral wholes to which they contribute form part of the best possible kind of world. I want now to argue that such an approach is needlessly ambitious, and imposes an unnecessary burden of proof upon the theodicist. Given our general strategy, it is important to be clear on this point. For our assessment of what the theodicist needs to show in relation to the various integral wholes which feature in this first type of theodicy will, of course, make a difference to our estimation of which evils remain to be understood in terms of the ideas of divine inscrutability and deficiency of divine power.

In approaching our topic, I shall draw upon the theory of social justice propounded by John Rawls. In brief, Rawls proposes that we may assess the justice of a social system by adopting what he calls the 'original position'.[13] To adopt the original position, we have to imagine ourselves comparing a given social system with various other such systems, while supposing that we do not know which particular social role we would play in any of these societies were they to be actualised, and do not know the endowments of character, intelligence and so on, which we would have in any of these cases. If a given system might have been chosen in a free and informed way from behind such a 'veil of ignorance', Rawls suggests, then we may suppose that it is just. The point of the 'veil of ignorance' device is, of course, to suggest a way of assessing questions of justice which prescinds from the particularities of one's own situation, so that one considers the issues simply as a rational agent, without allowing any self-interested concern to distort one's perception of what would be best.

Now, by extension, we might envisage an original position where it is not merely the social system that is up for choice, but the more general character of our world. Thus we may envisage choosing between worlds with different sets of natural laws, or worlds where human beings have different ranges of natural endowment, and so on. Of course, in constructing a theory of social justice, there is no point in treating these further factors as variables, in so far as it lies beyond our power to make any difference to the human situation in these respects. However, if we are addressing the problem of evil, and wondering not so much about which social arrangements may be compatible with a human justice, but rather about which worlds may be compatible with a divine justice, then we may well wish to generalise Rawls's proposal in this sort of way.[14]

Of course, Rawls's proposals have proved controversial. However, my intention here is simply to draw on the notion of an original position. This notion seems to me to capture rather well our sense that social justice depends upon treating the interests of other people as seriously as our own; of course, the point of the original position idea is to suggest a vantage point upon human society from which we cannot distinguish between 'our' interests and 'theirs'. There seems to be enough of a consensus about the relevance of this sort of idea to questions of social justice to ensure that a Rawlsian approach to the problem of divine justice, when it is implemented in this general way, is unlikely to provoke objections simply on grounds of method.

So the question we need to consider is this: could a world such as ours be the object of rational choice in the original position (where the choice is radicalised in the way I have indicated, so that it includes worlds of varying natural laws, and so on)? If we feel able to answer 'yes', then we have some reason to grant that our world is compatible with a divine justice since it could have been chosen by its inhabitants in an informed way, and without regard to their own interests at the expense of those of others. Now the answer we give to this question will depend of course upon the scope of our choice. Given the opportunity to inhabit only one world, I should presumably choose to inhabit the best of the various worlds open to me (or one of the best, in the case where several worlds are jointly best). But given the opportunity to inhabit several worlds successively, it is far from clear that I should choose only worlds of the best kind. On the contrary, in this case, I would surely have some reason to inhabit other kinds of world, which offer rather different kinds of experience from those available in the best kind of world, and which would thereby enrich my life overall. In short, once we relax the assumption of being able to inhabit only one world, then the notion that only a world of the best kind can be an object of rational choice begins to look doubtful. If that is so, then the assumption which we have found embedded in the theodicies of Hick and others will also be open to question.

Before pursuing this idea further it is worth recalling that in general monotheists have believed that there is a life after this one; so the supposition that this world is not the only theatre of human experience is anyway an integral part of monotheistic faith in its traditional forms. Of course, this is of no concern to the natural theologian *qua* natural theologian, but it is significant given the proper concern of natural theology to throw some light on patterns of belief which are practically speaking available to people, rather than providing a merely possible account of the nature of things. It is true that the traditional monotheistic scheme does not use the idea of a succession of future lives, by contrast with the reincarnational approach favoured by eastern faiths. However, if the afterlife is said to be in time, then it will presumably offer an infinite extension of our present experience; and even if not in time, it is presumably held to involve a rich extension of our experience in this life.

Moreover, the idea of a further life also holds some plausibility from the perspective of natural theology - and not merely because of the possible role of such an idea in constructing a theodicy. More fundamentally, such an idea seems a natural extension of the thought that the world's maker relates to his or her creatures providentially; and this thought is implicit in various natural theological arguments, including the argument from design. So I suggest that the hypothesis of further human experience beyond the bounds of this life is likely to have a reasonably secure place within the theistic scheme, whether that scheme draws upon 'revelation' or upon natural theological considerations. If that is right, then the notion of an original position which comprises a rich set of possibilities for experience seems to be one which theists can legitimately use, without facing the charge of artificially and over-elaborately extending their basic hypothesis in order to accommodate counter-evidence. For ease of exposition, I shall continue to talk of choosing from worlds, allowing that this way of talking can be translated back into a more strictly theistic scheme for the reasons we have noted.

In order to appreciate the full implications of this understanding of the original position framework, let us take the notion of an unrestricted choice of experience to its limit. Suppose then that I can choose from worlds which are infinite in number and variety, and am given the opportunity of inhabiting successively as many of these worlds as I like. In that case, we might think, it would be rational for me (not rationally obligatory perhaps, but rationally permissible) to choose at least some worlds whose integral wholes are in at least some cases only just better than not. (Again, an integral whole will comprise evils and goods where the evils are the logically necessary preconditions of the goods.) After all, an integral whole which is only just better than not will still contribute something to my well being, and under conditions of unrestricted choice, the choice of such a whole will in no way detract from my ability to enjoy further integral wholes which offer a more significant surplus of good over bad.

I conclude then that there are reasons for doubting whether our first kind of theodicy requires the sort of assumption which seems to figure in many presentations of it. For instance, it is by no means evident that a theodicy needs to show that the integral whole which comprises significant-freedom-and-moral-evil is better than the whole which comprises limited-freedom-and-no-moral-evil, or that the whole which comprises initial-moral-immaturity-and-subsequent-growth-into-maturity is better than the whole which comprises initial-and-enduring-moral-maturity. In fact, given that there are reasons in natural and revealed theology for thinking that the afterlife experiences of human beings (however they are conceived in detail) will be rich in variety and extent, the presumption must surely be that a theodicy needs only to establish that a given integral whole is better than not.

We could cite a parallel from economics here. Given an average income, I will need to exercise some care in my choice of purchases; in the normal case, I will want to be sure that any significant item of expenditure will benefit me (or others) quite considerably. But in the absence of any financial constraints, I will have good reason to make any purchase providing that it contributes something overall (however little) to my well-being. In the language of economists, monetary cost only represents a real cost if the spending of money carries an opportunity cost (in other words, if the spending of money restricts my opportunities for future consumption); it follows that if expenditure carries no opportunity cost, then I might as well purchase anything which yields some net benefit, however small. Analogously, if I can inhabit as many worlds as I like – in other words, if my choice of worlds carries no opportunity cost – then I will have adequate reason to choose a world (or at any rate an integral whole) on condition that it contributes something to my well-being overall. It is worth noting that on this general approach, the goods which are needed to compensate for various evils may in principle belong to some *future* life. This suggests that the theodicist may not need to identify a given integral whole simply by reference to the character of our present world. However, for ease of exposition, I shall generally abstract from this possibility in what follows.

I want next to consider some objections to this understanding of what a theodicy needs to establish. One issue which may give theists reason to show some caution in adopting the idea of limitless possibilities for further experience relates to the thought that the meaning of our lives actually depends upon their temporal finitude. Analogously, if someone were to have an infinite stock of money, their choices regarding expenditure would carry no significance, for they could not buy the wrong (or conversely, the right) things; or more exactly, they could not buy the wrong thing in the sense of restricting (for purely monetary reasons) their opportunities for future consumption. The theodicist can accommodate this point most simply by upholding the idea of an extended – not altogether unbounded – range of possibilities for future experience (allowing that such experience may still be temporally infinite). This idea seems to be enough to generate the conclusion that at least some evils (and perhaps many, depending on the details of the case) will be compatible with the justice of God in the case where they contribute to integral wholes which are only just better than not. For granted a restricted but still extensive range of integral wholes from which to choose in the original position, a person may have enough reason (not necessarily a compelling reason) to choose some wholes which are only just better than not, in so far as these wholes will contribute to the overall richness of a life. Notice also that in the ordinary theistic scheme, heaven is said to be a radically different (because radically better) 'place' than this world. This suggests that the afterlife envisaged by theists will not significantly undermine the meaning of our choices in this world, since the choices available in such a radically different life will presumably be of a correspondingly different kind.

A second objection might maintain that this general approach makes resolving the problem of evil if anything too easy for the theist's own good. It may be said: surely such an approach will render so many worlds consistent with a divine justice that the basis of theistic belief will be weakened in other respects. In particular, it may be alleged, the argument from design will be undermined, for that argument depends on the assumption that certain outcomes are more likely if there is a God than if not; and this assumption will be in question if we can reconcile too great a range of possibilities with the divine goodness. To put the matter briefly, too successful a theodicy may well damage the predictive power of the design hypothesis.

For example, someone might reason as follows: 'If I have good reason to choose any world which is simply better than not (or more exactly, any world each of whose evils is subsumed within an integral whole which is better than not), then why should I not choose a world which is largely devoid of natural beauty? Of course, other things being equal, a world of this kind would be inferior to a beautiful world, but according to the theodicy under discussion, any world which is better than not is a possible object of rational choice.' The proponent of design can offer a simple reply to this line of reflection by noting that it will not apply to any feature of the world which is a necessary condition of human life. Even if I have reason to choose to inhabit a world which is aesthetically unappealing, in the nature of the case I cannot have reason to choose a world which I cannot inhabit: such a world falls outside the scope of my choice. Hence the arguments from life, sentience and concept use, which we considered in Chapter 2, are undisturbed by this objection.[15] Moreover, the theodicist might maintain that while an unattractive world may be compatible with the divine goodness, it remains less likely on the design hypothesis than otherwise. If we grant Tennant's suggestion that an unattractive world is overwhelmingly likely in the absence of design, then this suggestion will follow directly. (However, I am inclined to think that Tennant's proposal needs to make certain concessions to the sociobiological perspective.) Or again, we might note that a designer presumably has more reason to create attractive worlds than unattractive worlds; so that if a designer makes many worlds, there are likely to be more examples of the first kind of world. So even on the assumption of limitless possibilities for future experience, there remains some presumption that, on the theistic scheme, we are more likely to find ourselves in an attractive than an unattractive world.

However, while this reply may help to preserve the force of the argument we examined in Chapter 1, it may also make the supposition of no opportunity cost less effective as a response to the evidential form of the problem of evil. For the reply concedes that even if certain evils (or flaws such as unattractiveness) are compatible with the theistic scheme, they may be rather unlikely on that scheme. The theodicist can respond to this challenge by invoking the distinction between these two claims:

1 Any given integral whole is likely to prove significantly better than not.
2 Every integral whole is likely to prove significantly better than not.

Even if the theistic scheme implies (1), it seems it does not imply (2). And as long as there remains some reasonable prospect of at least some integral wholes proving to be only just better than not, given the truth of theism, the general strategy we have been considering will remain relevant as a critique of the tendency we have noted in the writings of Hick and others, in so far as they assume that in every case the theodicist should aim to establish that an integral whole is better than its alternatives in terms of general type.

So far I have been concerned simply with the issue of how good an integral whole should be if it is to be consistent with the goodness of God. I have not claimed that the world satisfies this condition, whatever it may be, but simply that philosophers of religion regularly impose upon the theodicist needlessly high standards of proof. Next, I want to extend this approach by looking at one example of an integral whole.

An example of the integral whole approach

Standard formulations of our first kind of theodicy appeal to the connections between evils and, for instance, significant human freedom, or the potentiality for moral growth. In this section, I shall argue that another approach is possible, where evils are seen to make possible a more fundamental kind of good, namely the good of our existing at all. This approach will offer a further perspective on the question of how good an integral whole must be if it is to be consistent with the purposes of a benevolent God.

My discussion of the original position idea takes for granted the conceivability of our existing in another, better world. However, given the close connection between our experience and the sort of people we are, it seems we should say that we, as the people we concretely are, are part and parcel of this world. Think for instance of how difficult it is to imagine replicating a particular individual, considered concretely, in a different historical epoch from their own. Someone born in our time with the genes of a Thomas More or a Catherine of Siena would surely be radically different from their historical counterpart in terms of personality and commitments. This reflects, I suggest, a conceptual truth, about the relation between experience and personal identity considered concretely. But if it is difficult to conceive of replicating an individual, considered concretely, in a later historical epoch within this world, how much more difficult would it be to replicate ourselves, considered concretely, in another, radically different world, and in particular in a world devoid of the pervasive and profound evils of our own world. Considering that the people we love are not just bundles of genes, but concrete individuals, this thought is a powerful one, I suggest. It invites us to think that in so far as we can discern the meaning of evil, which is perhaps not very far, its meaning has to do, at least in part, with the making possible of certain forms of life, or equally of certain individuals considered concretely. If that is so, then we can begin perhaps to see how evil could in a paradoxical way betoken the presence of a radically generative love, which affirms persons in the sense of giving them existence. To put the point briefly, I am suggesting that our vulnerability to hurt, sickness and to death (in short, our vulnerability to evil) so deeply conditions our relations to one another and to our surroundings that a world without these things would be a world in which human life, considered concretely, would not be possible.

Robert Adams has argued that evils may plausibly be regarded as the metaphysically necessary conditions of our existence, in so far as they make a difference historically to the 'combinations of . . . people and marriages' which arise, and thereby a difference in terms of which people are born.[16] On this view, evidently, personal identity is tied in a broadly logical way to an individual's genetic make-up. Adams' suggestion offers another way of developing the thought that there is a logically binding connection between evils and our very existence. However, this strategy is vulnerable to the apparent fact that even if my existence is logically conditional upon the union of the very sperm and egg that in fact gave rise to my beginning, God could still have brought about my existence independently of evil, by creating that sperm and egg miraculously, so circumventing any need for the causal history which in fact preceded their coming to be. To this it may be replied that while God could of course create a sperm and egg of the same type independently of the causal history of the world, this is not to say that God could create that very sperm and egg without the prior history of the world. To meet this difficulty, we might suppose more exactly that God could have allowed cosmic history to take its course until 'Adam and Eve' (or whoever the first human beings may be) appeared. He could then miraculously have removed appropriate sperm and eggs from them and miraculously have caused them to be united, and so on for further generations, in such a way as to bring into being the very individuals who have in fact come to be. On this scenario, it seems we do have some reason to suppose that it is the very individuals who have existed in our world who would come to be, and not merely individuals like them.[17]

Keith Yandell is another philosopher who has appealed to the connection between evils and the conditions of personal identity in an attempt to address the problem of evil. He makes use of the following principle:

> (A) Were a person not to have faced the moral situations and virtue circumstances that in fact she faced, she literally would have been a different person – not the same person with a different character, but another person.[18]

Yandell offers two readings of (A). According to one reading, one's 'participation' in morally significant situations determines the person one is; according to the other, it is one's particular response to such situations which determines the person one is. From (A), read in either of these ways, it follows, Yandell suggests, that 'if one is grateful that a loved one was the person she was, one cannot consistently bemoan her having faced the evils she faced'.[19] Yandell also notes that an argument of this general form remains persuasive, as a response to the problem of evil, even if we adopt a less radical thesis, according to which one's response to evils fixes not one's identity, but one's character.

I am inclined to side here with Adams in supposing that the metaphysical conditions of a person's identity are tied to their beginnings, rather than to what happens to them or what they do subsequently. However, as Yandell suggests, it doesn't especially matter what line we take on this issue, in the present context, providing that some connection (of a broadly logical kind) is granted between evil and a person's identity or character, and providing that identity or character are deemed significant. Moreover, once we adopt this general approach, we should not be confined, I suggest, to the character of a person considered from a moral point of view. We should also bring into the reckoning a person's aesthetic preferences, sense of humour, and so on: in other words, all those features of the personality which seem significant for who the person, considered concretely, is. To this extent, I want to endorse Yandell's position, but at the same time to broaden it, so that non-moral features of the person are also given due weight.

There is, I suggest, no general rule which we can adopt here, in order to identify which features of a person's concrete identity are significant. Plainly some are not. For instance, in general it matters little whether I am woken by the alarm at 7.00 or at 7.01 in the morning (although of course there are circumstances where even this sort of difference would matter). Let us say that a person's concrete* identity comprises those features of her concrete identity which matter deeply for who she is. Now there is good reason to think that evils of the kind that figure in formulations of the problem of evil make a difference to people's concrete* identities. For instance, suppose that God makes a world without these evils, and populates that world with the very individuals who have existed in this world (allowing that this is possible, *pace* Adams), and suppose that in every other respect the conditions of our world are reproduced in this further world (suppose for instance that the same individuals get to know one another, assuming again that this is possible). In such a world, human beings will not be hurt or frustrated by one another, or by 'natural' evil; so in such a world, questions of morality will have no place (or at any rate, their place will be profoundly different). Given the importance of a person's moral stance in defining who they are, considered concretely, we might conclude that none of the individuals in our world would remain the same concretely* in this further world.

Later in his paper, Adams draws attention to the role of considerations of this kind. For instance, he recalls the story of Helen Keller and writes that:

> Her actual life – in its emotional as well as its sensory qualities, in its skills and projects, and doubtless in much of her personality and character – was built around the fact of her blindness and deafness . . . Her never having been blind or deaf would have been very like her never having existed. Why should she wish for that, given that she had reason to be glad she existed?[20]

To put the matter in our terms, Helen's experience of the world was so profoundly conditioned by certain evils in her personal history that in the absence of those evils her existence, considered concretely*, would not have been possible. This example offers a particularly striking illustration of how evils may be the logically necessary preconditions of a certain individual considered concretely*. However, a world in which evil is prevalent is also relevant to the concrete* identity of individuals who have suffered no great evil, whether themselves or in relation to those who are close to them. For instance, the acknowledged possibility of a life being cut short by natural evil is enough to condition one's attitudes towards one's own life and that of others profoundly, and thereby to shape who one is concretely* even if one has no firsthand experience of such evils, in relation to oneself or loved ones.

Adams also notes, rightly I think, that it may only be possible to accept certain evils as a condition of one's concrete* existence retrospectively. In other words, it may only be after a new concrete* identity has arisen, through having new experiences, and forming new friendships and projects, that one can accept the initial evils as an integral part of who one is concretely*. As Adams observes, this consideration offers the theist a reply to the evident fact that not all people can feel glad about their existence during the course of this life. Here the theist may appeal to the possibility of an eschatological vantage point upon one's sufferings, from which perspective they may seem to be acceptable as an integral part of one's concrete* identity.[21]

If we are persuaded by the idea that there are integral wholes of this kind (where the pervasive evils of our world are related to the good which consists in human life considered concretely*), then a number of consequences follow. First of all, this approach has a bearing on the question of whether theism implies that in general it will be possible to subsume evils within integral wholes which are significantly better than not. If we allow that our existence as the concrete* individuals we are is integrally tied to the existence of various evils, and that the resultant integral wholes are for all we know only just better than not, and if each of us supposes (as each of us surely does) that God had adequate reason to make him or her, then we are committed to the view that, in at least some cases, an integral whole can be consistent with the goodness of God providing simply that it is better than not. Of course, the force of this sort of argument rests on our sense of the importance of the concrete* individuals whom we cherish, including ourselves. Given this sense, we surely do feel some temptation to say that if the bringing about of these concrete* individuals should turn upon the permitting of evils which are related to those individuals in integral wholes which are only just better than not, then the evils are indeed permissible (subject perhaps to the further condition that the balance of good over evil should be positive in relation to each individual). So this way of developing the first sort of theodicy can play a part in meeting an objection I noted earlier (drawing on a non-consequentialist approach to ethics); for it implies that the goods in this case are not only more than compensating, but also sufficient to justify the evil.[22]

Of course, this line of argument may leave us wondering, again, about the viability of the design argument. What if the existence of various concrete* individuals can be secured only through the creation of an unattractive world, for instance? Again, I suggest that a design argument of the fine-tuning variety is not compromised by this thought, while an argument in Tennant's style will retain some plausibility here, as long as we grant that an attractive world remains at any rate more likely given design than otherwise. Again, this strategy does detract from the ability of this approach to theodicy to rebut the evidential form of the problem of evil, but the proponent of design is again free to urge that the design hypothesis predicts only that any given whole is likely to be significantly better than not, and not that every such whole will be.

The thought that there is a conceptual connection between the kind of world we inhabit and who we are, considered concretely*, also carries implications for the opportunity cost approach. It suggests that even if I am given an unrestricted choice of worlds, I will still face opportunity costs, because the decision to inhabit world *x* before world *y* rather than vice versa may carry consequences for who I am concretely*, and therefore consequences for the kinds of experience which are open to me in later worlds. However, this thought does not, I think, undermine the basic drift of our earlier argument. We can allow that my choice of worlds will make a difference to who I am concretely*, while still supposing that I am free to choose a world providing that any evils to which its inhabitants (considered concretely*) are exposed can be subsumed within integral wholes which are overall better than not.

Recent discussions of the problem of evil often advert to a particularly difficult test case which William Rowe has posed for the theist. This case concerns a fawn which is trapped in a forest fire, and subject over some days to an agonising death. Rowe notes that 'there does not appear to be any greater good such that the prevention of the fawn's suffering would require either the loss of that good or the occurrence of an evil equally bad or worse'.[23] In response to this proposal, the theist will at least want to explore reflections of the following kind. Suppose that the world is so structured that animal suffering of the kind which involves intense and protracted pain is no longer possible. (Such a generalisation seems to be what Rowe is inviting. For presumably he is suggesting that any instance of such suffering will call into question the goodness of God.) In such a world, after suffering an injury, an animal would find itself free from pain of any intensity shortly afterwards. But of course that might not be to the animal's benefit. It might mean for instance that the animal would further damage some already injured body part (since it would lack any warning in the form of enduring pain that the part needs protection). So suppose instead that God makes a world in which some other mechanism serves to ensure that the animal will protect the injured body part: suppose that there is a natural regularity according to which injured animals behave in a way which will prevent further injury, without pain providing any cue. Indeed, we might suppose that if God has adequate reason to establish some such natural regularity, then God has adequate reason to introduce a further regularity which will ensure that animals avoid injury in the first place, without the experience of (or prospect of) pain serving to shape their behaviour.

But the experience of being, for instance, a deer under such conditions would be radically different from the experience of being a deer in a world such as ours. (Here I simply assume that it would be possible for deer to exist under these idealised circumstances.) Some might suppose furthermore that a deer's existence under such circumstances would be concretely* quite different, which in turn suggests that its existence in a world such as ours may after all be the condition of a significant good. Moreover, a world of this idealised kind would be quite different from our world in various other respects. In establishing various regularities relevant to providing a functional substitute for animal pain, God would have to reshape the character of natural regularity more generally. The consequence of doing so would presumably include the fact that human beings (as animals) would also be free from pain. And in turn this would make a difference to human lives considered concretely*. To resist this implication, we might suppose that God acts in this regard not in terms of general regularities but miraculously, so that human beings for instance, but not other animals, are able to experience pain. But in turn that would call into question the causal unity of the world, which itself would have profound implications for human beings' sense of the world's meaning (assuming that they recognise this lack of causal unity), and therefore for their lives considered concretely*.[24] It is worth emphasising again that these considerations are not meant to suggest that we cannot conceive of better lives than our own (pain-free lives, for instance), nor even that we cannot conceive of ourselves enjoying such lives. The suggestion is just that our lives considered concretely* may be tied to a world of the general character of this world, and that these lives may be better than not. I conclude then that the proposal we are considering seems to have some bearing on Rowe's problem. But I do not claim to have identified a sufficient theistic explanation of the evil of the fawn's suffering.

I have been arguing that the first of our approaches to theodicy requires us to consider whether evils can be subsumed (with some reasonable likelihood) within integral wholes which are better than not. If that is so, then philosophers of religion have, in some cases, imposed needlessly stringent standards of proof upon the theodicist, in so far as they have required a theodicy to show that integral wholes comprising good–and–evil are significantly better than not, or at any rate better in terms of general type than their alternatives. I have still not said anything explicitly about the charge that this first sort of theodicy is problematic from a spiritual point of view. Before addressing this issue, I want to say something about the other two kinds of theodicy I introduced at the beginning of our discussion, for these approaches also have some relevance in this regard.

Divine inscrutability and divine power

At more or less this point, I suggest, philosophical argument of the kind which seeks to provide a positive explanation of evil reaches its limit. There is scope for argument, of the kind found in the philosophy of religion literature, about which evils make possible which goods. But once these issues have been clarified, and once we have addressed the question of how good any such integral whole has to be, we are faced with what we might call (following Wittgenstein) an 'absolute judgement of value': in other words, a value judgement which cannot be further clarified by the citing of various non-evaluative considerations.[25] Should we suppose that the world is evidently better than not (in respect of each of its integral wholes)?[26] And if we do feel able to suppose that this is so, will we also grant that this fact constitutes a sufficient justification of the evils in question? In answering these questions, each of us must consult his or her own experience of the world, and the experiences of others, in so far as we feel able to grasp empathically the way things appear to them. A satisfactory treatment of the problem of evil, I suggest, should lead us to see that the problem is ultimately a problem of this kind: one where the difference between believers and others is rooted in a fundamental difference of evaluative response to the world. Such an understanding seems preferable to one which proceeds as though the introduction of some new technical apparatus might resolve the problem of evil at a stroke, as though it were fundamentally a problem in logic rather than a problem in life.

My own view is that not all evils can be adequately accounted for by means of this first approach. Surely there is something which remains to be understood on the theistic scheme, even when full account has been taken of the various integral wholes within which evils may (from our perspective) be inserted. (Again, this conclusion can be accorded a somewhat a priori character: given the transcendence of God, the theist has good reason to doubt whether she *could* have a complete positive explanation of evil.) So at this point, I would consider the possibility of strengthening this first sort of theodicy by reference to the idea of divine inscrutability. Again, in this way, we will also be able to meet the charge that the more-than-compensating-goods approach to theodicy attributes to human beings too elevated an understanding of the divine purposes.[27]

The hypothesis of divine inscrutability seems to find ready application as a way of buttressing the integral wholes theodicy. To set out some of the main points briefly, it seems our understanding of the full extent of the various integral wholes within which the world's evils may be situated is bound to be limited, even if we confine our attention to integral wholes which extend no further than this world. Chaos theory has taught us something about the way in which small-scale events may have a large-scale, cumulative impact. And in the same way, we should suppose, even relatively small-scale events in an individual's life will have effects which stretch cumulatively and from our perspective indeterminately into the future. For instance, it may be that the reading of this chapter will (eventually) bring you all sorts of benefits. Notice that even when these benefits arise, their connection to the reading of this book may remain quite unknown to you. There is a serious point to be made here: we surely cannot reasonably imagine which harms may be avoided or benefits secured even in relation to the fine detail of our lives. For this reason, it seems to me, we should not expect to be able to gauge with any precision the effectiveness of our first sort of theodicy: even supposing hypothetically that a given evil is in fact subsumed within some larger whole which is overall good (and even supposing that all of the goods in question have already arisen, within this world), there is no reason to suppose that from our merely human vantage point we will be able to grasp that this is so. Here is one context where the appeal to divine inscrutability seems legitimate, and even inevitable.[28]

Of course, the first sort of theodicy claims that various evils are the *logically necessary* concomitants of various more than compensating goods, not merely that they are the necessary concomitants of those goods from the point of view of a particular set of contingent natural laws. And it may appear that the evils we encounter, even when they are embedded within cumulative sequences of events of the kind envisaged in chaos theory, do not constitute the logically necessary preconditions of the goods which follow on from them, even if they are the physically necessary preconditions of those goods. But here again, I think, a certain humility is in order about the extent of our ability to identify the relevant integral wholes. For instance, as we have noted, cosmologists tell us that there is an intimate connection between various fundamental characteristics of the cosmos at the time of the Big Bang and the suitability of the universe for the emergence of life. This suggests that in general the conditions which must be satisfied by any genuinely viable physical cosmos are more restrictive than we might at first suppose. Of course, in the style of a cartoon strip, we could imagine a universe which is greatly different from ours in terms of its initial conditions but which even so proves consistent with the development of life. But imaginability in this sense is not, it seems, a measure of real possibility.[29] Possibility in the sense of imaginability gives no thought to whether events could follow from the interaction of real things whose natures are reasonably stable over time. Presumably God has reason to create a universe in which there are real individuals, and not a cartoon strip kind of universe in which in principle anything can follow anything else, depending on the whim of the script writer. So here is another connection in which appeal to divine inscrutability, as a way of bolstering the first sort of theodicy, seems appropriate. Not only can we not envisage the ultimate consequences even of small-scale events; even if we could do so, we would struggle to say to what extent these consequences reflect logical constraints (or more exactly, constraints to do with 'real' possibility) rather than the constraints imposed by a particular set of contingent natural laws.[30]

Notice that this account also carries implications for the argument from design. For instance, it may lead some to suppose that for all we know, a radically unattractive world is not a real possibility, even granting that it is, clearly, an imaginable possibility. As we saw in Chapter 1, Tennant's argument from beauty seems to depend on the claim that an absence of beauty, or more radical forms of aesthetic failure, is a real possibility. Indeed the argument moves from a study of human agency to the claim that the existence of an unattractive world is not merely a real possibility but overwhelmingly likely, in the absence of design. So Tennant's version of the design argument seems to require the claim that the boundaries of real possibility are not all that restrictive. This seems to me plausible, at any rate in relation to the world's aesthetic properties. But of course, this understanding of the nature of real possibility will limit the effectiveness of this particular response to the problem of evil (for it will suggest that the imaginability of a world which is like ours except in so far as it lacks various evils may well be a measure of the real possibility of such a world). Here again we find that, in the name of self-consistency, the proponent of design is required to forfeit certain radical responses to the problem of evil. However, the proponent of design remains on strong ground in relation to the phenomena of fine-tuning, I suggest. So far as I can see, there is no reason to suppose that constraints of real possibility significantly restrict the set of possible universes, where universes are distinguished in terms of their expansion rates, or the values of their forces, in the ways proposed in the fine-tuning argument.[31]

These two ways of introducing the idea of divine inscrutability do not depend on the thought that the divine value system is inscrutable to us. They appeal only to evident limits upon our powers of computation, in respect of the ultimate consequences of events, and in respect of the extent to which these consequences are constrained by what is really possible. But there is also some reason to suppose that, if there is a God, then we will not be able to grasp in full his or her evaluative ideals (or goals), any more than children can reasonably aspire to grasp all the evaluative ideals of their parents, however appropriate and fundamental those ideals may be. This is a further consideration the theodicist should introduce when making appeal to the idea of divine inscrutability. Again, we have reason to accord a fairly limited role to this sort of idea, in order to preserve the belief (of theists and others) that our understanding of the evaluative significance of our choices is not radically mistaken.

Stephen Wykstra has appealed to this sort of consideration when replying to William Rowe's example of the fawn which we noted earlier. He comments: 'If outweighing goods of the sort at issue exist in connection with instances of suffering, that we should discern most of them seems about as likely as that a one-month-old should discern most of his parents' purposes for those pains they allow him to suffer – which is to say, it is not likely at all.'[32] In turn, this suggests, according to Wykstra, that our inability to identify the goods which might be served by the fawn's suffering has no tendency to establish that there are no such goods. It seems to me that Wykstra's reply is effective, providing it does not amount to an insistence on our radical ignorance of evaluative questions, lest we call into question the point of human choice in accordance with humanly recognised evaluative standards. Distinguishing between the limits on (a) our evaluational and (b) our computational capacities can help here. This distinction suggests that our inability to assess questions of divine justice may not spill over into an inability to assess moral questions in the human sphere, for the computational problems which arise in this latter case are presumably nothing like so formidable. (For instance, I take it that often enough we can reasonably foresee the outcome of human choices.) Moreover, the argument I have sketched does not rely simply on the thought that there is bound a priori to be a deep disparity between divine and human understanding. It also notes that established facts about the world (those recorded in chaos and cosmological theories) should alert us to the limitations on our ability to ascertain the goods which evils may make possible.

Once these various ways of reinforcing the argument from integral wholes, in terms of the idea of divine inscrutability, have been introduced, should we then conclude that the theist has said as much as needs to be said or can reasonably be said on our topic? I think that one further approach is also worthy of mention. Here we turn to the thought that there may be contingent constraints on God's powers.

According to some commentators, theism depends for its epistemic standing on the belief that God is omnipotent, omniscient, and so on: or to put the matter in the terms of Anselm's succinct formula, on the belief that God is that than which nothing greater can be conceived. For instance, the ontological argument maintains that God, so conceived, necessarily exists, and can therefore be known to exist quite apart from the empirical evidence; and even theists who are sceptical of this argument have supposed that the prior probability of theism depends crucially on the assumption that God's knowledge and powers are without limit. However, the argument from design is not evidently committed to the thought that the world's source must possess all the omni-properties. Of course, some will object that a designer who falls short of having all the omni-properties is not properly considered divine at all. However, I shall defer consideration of that issue until we discuss the nature of worship, in Chapter 6.

Suppose we concentrate on the question of whether evil in particular provides the theist with good reason to suppose that God's powers are subject to contingent limitations. Clearly, this supposition will strengthen a theodicy, in so far as it implies that a particular combination of good and evil may represent an integral whole for the designer, even if the evil is not a logically necessary condition of the good. However, overall it may be doubted whether this approach extends any significant advantage in addressing the problem of evil, since it has a tendency to undermine the second of the theodicies we have discussed. For reducing the scope of God's power (and knowledge) will call into question the divine transcendence; and as God's transcendence is eroded, so the notion of divine inscrutability will become correspondingly more difficult to sustain. I suggest then that this approach may be adopted by those who have other reasons (not related to the problem of evil) for supposing that the world's source is finite; it is not clear however that there are sound reasons for making use of the notion of contingent limitations on divine power solely as a response to the problem of evil.

Some applications

I want to draw this discussion to a close by looking at some implications of the theodicy I have been outlining. I shall consider two issues in particular. First of all, in the Introduction, I suggested that if there is a God, then atheism seems to be a part of the divine dispensation (albeit that atheism represents, until recent times, very much a minority reading of the meaning of human experience); and I promised to say a little more about how this fact might be reconciled with a theistic perspective.

The discussion of this chapter suggests one approach to this issue. It might be said that if the fundamental question for theodicy is whether it is better than not that the world should be, it appears that a world in which there are conscientious atheists is evidently compatible with the existence of God: for there is surely no doubting that the lives of atheists are worth something *in respect of their atheism.* Here is one case where a re-orientation of perspective away from questions of the kind 'Is atheism better than its alternatives?' towards questions of the kind 'Is atheism in and of itself a good?' may produce a straightforward response to problems which have vexed some theists.[33] Similarly,we might argue that a person's atheism may be a component of her concrete* identity, or more generally that a world in which conscientious atheism was not possible would be so radically different from our own that the concrete* existence of many people – believers and non-believers – would no longer be possible. Of course, conceding the possibility of authentic atheism on the theistic perspective (that is, atheism which cannot be ascribed to a failure of will or intellect) in turn carries implications for the proper ambitions of natural theology. If atheism is legitimate in this sense, then there is no necessary connection between the truth of theism and the possibility of a universally persuasive natural theology. But of course this leaves open the possibility of a natural theology whose objectives are more modest.

Turning to the second issue, as I have noted, theodicy can sometimes seem like a rather unspiritual business: a matter of supposing that one will receive from God various rewards in exchange for putting up with a basically unsatisfactory world. We might think that a properly religious response to the world is rather one of accepting the will of God, whatever it may involve. I suggest that the theodicy I have been developing can meet this sort of concern, since it makes only limited use of the 'pay-off' idea.

This idea is most evident in the first of our types of theodicy, where various evils are said to make possible various goods. However, the version of that theodicy which I have sketched invites us to think that the question the believer needs to ask is not really: what will I get out of this? (For instance, will I get moral development of the kind Hick envisages?) On the approach I have taken, the good in question may be simply myself (and other selves) considered concretely*. If we revert to the idea that an integral whole is compatible with the goodness of God providing simply that it is better than not, this suggests that the question we need to ask is more like this: are these selves, considered concretely*, overall worthwhile? Such an approach seems to cohere rather well with the spirituality of the 'ordinary believer', in so far as it is the lived experience of being able to accept one's life concretely* (and not the prospect of some pay-off) which forms the bedrock of the believer's trust in God. In other words, such an approach to theodicy seems to draw upon the very sense of meaning that is relevant in ordinary religious life as a way of coping with evil; and to this extent, I suggest, it can withstand the charge of falling prey to concerns which contradict the spirit of religious commitment.

The second form of theodicy also leads in the direction of such a spirituality, in so far as it draws attention to the limits on our ability to perform the calculations or identify the values which are relevant to theodicy. To this extent, it does not lead us to reason: 'I'll put up with all of this on condition of such and such a pay-off'. Rather, it invites an acceptance of the finitude of our own perspective, and our inability to judge what would satisfy our deepest desires. If we adopt the third form of theodicy, similar consequences will follow, I suggest. For if there are contingent limits on divine power, we cannot reasonably claim to know just where they fall. Here again, it seems we are quickly driven to acknowledge the limits on our own understanding.

If we wanted to pursue this line of reflection in a radical way, we might choose to surrender the original position framework I have been using. That framework takes us back to the notion of a pay-off to the extent that it leads us to suppose that our existence in this world will find compensation through our existence in another, better world. The heroic approach here would dispense with the thought of an afterlife, and suppose that this world is to be accepted not so much as a theatre of human development, or on the understanding that further and better experiences will ensue, but simply as a space in which imperfect individuals like you and me can exist. More particularly, it might be said that our very existence betokens God's love for us as the concrete* individuals we are, and that is enough to make our lives worthwhile. Again, I doubt whether abstract argument can do much to recommend such a perspective. This is not to say that it is unacceptable, only that in reaching a verdict upon it, we will need to defer once more to an absolute judgement of value.[34]

Conclusions

In this chapter I have continued our examination of the basic thesis of this work: that the world exists because it is good that it should exist. I have argued that this thesis is not evidently overturned by the evils and disvalues of the world, providing we make proper use of the integral wholes idea and the notion of divine inscrutability. In keeping with the general theme of our discussion, I have tried to clarify just how good an integral whole must be if it is to be a fitting object of God's creative activity; and I have argued that in at least some cases, an integral whole may be consistent with the purposes of a benevolent God providing simply that it is better than not. I have also tried to broaden the integral wholes theodicy so that it takes account of the relationship between evils and the possibility of human life considered concretely. This sort of approach invites us to keep our attention focussed on the qualities of this life, rather than speculating about the ways in which a further life might provide some compensation for the evils undergone in this life. A further concern of this chapter has been the relationship between theodicy and the argument from design. I have argued that these are consistent projects, providing that the theodicist invokes certain ideas in moderation. For example, she should accord a limited role to the thought that the divine value system and the nature of real possibilities lie beyond our ken.

I have still not offered any precise verdict about the extent to which (if at all) disvalue undermines the case we have examined in Chapters 1 and 2. This is partly because there is an ineliminable element of personal judgement in these matters; so there is little possibility of reaching a consensus about where exactly the balance of argument lies. Moreover, I want to argue in due course that acceptance of our basic thesis is compatible with quite a range of views concerning the epistemic status of the design hypothesis. Before developing that suggestion however, I shall offer, in Chapter 4, one further response to the problem of disvalue. In the present chapter I have concentrated on the problem of evil in relation to human life; in Chapter 4, I shall extend this discussion by examining disvalues in 'nature'.

4 Theodicy in an ecological mode

Introduction

The general theme of this book is the goodness of the world. In this chapter, I want to consider this theme from a further perspective by drawing on the emerging disciplines of environmental ethics and ecology. As I hope to show, these disciplines throw new light on the values in nature, and can therefore contribute to our defence of the claim that the goodness of the world is its reason for existence.[1]

In the world of business and public policy, we have become familiar with the idea that any major undertaking should be accompanied by an 'environmental impact statement'. In recent years, theologians have conformed to this trend, by seeking to show that Christian commitment is an undertaking which has (or ought to have) beneficial implications for our relations to the natural world.[2] Of course, they have been spurred on in this endeavour by the suggestion that there is some sort of strain between Christian belief and ecological sensitivity, and more particularly by the charge that the Christian worldview (coupled perhaps with the Greek metaphysic in which it has been cast) is in some significant measure responsible for our current ecological predicament, whether on account of its tendency to think of matter and spirit antithetically, or for some other reason.[3] The issues I address in this chapter will have some relevance to this larger topic, concerning the consonance or otherwise of Christian belief and a properly informed environmental ethic. But I shall be considering more specifically the question of whether the perception of the non-human world which emerges in the writings of ecologists and environmental ethicists throws into new relief two issues in natural theology: the nature and extent of the world's goodness, and the character of the impediments which may obstruct our discernment of its goodness.

The main focus for my discussion will be (once more) the work of Holmes Rolston III, whose seminal writings in environmental ethics have done much to shape discussion in the field. The theological resonances of Rolston's work are surely not coincidental. He has a doctorate in Theology and Religious Studies from the University of Edinburgh and is ordained in the Presbyterian church (USA). However, his theological interests are rarely explicit in his writing on environmental ethics.[4] And where he has made connections between his theological concerns and his ethics, he has not, so far as I am aware, sought to bring out the particular connections which form the subject matter of this discussion.

I ought to begin with a brief point of terminological clarification. Ecology is of course a science, concerned with the description of the complex structure of ecosystems; and accordingly, we might suppose that ecologists as such make no explicit value claims.[5] On the other hand, environmental ethicists plainly do make such claims about the nature of our relations to the natural world, and in so doing they customarily draw extensively on the writings of ecologists. In considering the possibility of an ecologically informed theodicy, I am as much interested in the possibility of an environmental ethically informed theodicy. In other words, I am interested in the evaluative significance assigned to the findings of ecologists by environmental ethicists in general, and by Rolston in particular. So for the purposes of this discussion, I shall not draw a sharp distinction between the two disciplines: by ecology will be meant ecology as interpreted by Rolston and his colleagues in the context of constructing an environmental ethic. The blurring of this distinction would meet with Rolston's approval, I think. He grants that the environmental ethicist does not merely reiterate the work of ecologists, but also notes the difficulty of distinguishing between the ecological 'facts' and the environmental ethical 'values'. For instance he comments that:

> What is ethically puzzling, and exciting, in the marriage and mutual transformation of ecological description and evaluation is that here an 'ought' is not so much *derived* from an 'is' as discovered simultaneously with it. As we progress from descriptions of fauna and flora, of cycles and pyramids, of stability and dynamism, on to intricacy, planetary opulence and interdependence, to unity and harmony with oppositions in counterpoint and synthesis, arriving at length at beauty and goodness, it is difficult to say where the natural facts leave off and where natural values appear. For some observers at least,

> the sharp is/ought dichotomy is gone; the values seem to be there as soon as the facts are fully in, and both alike are properties of the system.[6]

My attempt to relate the environmental ethical (cum ecological) perspective and the issues in natural theology I have distinguished will focus upon two features of this perspective in particular. First of all, I shall draw upon the tendency of ecological thought to represent the world in holistic terms, that is, its tendency to understand things in nature by reference to their place within a complex web of such things. And secondly, I shall be interested in the non-anthropocentric scheme of values which is characteristic of the writings of many environmental ethicists, Rolston included. These two doctrines are of course related. If we think holistically about the place of human beings in nature, then immediately we are likely to suppose that their well-being is tied to the well-being of other creatures and to the normal functioning of various non-biological processes. On this view, we are likely to suppose that human interests and the interests of the wider 'biotic community' have a tendency to coincide, so that an enlightened anthropocentrism will find expression in a concern for the flourishing of non-human life forms and for the integrity of the ecosystem more generally. Rolston takes this theme a step further, arguing that things in nature have an intrinsic value, and are not to be valued simply on account of their usefulness in promoting human well-being. However if our holism is radical enough, there may not be much difference between these two perspectives (those of 'deep' and 'shallow' ecology) in terms of their implications for human conduct. But I shall return to Rolston's understanding of natural value shortly. At this juncture I wish simply to draw attention to the fact that I shall appeal to the holism and non-anthropocentrism of Rolston's thought in making a case for the possibility of some sort of fruitful conversation between environmentalists and natural theologians.

It might seem easy enough to connect a commitment to the fundamental goodness of the world and the concerns expressed in the ecological perspective. After all, this perspective is conventionally taken to include the demand that human interference in the natural world should be restricted; and in turn that may seem to imply that nature is good when left to run its own course, and even that 'wild nature' as such cannot be improved upon (not at any rate by us). I shall argue that the writings of Rolston and others provide a way of articulating this basic insight. I begin by noting a number of interpretations of the natural world, some of which draw their inspiration directly from the natural sciences, which pose a challenge to any belief in the goodness of the world. I shall then seek to read Rolston's work as an ecologically informed rebuttal of this challenge.

David Hume is the most celebrated philosophical critic of the design argument, and not surprisingly his objections to the argument reflect a negative assessment of the basic tendencies of the natural world. Thus, in the person of Philo, he remarks that when we consider the world of living things, we discover that:

> The whole presents nothing but the idea of a blind nature, impregnated with a great vivifying principle, and pouring forth from her lap, without discernment or parental care, her maimed and abortive children.

And he infers that:

> the original Source of all things [or nature itself we might add] . . . has no more regard to good above ill than to heat above cold, or to drought above moisture, or to light above heavy.[7]

In brief, Hume's complaint is that nature is indifferent to the well-being of her creatures. This sort of negative evaluation of the natural world is echoed in the writings of other philosophers. John Stuart Mill observes that nature presents an 'odious scene of violence'.[8] And William James also finds fault with nature considered as a whole, drawing a conclusion about how we should behave in relation to the natural world which is strikingly contrary to the sort of conclusion typically favoured by environmental ethicists:

> Visible nature is all plasticity and indifference, – a moral multiverse . . . and not a moral universe. To such a harlot we owe no allegiance; with her as a whole we can establish no moral communion; and we are free in our dealing with her several parts to obey or to destroy, and to follow no law but that of prudence in coming to terms with such of her particular features as will help us to our private ends.[9]

Scientists as well as philosophers have lent their voice to the view that nature is indifferent to life, and if viewed as a work of contrivance, then badly contrived. Thus Darwin wrote that the process of natural selection was 'clumsy, wasteful, blundering, low, and horribly cruel'.[10] And Stephen Jay Gould has commented that: 'Odd arrangements and funny solutions are the proofs of evolution – paths that a sensible God would never tread'; citing an example, he notes that: 'Orchids were not made by an ideal engineer; they were jury-rigged from a limited set of available components.'[11] Similarly Francis Crick remarks that biology has no 'elegance', in view of the haphazard nature of evolutionary change.[12]

Of course, it is sometimes supposed that nature is not properly the subject of any kind of evaluative assessment except in so far as it impinges upon the lives of human beings. And sometimes the problem of 'natural evil' as discussed by philosophers of religion takes this form. But in these quotations, it seems that exception is being taken to the natural world in virtue of its own inherent character, independently of its bearing upon human well-being. (This is true even of the quotation from Hume, since he seems to be concerned with life in general, and not merely with human life.) Thus the natural world is said variously to be 'blind', 'odious', 'a harlot' to whom we owe no allegiance, 'clumsy' and 'cruel', 'odd' and 'funny', and inelegant. I take it that these value judgements if understood as characterisations of the fundamental bent of the natural world are incompatible with, or at least place under serious strain, a natural theological understanding of the world's significance. Certainly they are incompatible with the version of the design argument which I have sought to defend, which rests upon a conviction that the world is manifestly good; but such a bleak assessment of the non-human world also seems to pose a challenge to theistic belief more generally, including those forms of belief which do not depend upon a claim to discern the workings of providence in any detail.[13]

Now the writings of environmental ethicists are also standardly opposed to this sort of assessment of the natural world. For instance, Rolston cites with evident approval the following case. In the winter of 1981–82, the bighorn sheep of the Yellowstone National Park caught conjunctivitis. The park officials, Rolston notes, judged that 'the disease was natural and should be left to run its course', despite knowing that many of the herd would die if not treated.[14] The decision not to intervene here was not based, it seems, upon an inability to treat the sheep effectively, but on the sense that in the long run, the natural order would hit upon some optimal outcome by the working out of its own processes. A host of philosophically charged issues arise at this point, among them the importance of sentience as a criterion of value, and the relationship between our dealings with the natural world and our dealings with one another in the realm of 'culture'. But here I note simply that Rolston's judgement, and the judgement of the park officials, seems to reflect a much more affirmative understanding of the behaviour of the natural world, even in cases of disease and suffering, than the views I recorded above. This suggests that we should take seriously the possibility of some kind of affinity between ecology, understood in a broad, Rolstonian sense, and natural theology. I want now to explore this possibility in rather more detail.

Towards an ecological theodicy

Rolston's writings contain a wealth of material which is relevant to this general topic. Indeed, just about everything he says has some bearing upon it. So I shall have to be highly selective in this report on the implications of his views for the possibility of an ecologically informed natural theology. In general terms, Rolston's case for a positive valuation of the natural world has two points of focus: first of all, he requests a broadening of our perspective so that natural phenomena are considered in their ecosystemic context; secondly, and relatedly, he invites us to develop new value concepts for the purpose of understanding the richness of the natural world. These two themes take us back to the holism and non-anthropocentrism of his perspective. His desire to understand natural phenomena in a broader context flows from a holistic conception of their significance; and the desire to frame new categories of value is related to his sense that our existing categories are rooted in specifically human forms of value, or at any rate in the values which we associate with sentience.

Turning first of all to the question of holism, Rolston argues that the Darwinian paradigm is not so much mistaken as partial. Once we extend our focus away from the individual creature, beset by problems of predation and competition, towards its setting within an ecosystem, we will find that new forms of 'order', 'harmony', and 'stability' come into view. 'In post-Darwinian nature', Rolston remarks, 'we looked for these values in vain, while in ecological description we now find them; yet the earlier data are not denied, only redescribed or set in a larger ecological context'.[15]

There are many examples of this general approach in Rolston's work. Here are a few. For instance, from a purely local perspective, it may seem wasteful that most species produce a surplus of young. But viewed in ecosystemic context this surplus appears, according to Rolston, as a necessary condition of mutational advance: granted that no species can expand in numbers indefinitely, there must be a surplus of young if there is to be selection across mutants; and in turn, it is only if there is selection in relation to mutants that a species will be able to track effectively changes in its environment, and to contribute towards the evolution of more complex life forms.[16] Moreover, Rolston suggests, the surplus is not wasted for a further reason, because it sustains the lives of other creatures. What is waste in the rabbit life stream is a resource in the coyote life stream; and in general, Rolston suggests, 'wherever there is available free energy and biomass, a life form typically evolves to exploit those resources'. Thus 'Nature's exuberance', he writes, 'is also nature's economy'.[17] These observations surely go some way towards tempering Hume's judgement that the 'great vivifying principle' of nature is indifferent to the needs of creatures; on the contrary, it appears that there is a systematic connection between nature's abundance and her ability to sustain existing life forms, and to evolve new life forms which are capable of flourishing in their environments.

Turning to another example, pain may appear to be a further instance of nature's disregard for her offspring. Again, on Rolston's view, this impression changes when we enlarge our focus. Thus while it is true that in a particular instance, a creature may suffer and derive no benefit from its suffering, in general the evolutionary process will pare away any capacity for pain that does not confer some sort of benefit on average to the many members of the species. Moreover, on Rolston's view, pain, like the surplus of young, proves to be related to the tendency of the evolutionary process to evolve more sophisticated life forms. Thus he writes that:

> In natural history – whatever might be true in other imaginable worlds — the pathway to psychosomatic consciousness, the only kind of experience we know, is through flesh that can feel its way through the world.[18]

Again, these remarks must count against, even if they do not dispel altogether, the thought that nature is 'cruel'. On this view the pain creatures undergo plays a systemic role, in preserving the species, and in permitting the emergence of new and higher life forms.

So far I have considered the bearing of Rolston's work on the charge that nature is wasteful and cruel, and in these respects indifferent to the flourishing of life. The other charge which figured prominently in our earlier discussion was that nature is 'blind', and therefore develops haphazardly, if at all. Of course, this thought is connected with the discovery that genetic mutations are random.

Here again, Rolston accepts these claims as a description of individual things, but reaches a different evaluative conclusion, by setting these localised truths within a broader context. In particular, he proposes that mutational randomness favours non-randomly the development of better adapted life forms. Thus he writes that:

> We do not here wish to cast out the randomness (or the conflict); we want to recast it in a bigger picture. Randomness is not valueless noise in the system. Rather, embedded within systemic principles of order, it is a value generator, a value transformer.[19]

Moreover, the random searching out of new adaptational possibilities is selectively focussed. As Rolston observes: 'Only those variations are tested and selected that are more or less functional. The organism typically only probes the nearby space for possible directions of development.'[20] This suggests not so much a chaotic lurching from one possibility to another as a systematic examination of the various potentialities of the natural order. Far from being unreliable as a problem solving method, mutational variation has even been taken as a model for various computer-based problem solving strategies.[21] Of course, this leaves the objection of Gould and others that the whole process is rather ad hoc. But on this point Rolston counters that the historical character of evolutionary development is itself valuable: indeed 'it is more valuable', he writes, 'to have history plus value as storied achievement than to have "elegant" optimal value solutions without history, autonomy, or adventure'.[22]

Evidently, there is a mass of material here which is broadly relevant to the question of the goodness of the natural world, and relevant in particular to the thought that it is not fundamentally wasteful, cruel or (in any pejorative sense) blind. Rolston's approach to these topics is naturally viewed as a generalisation of the integral whole approach to theodicy, which we discussed in Chapter 3, in so far as he seeks to situate evils or disvalues within larger states of affairs which are overall good. But of course, his system is also non-anthropocentric; on this view, the process of 'soul-making' is not limited to the transformation of human beings, but extends to the natural world in general. Thus pain and death, when understood ecosystemically, prove to be a condition not merely of renewed human life, but of the flourishing of new life forms. At times, the Hickian overtones of this approach are unmistakable. For instance in his discussion of the pasqueflower, Rolston writes that 'the floral diversification of our temperate climates is very much a product of winters alternating with summers. This pasqueflower springs forth in its particular form of early beauty [the time of its flowering is recorded in its name] as much because of winter as to spite it; it buds and blossoms because it is blasted.'[23] And unusually, he permits himself to note the obvious theological resonances of this fact (implied of course in the flower's name). 'The way of Nature', he comments, 'is, in this deep and earthen sense, the Way of the Cross'.[24]

By showing how we might generalise the soul-making theme, Rolston's work also throws at least some light on William Rowe's much discussed test case for theodicy. As we saw in Chapter 3, Rowe suggests that the agonising death of a fawn following a forest fire (caused by a lightning strike) is apparently pointless.[25] Rolston offers this ecosystemic understanding of fire:

> Consider how our attitudes toward fire have changed since being informed by ecology. Fire sanitizes and thins a forest, releasing nutrients from the humus back into the soil. It resets succession, opens up edging, initially destroys but subsequently benefits wildlife. It regenerates shade intolerant trees.

And he concludes that 'the temporary upset is integral to the larger systemic health'.[26]

Of course, this is hardly a decisive refutation of Rowe's case. We may want to ask: granted that fires can benefit a forest, why should deer have to be exposed to fire? Or again and more fundamentally: granted that various benefits for the wider ecosystem follow on from the particular incident Rowe describes, is there not a possible world in which deer are exposed to fire but do not suffer, and even survive? This question of whether the values and disvalues which Rolston understands holistically are bound together by relations of logical necessity, or only by relations of contingent, natural necessity, is too large an issue to be pursued here. But I venture the view that we cannot confidently say that the connections in question are not broadly speaking logical. After all, as we have seen, recent developments in cosmology have drawn our attention to the delicate relationship between the large-scale character of the universe and the possibility of its giving rise to life. And this discovery should make us wary of supposing that we can coherently envisage a material world in which sentient things behave in a broadly regular way, in accordance with their natures, but in which deer (or their counterparts) are not burned, or do not suffer when burned.[27]

So far I have been talking about the holistic dimension of

Rolston's approach to the value of the natural world. The second general strategy which Rolston commends, as a means to understanding the value of nature properly, is a re-thinking of our value concepts. Of course, this further strategy is related to the first. It is because we are not used to thinking ecosystemically that our existing value concepts lead us to understate the goodness of the world in various respects, and in particular to overlook the goodness which attaches to ecosystemic wholes.[28] I shall give just one example of the stretching of our value concepts that is needed, on Rolston's account. This example is of particular interest to us given our earlier discussion of Tennant's argument from design from natural beauty. According to Rolston, if we are inclined to doubt the natural beauty of the world, this may reflect a deficiency in our value concepts, rather than any fault in nature.

Rolston notes the common view that the natural world is in general beautiful, in a pictorial sense. (The tradition of landscape painting is one obvious manifestation of this sort of response to nature.) But he goes on to note that this claim can be challenged, since any given landscape will be full of dying and disfigured things. Surely it is difficult to uphold the claim that nature is in general beautiful once these further features are brought into view? Characteristically, Rolston's reply to this challenge invokes the ecosystemic perspective. Decay and predation, and pain, are all ecosystemic preconditions of various forms of flourishing. Thus 'ugliness, though present at times in particulars, is not the last word. Realists with a "depth" past a "flat" vision can "see" the *time line* as well as the *ugly space* immediately present; they know that regenerative forces are already present, that over time nature will bring beauty out of this ugliness, and that this tendency is already present and aesthetically stimulating now.'[29] Thus our pictorial sense of beauty is only partially adequate to the beauty of nature; seeing this beauty requires an enlarged, ecosystemic aesthetic sensibility. Clearly, this sort of understanding of the value of nature, one which does not gloss over the suffering and ugliness of the world, but sets it in an ecsosystemic context, is not merely Panglossian. As Rolston notes, the world is not a 'jolly' place, and if it is beautiful, its beauty is of a 'somber' kind.[30]

Rolston's suggestion that our value concepts are sometimes inadequate for the purpose of mapping the value of nature carries a further implication which has some relevance for our discussion. What if we should find that in some respect we simply cannot value the world? Rolston's approach implies that this failure may reflect not so much a deficiency in nature as a deficiency in our concepts.

(There are echoes here of course of Wykstra's reply to Rowe's problem in relation to the suffering fawn; analogously, we may say that our failure to see any value in the fawn's suffering is unsurprising, even supposing there is such value, given our history of needing to reform our concepts when trying to understand the value of nature.)[31] In view of his own experience of uncovering new forms of value through the closer study of nature, Rolston finds himself reluctant to admit that his failure to find the world valuable in a given respect clearly indicates a failure in nature. Thus he reflects on the limitations of the ecosystemic method, thus far, in these terms:

> We shall surely not vindicate the natural sequence in every detail as being productive of ecosystemic health, and therefore we cannot simplify our ethic to an unreflective acceptance of what naturally is the case. We do not live in Eden, yet the trend is there, as ecological advance increasingly finds in the natural given stability, beauty, and integrity, and we are henceforth as willing to open our concepts to reformation by the world as to prejudge the natural order.[32]

The implication of Rolston's position here is perhaps rather that we do not clearly live in Eden, but might do so, for all we can tell.

So far I have been arguing that Rolston's holism and his ecosystemic (non-anthropocentric) conception of value provide a useful framework for re-thinking certain familiar issues to do with the goodness of the world. This framework is particularly relevant to discussion of a generalised form of the problem of evil, one which finds that the natural world is flawed in the ways we have noted. So far as I can see, it does not lend itself directly to an argument from design; for instance, it does not, without further elaboration, establish the improbability of this state of affairs independently of contrivance or knowing guidance of some sort. It offers rather a basis for the view that the natural world is consonant with a theistic scheme, rather than requiring to be explained in those terms.[33]

I turn now to the second of the general themes I identified at the beginning of this discussion, namely the issue of why we should fail to discern in full the value of the world, if we do. I have already noted one approach to this question which is suggested by Rolston's work, namely the thought that our value concepts fail to register certain systemic features of the world's goodness. But there is a further line of reflection in Rolston's writings which can usefully be brought to bear on this issue.

Failing to see the value of the world

To understand the value of nature, it is necessary then to be ecologically informed. But in Rolston's view, it is also necessary to have extensive first-hand experience of nature. So as with other spheres of evaluative judgement, it seems that making appropriate value judgements in relation to nature depends not just, nor even primarily, upon having a relevant body of theory, but upon close familiarity with a range of particular cases. Hence Rolston can write that: 'The recommendation that one ought to value these events [in nature] follows from a discovery of their goodness in place, which is not so much by argument as by adventure that experiences their origins, structures, and environmental locations.'[34] So here is a further reason why some of us fail to appreciate fully the value of nature: we may be lacking not only in the requisite ecological theory, but in relevant experience.

Moreover, Rolston is clear that such experiences have a profound importance in determining our sense of ourselves and the significance of human life. In fact, on Rolston's account, this particular sphere of evaluative experience is not really optional, for purposes of developing fully as a human being. Thus he notes that our experiences of nature are recreational in the deepest sense: 'Something about a herd of elk grazing beneath the vista of wind and sky, or an eroded sandstone mesa silhouetted against the evening horizon, *re-creates* us.'[35]

The ability of nature to play this re-creating role is rooted in our evolutionary past. As Rolston notes: 'Given evolutionary theory, genetics, biochemistry, and more lately, sociobiology, it is difficult to think that our emotions have not been shaped to fit us for the natural environment.'[36] Accordingly, there are occasions when our felt affinity with certain scenes or situations in nature seems to amount to a biological reflex.[37] However, it is also clear that on Rolston's view, this re-creation of the self through its exposure to the natural world is a quasi-moral achievement. Thus it needs to be worked at, and requires the kind of self-emptying that we associate with moral insight. I want now to elaborate a little on how experience of nature can play this role.

In a memorable passage, Iris Murdoch writes of how observing a scene from nature can liberate a person from egocentric concerns:

> I am looking out of my window in an anxious and resentful state of mind, oblivious of my surroundings, brooding perhaps on some damage done to my prestige. Then suddenly I observe a

> hovering kestrel. In a moment everything is altered. The brooding self with its hurt vanity has disappeared. There is nothing now but kestrel. And when I return to thinking of the other matter it seems less important.[38]

This is the sort of experience that Rolston seems to have in mind when he supposes that experiences of nature can contribute towards a morally significant redefinition of the self's concerns. On Rolston's view too, this sort of self-transcendence requires a sensitivity to the worth of things in themselves, quite apart from their ability to further the projects of the egocentric self.[39] Thus he writes that: 'Wild nature is a place of encounter where we go not to act on it, but to contemplate it, drawing ourselves into its order of being, not drawing it into our order of being.'[40]

It is perhaps significant that Rolston talks here of 'drawing ourselves' into an appreciation of the intrinsic worth of nature, implying that this sort of appreciation may well require effort and a training of our powers of attention. (By contrast, the particular example I have cited from Murdoch suggests a spontaneous response.) At this juncture, Rolston characteristically asks for an ecosystemic reworking of another of our value concepts, this time that of the self. Thus he writes that in such experiences of nature, 'the "self" has been so extended as to be ecosystemically redefined.' Hence: 'The human welfare which we find in the enriched ecosystem is no longer recognizable as that of anthropocentrism.'[41]

So on Rolston's view a proper appreciation of the value of nature depends upon some familiarity with relevant ecological theory, and upon a willingness to immerse ourselves in experience of nature, and lastly and most challengingly upon the willingness to allow our sense of self to be stretched by coming to recognise the inherent value of natural things. Accordingly, the failure to appreciate the value of nature may arise from a failure in any of these respects. But in this connection, I want to stress the importance of the final condition of proper evaluative insight: the ability to escape to some extent from the egocentric perspective. The implication of Rolston's view here is that it is unsurprising that often enough we do not fully grasp the value of the natural world, because doing so would require something akin to a moral conversion. Indeed, this conversion is if anything more radical than the conversion which is (directly) relevant in our relations with other human beings, in so far as the natural world often presents itself as a threat to our well-being. Thus he writes:

> That we should struggle against storm and winter is not here denied, nor that we may need to oppose wolves and thistles, rattlesnakes and the malaria mosquito. But we add that we can respect the alien not only in its autonomous otherness, but even in its stimulus, provocation, and opposition.[42]

As Murdoch's example indicates, the capacity for this sort of self-transcendence while it is directly relevant to our relations with the natural world, also carries indirectly implications for our relations to one another, by helping us to relativise the egocentric perspective.

Conclusions

I have tried to show how the holism and non-anthropocentrism of Rolston's environmental ethics offer a new vantage point upon the goodness of the natural world, and upon the question of why we may sometimes struggle to recognise the full extent of its goodness. I do not suggest that invoking Rolston's account clearly settles these questions in favour of the natural theological perspective. It does not. But it supplies a range of data and conceptual resources which are of fundamental relevance to these matters.

Clearly, a more detailed incorporation of Rolston's approach within a natural theology would need to address a range of issues which I have only touched upon, if I have mentioned them at all. Some philosophical critics will press the question of whether Rolston's value system is excessively consequentialist, in trading off the well-being of (current) individuals against those of species, and those of species against those of ecosystems. At any rate, we will certainly want some assurance that his evaluational holism in the natural sphere will not spill over into a kind of totalitarianism in the domain of interpersonal relations.[43] On the other side, more radical environmentalists will maintain that Rolston has conceded too much to the anthropocentric viewpoint, by allowing that 'the highest value attained in the system is lofty individuality with its subjectivity, present in vertebrates, mammals, primates, and pre-eminently in persons'.[44] His view is also open to theological critique of course. Some will object that his thoroughgoing affirmation of the natural world is inconsistent with Christian teaching, because it does not take seriously enough the doctrine of the Fall, or does not leave open the possibility that the natural world will be subject to radical improvement at the eschaton.[45] In my own view, Rolston's approach is not overthrown by any of these considerations, though it may need fine-tuning in the light of such concerns. At the least, it offers a way of broadening traditional philosophical discussions of the problem of evil, in a way which takes account of disvalues which are independent of any hurt done to human beings, and draws attention to the multiple achievements – conceptual, experiential, and (broadly speaking) moral – which are presupposed in any informed response to these issues.[46]

We have now considered the 'problem of evil' from a range of viewpoints. I have argued that the integral whole approach to theodicy throws some light on the compatibility of evil with the claim that the universe is fundamentally good; and I have tried to develop such a theodicy in ecological terms, and in relation to the thought that certain evils may be the precondition of our existence considered concretely. I have also noted that no theodicy should expect to provide a complete rationale of evil, in part because of the disparity between divine and human understanding, and in part because of the goodness of the integral wholes associated with authentic atheism. If this is so, then any defence of the claim that the world's goodness is its reason for existence must paradoxically stop short of supposing that this claim is demonstrably true.

Different people will of course have different views about the plausibility of the case I have been assembling in Chapters 1 to 4. I want to argue next that a commitment to the fundamental goodness of the world, and to the idea that its goodness is its *raison d'être,* remains rational even if the epistemic case should fall some way short of certainty. There are a number of ways of developing this idea, but I shall draw on the notion that there are moral (non-epistemic) reasons which favour the adoption of some such commitment.

Part III

Moral commitment to the goodness of the world

5 A non-epistemic case for trusting in the goodness of the world

Introduction

So far, I have examined parts of the evidential case both for and against the thesis that the goodness of the world is its reason for existence. I have argued that the aesthetic qualities of nature together with its tendency to produce richer and more complex forms of existence provide a solid foundation for this thesis, and that the various disvalues in nature do not count decisively against it. I am not going to offer any precise verdict on the overall persuasiveness of this case, for two reasons. First of all, it seems inevitable that some people will find that these arguments fall short of establishing beyond reasonable doubt that the goodness of the world is its *raison d'être.* Again, I suggest that this fact is itself in some degree predictable on natural theological grounds, and should therefore be anticipated within any overarching natural theological case. Secondly, I suggest that establishing the reasonableness of belief in our thesis does not depend upon showing that the hypothesis of design is clearly more probable than not. In particular, once the force of moral considerations is taken into account, it seems enough to show that the balance of epistemic considerations is not clearly against this hypothesis. My object in this section is to offer some support of this understanding of the burden of proof which the proponent of design must assume.[1]

This discussion has another purpose too. At various points already, I have alluded to my concern to find connections between natural theology and the considerations which seem to inform religious belief in practice. Now it seems clear enough that there is a marked correlation between the religious beliefs of human beings and their communities of origin. This suggests that an account of the rationality of religious belief which is sensitive to the actual processes of belief formation should say something about the role of community participation in the adoption of such beliefs. Moreover, I suggest that many people hold religious beliefs partly out of a sense that, in doing so, they are showing trust in the ultimate nature of things, and that such trust is, other things being equal, morally appropriate. In these respects, it seems to me, the considerations which move people to believe often have a moral dimension. And this fact should surely be explored in any assessment of the reasonableness of religious belief *in practice*.

So the twofold purpose of the discussion of this section is to consider what burden of proof the natural theologian is reasonably required to bear, and to do this by mapping out a role for pragmatic considerations in the justification of religious belief. Our discussion so far has adopted an evidential perspective and, predictably, that discussion has proved to be somewhat indeterminate, to the extent that it has not supplied reasons for belief which every reasonable person ought to find compelling. My suggestion in this chapter is that we can bring these matters to a clearer resolution by supplementing these evidential considerations by reference to the social and moral dimensions of religious belief. This project represents an extension of our ongoing concern to ground the arguments of natural theology in familiar evaluative commitments. In this case, the commitments in question will be moral or interpersonal. Although the argument I offer will be pragmatic rather than epistemic, there is still good reason to consider it an exercise in natural theology, in so far as it does not depend on appeal to the scriptures or 'revelation' of any particular faith tradition. It is worth emphasising that the arguments of this chapter do not enable us to bypass the evidential case we have discussed in Chapters 1 to 4; for they will apply only if there is a reasonably robust evidential case for the claim that the goodness of the world is its reason for existence.

So far, I have said a little about the issue I wish to consider in this chapter, and a little about the method I intend to follow in the process. Before moving on to the main body of the discussion, I would like to introduce just briefly a classic paper which takes up these same concerns in a rather similar fashion. In particular I want to say something about William James's essay 'The Will To Believe'.[2] In this paper, James argues that in cases where intellectual enquiry alone is incapable of settling the truth or falsity of two competing hypotheses, we are justified in preferring one over the other providing that the choice between them presents us with 'a genuine option', that is, as he puts it, a choice that is 'living', 'momentous' and 'forced'.[3] To say that an option is living for a particular individual is to say that she is psychologically capable of adopting either of its constituent hypotheses. Here James is trying to bring out the fact that sometimes a person is unable to adopt a belief not so much because of objections of a logical or evidential kind, but more fundamentally because it has no purchase upon her imagination. In this sense, we may say that the religious belief system of Australian Aborigines may not be a live possibility for me, not merely because of my ignorance or because of theoretical reservations I might entertain in relation to their worldview, but because my imaginative and affective life, as well as my intellectual commitments, are too far removed from theirs. To say furthermore that an option is momentous and forced is to say in turn that it involves a choice of fundamental importance, from which significant benefits might flow, and to say that its constituent hypotheses are logically exhaustive (so that there is no possibility of preferring some other hypothesis to those proposed in the option).

We can see what James is driving at here. His thought is that if a question cannot be resolved by intellectual enquiry, and if you have to take a stance on one side or other (because the option is 'forced'), then you are surely justified in determining which way you will jump by reference to practical considerations (given that the option is 'momentous'). James takes it that the hypothesis proposed by religious belief does form part of a genuine option for the group he is addressing. (He is speaking to the Philosophical Clubs of Yale and Brown Universities; he notes that for this group the relevant belief system is Protestant Christianity.)[4] The question of whether or not to subscribe to religious beliefs is momentous, because even in this life many important benefits will follow on from the adoption of such beliefs; it is forced, because agnosticism places these benefits as surely out of our reach as disbelief; and it is live in so far as we (or at least the members of James's audience) are indeed capable of holding religious beliefs, and giving them a role in regulating our lives from an imaginative and affective point of view. Moreover, according to James, the truth or otherwise of religious beliefs is not capable of being settled by intellectual enquiry. Under these conditions, he suggests, we are entitled to let our 'passional nature' decide our response to the religious hypothesis; in other words, we are free to invoke 'the will to believe'.

To this it may be objected that if the evidence is insufficient to establish the truth or falsity of a hypothesis, then the rational response is suspension of judgement. But James argues that the determination to suspend judgement in such cases is itself a 'passional' commitment. Thus he writes:

> To preach scepticism to us as a duty until 'sufficient evidence' for religion be found, is tantamount . . . to telling us, when in the presence of the religious hypothesis, that to yield to our fear of its being error is wiser and better than to yield to our hope that it may be true. It is not intellect against all passions, then; it is only intellect with one passion laying down its law.[5]

James himself considers that, in this context at least, the gaining of truth is more to be prized than the avoidance of error. In turn, this reflects his empiricist sense that 'objective evidence and certitude' are not realistic ideals of human enquiry.[6] Given this empiricism, the suspension of judgement rule is, he thinks, practically unsustainable, and itself contrary to reason, in so far as it excludes the possibility of gaining truth where it might be found:

> I, therefore, for one, cannot see my way to accepting the agnostic rules for truth-seeking, or wilfully agree to keep my willing nature out of the game. I cannot do so for this plain reason, that *a rule of thinking which would absolutely prevent me from acknowledging certain kinds of truth if those kinds of truth be really there, would be an irrational rule.*[7]

I do not want to endorse James's account in all its detail. It may be that his 'empiricism' enjoins excessive scepticism about the nature of human understanding, and it may be that his emphasis on the practical benefits of religious belief runs the risk of grounding religious commitment in merely self-interested concerns. However, James's approach is of interest to us because it takes up, in an engaging way, a number of the issues to be considered in this chapter. First of all, it raises the question of how much evidence is needed if religious belief is to be rationally tenable. James's answer is in brief that a state of epistemic parity is sufficient, providing that the belief forms part of a genuine option and providing that intellectual considerations alone are incapable of resolving the issue. Moreover, James's account is sensitive to the role of psychological considerations in the formation of religious belief. Where we stand on the question of religious truth is likely to depend, he intimates, upon our psychological disposition: for some of us, such belief will seem attractive, and the life it makes possible will seem to confer genuine benefits; for others, this will not be so. So James's discussion takes into account the existential dimension of religious commitment: the fact that such commitment is made not merely on theoretical grounds, but for the sake of participation in a certain form of life.

My simplest recourse at this point would be simply to embrace James's account, and to conclude that if the evidence is not clearly against the design hypothesis (a claim which may be sustained, I suggest, in the manner of Chapters 1 to 4), and if it seems unlikely that intellectual enquiry (in this life) will ever determine (beyond all reasonable doubt) its truth value, then we can, with integrity, allow our stance on the issue to be decided by our 'passional natures'. But instead I shall try to develop a further pragmatic account of the justification of religious belief. My account will follow James in giving an important role to personal decision in the formation of religious belief, so downplaying the role of abstract, argumentative inference. And, with James, I shall argue that a state of epistemic parity may be sufficient for the justification of religious belief: in fact on this point, my perspective will be, if anything, more radical than his. So my approach will follow James's example in looking to non-epistemic considerations as a basis for religious belief. But whereas on his view these considerations appear mostly to be prudential (though there are hints of another perspective), on my approach they will be moral. So my account, I think, stands independently of James's proposal, but is related to it in these various ways. I hope this prefatory discussion of James's approach will help to bring out the distinctiveness of what I want to say on these topics, as well as drawing attention to the continuities between my proposal and at least one earlier treatment of these issues. Again, in the present context, the point of the following discussion is to provide some account of the conditions of justified belief into which we can insert our reflections in Chapters 1 to 4.

A moral, communitarian case for religious belief

Richard Gale has proposed that in certain circumstances, we are justified in upholding the good character of another person even if we should lack an epistemic basis for this claim.[8] Suppose for example that my parents stand accused of some serious offence, and deny the charge. If the epistemic considerations known to me fail to settle the question, then we should suppose, according to Gale, that rather than suspending judgement I ought to uphold my parents' innocence, not merely in the sense of protesting to others that they are innocent, but in the sense of believing as much myself. Clearly, believing in this sort of context is not a matter of judging that on the available evidence, a certain proposition is more likely to be true than any of its alternatives. It is rather a matter of, for instance, resolving to entertain feelings towards my parents of the kind that would be in keeping with their being innocent; and in general, it is a matter of allowing the idea of their innocence to regulate my feelings, imagination, and conduct. Belief in this sense is evidently, in some circumstances, voluntary.[9] (We may include here the case of indirect voluntariness: it may be that I can induce a belief by performing various actions which are known to give rise reliably to the belief.)[10]

Of course, because I know my parents well, I may have a fund of evidence, not available to others, which gives me from an epistemic point of view good reason to believe in their innocence, even when from the perspective of others there is no epistemic case in their favour. But for present purposes, we are envisaging the case where epistemic considerations are indecisive even for me. In such a case, according to Gale, I have a moral, trust-relationship reason for believing in my parents' innocence, rather than merely suspending judgement on the question. We might wonder whether this sort of moral consideration will count when the epistemic considerations known to me are on balance against my parents. If the epistemic case, although against them, is not so strong that believing in my parents' innocence ceases to be a 'living' possibility for me, then we might suppose that I still have an adequate (though not compelling) moral reason for believing in their innocence. In these circumstances, we might not wish to say that I am *obliged* to believe in their innocence; but we might still suppose that my doing so would be *commendable*, and in this sense justified.

In sum, Gale's suggestion is that in the context of trust relationships, that is, relationships of the kind which arise within family life, or more generally in our dealings with people where there has been a deep exchange of trust, there can be moral reasons for upholding beliefs which are integral to the relationship as a trust relationship; and these moral reasons can adequately justify a belief independently of any epistemic case in its support.

I suggest that most of us acknowledge the legitimacy of Gale's account in our ordinary habits of belief formation. But his proposal is also capable of being given a more theoretical justification. Once we have promised to do something, we have, of course, a moral reason for doing it. And by analogy, we might say, when we enter into a trust relationship with someone, we in effect (usually in a non-verbal way) promise to uphold her integrity. So once in such a relationship, we have a moral reason for upholding that person's integrity, a reason which will be adequate to ground our belief in her integrity even in the absence of epistemic support. Granted that this sort of moral consideration can be invoked quite properly in circumstances of this kind, we may be interested to know whether it, or something analogous to it, can play a role in the justification of religious belief in particular.

Gale notes that this approach to the justification of belief has, in some cases, more radical implications than James's account of the conditions of non-epistemic justification. For instance, on James's view, it seems I would not be entitled, let alone obliged, to uphold my parents' innocence in the circumstances I have described; instead I ought to suspend judgement, assuming that the issue is capable of being settled by means of an empirical enquiry.[11] (Recall that on James's view the will to believe can find proper employment only where an option 'cannot by its nature be decided on intellectual grounds'.)[12] Granted that James's account of the conditions of non-epistemic justification carries rather different implications from an account which rests on the trust-relationship case, we have good reason to consider whether this latter case offers a further way of developing a non-epistemic account of the justification of religious belief. This is what I propose to do.[13]

One further preliminary clarification is in order. James's account is explicitly a response to W. K. Clifford's proposal that 'it is wrong always, everywhere, and for anyone, to believe anything upon insufficient evidence'.[14] More recently, this principle has been criticised by Alvin Plantinga and others, who have argued that religious belief may be 'properly basic' (in other words, held legitimately without 'evidence', that is, without being inferred from any other belief).[15] Plantinga's case rests upon an analogy between religious beliefs and ordinary perceptual beliefs: in each of these cases, he thinks, a belief may be held with grounds and yet basically. So his case remains epistemic, although it is non-evidential. My discussion will offer another approach to the thought that religious beliefs may be properly basic, in the sense of being warranted independently of any evidential case in their favour. In this context, the justification will be moral rather than epistemic, and the analogy will be with beliefs which contribute towards our participation in a trust relationship (and not with perceptual beliefs). I shall now set out such an approach.

Stephen Wykstra has argued that there are many clear exceptions to Clifford's principle in so far as many of our beliefs are held quite properly on the basis of testimony, where we have not cited, and perhaps could not cite, any evidence in their support (not even the fact that such and such a person's testimony is to be trusted for such and such reasons).[16] He offers as an example the belief that there are electrons, which most of us hold, and are entitled to hold, so he suggests, basically.[17] Wykstra is surely right on these points. Now, as Wykstra notes, religious beliefs are also held in this communitarian fashion (like most beliefs indeed), and to this extent they too will be exempt from Clifford's requirement that a belief should be held only on the basis of evidence. But we should notice in addition that in many cases religious beliefs are not merely absorbed from the general epistemic environment. Instead, they are given to a person by certain significant others; and the learning and adoption of these beliefs may help to constitute and maintain a trust relationship with these others. I shall argue that this fact may provide the basis for a moral justification of religious belief, which may be used to supplement the epistemic case (from testimony) to which Wykstra alludes.

Suppose we concentrate on the case where the handing on of religious beliefs is from parent to child. Now as we all know anecdotally, there are parents who would consider their child's refusal to adopt their religious views a breach of the trust relationship between them. In cases of this kind, it seems that as a matter of psychological fact, the child's acceptance of its parents' views is required for the persistence of the trust relationship between them. However, this sort of attitude seems likely to involve a distorted conception of a child's responsibilities to its parents. So let us grant that in general a child is under no obligation to accept the religious outlook of its parents. Nonetheless, her willingness to do so can play, for conceptual and not merely psychological reasons, an important part in deepening the trust relationship between them. Above all, this is because religious claims do not merely concern abstract metaphysical claims about the nature of things. More likely, they will amount to an integrated moral and metaphysical account of the significance of human life. It follows that my subscribing to the religious views of my parents carries a deeper significance for my relationship to them than my subscribing to their views on, for instance, the nature of electrons. For in adopting their religious views, I am implicitly affirming their understanding of the meaning of their lives. Conversely, to deny the religious scheme in terms of which they make sense of their lives would be to suppose that their understanding of themselves and their endeavours is mistaken and, most likely, mistaken in some fairly fundamental way; and in holding such a view about their self-understanding, I would be setting a significant limit on the potential depth of the trust relationship between us, although I would not (in a properly constituted relationship) be excluding all possibility of a trust relationship.

I suggest then that a willingness to adopt the religious views of one's parents or, more generally, of one's immediate community should not be made a precondition of participation in the corresponding trust relationships. To this extent, the case of religious belief offers only a partial analogy with the case we discussed earlier: believing in someone's good character is more evidently a genuine precondition of any trust relationship with her than sharing her religious beliefs. Even so, a willingness to adopt the religious outlook of significant others has a clearer connection to the endurance of a trust relationship than does, say, a willingness to adopt their beliefs concerning the nature of electrons, or the weather tomorrow, or in general to share their views on some merely empirical issue. These reflections suggest that in some measure (to a lesser extent than in the case of believing in my parents' innocence, in the circumstances we have discussed, but to a greater extent than in the case of sharing their beliefs about the weather tomorrow) we may have reason to hold a religious belief in the absence of evidence in so far as it plays a constructive role in our trust relationships with others. As Wykstra notes, in general we have reason to hold beliefs in the absence of evidence if there is testimony in their favour; but I am suggesting that we may have particularly good reason for holding religious beliefs in the absence of evidence, in so far as the testimony in this case is provided by people to whom we bear a trust relationship, and in so far as the holding of religious beliefs can contribute constructively towards the maintenance of these relationships. In this fashion, trust-relationship considerations may contribute in a non-evidential, non-epistemic way to the overall justification of religious belief.

For example, suppose I find, after conscientious enquiry, that there is a state of epistemic parity between theism and each of its alternatives.[18] Let us suppose in particular that this state of parity obtains after I have given due weight, in the non-evidential way Wykstra notes, to any testimony in support of theistic belief.[19] In this case, I suggest, if I have sound trust-relationship reasons for subscribing to theism, then these reasons will ensure that overall I have positive reason to be a theist. It is arguable that trust-relationship considerations can also make a difference when the epistemic balance is against theism (or some other religious outlook), providing that this imbalance is moderate. In the case I gave earlier, where my parents stand accused of some serious offence, I may have powerful reasons for believing in their innocence even in the face of fairly strong counter-evidence. However, as we have noted, it seems that in the context of religious belief, trust-relationship considerations carry a lesser weight, since the adoption of religious beliefs is not properly a precondition of one's participation in trust relationships. Nonetheless, I think we would be inclined to commend someone for adopting a religious belief in the face of moderate counter-evidence for the sake of honouring her trust-relationship commitments; and in this sense, we would consider her belief justified. But again, on the account I am developing, there can be no question of anyone being obliged to adopt the belief in these circumstances.

If we do take the view that I would be justified in holding religious beliefs even in the face of moderate counter-evidence, providing they contribute to my trust relationships, then this approach may well prove more radical than James's in a further respect. As I have noted already, the trust-relationship approach is more radical than James's in so far as it allows pragmatic considerations a role even where intellectual enquiry is able in principle to decide the issue; it may also prove to be more radical than James's in so far as James seems to have in view the case where there is epistemic parity between the religious hypothesis and its alternative, not the case where religious belief is in some degree epistemically disadvantaged.

If these observations are to the point, they suggest that standard philosophical discussions of the justification of religious belief are wrong to abstract from the richly interpersonal context in which religious beliefs are typically formed. If that is so, then in constructing a natural theology we should not confine our attention to theoretical considerations of the kind we have discussed in Chapters 1 to 4. In addition, we should take into account the web of trust relationships which surround a person. Of course, whereas theoretical considerations bear in the same way, in principle, upon all people, the relevance of trust-relationship considerations will vary from person to person, depending upon the nature of their community setting; so at this point the justification of religious belief will become a thoroughly individual matter, and will need to take into account the particularities of each person's circumstances.

These observations call to mind a comment of Wittgenstein's. In his lectures on religion, Wittgenstein remarks:

> If the question arises as to the existence of a god or God, it plays an entirely different role to that of the existence of any person or object I ever heard of. One said, had to say, that one *believed* in the existence, and if one did not believe, this was regarded as something bad. Normally if I did not believe in the existence of something no one would think there was anything wrong in this . . .[20]

Clearly, in these remarks, Wittgenstein is concerned with the social context of religious belief, noting that one can be blamed or praised for one's religious beliefs to a degree that would not be appropriate in matters of empirical belief. I suggest that praise and blame are indeed relevant here not only because religious beliefs have inherently a moral or evaluative character, but also because the acceptance or rejection of such beliefs may well play a part in sustaining or damaging our trust relationships with others. In other words, such beliefs are the object of praise and blame because of their importance for the life of a community.

Of course, in the spirit of the Enlightenment, we may well feel some discomfort about the social dimension of religious belief. We may sense that, if the community is given this sort of role in the inculcation of religious belief, then a religious tradition may become oppressive or a conduit of mere superstition. I hope I have guarded against such an interpretation of my approach, by noting that on this view trust-relationship considerations cannot oblige a person to hold a religious belief. Moreover, given the comparative weakness of trust-relationship considerations in the religious context, evidence and argument are sure to retain an important role in the justification of religious belief. Where the evidence is seen to be strongly against religious belief, it is unlikely, as a matter of psychological fact, that trust-relationship considerations will carry sufficient weight to make the adoption of religious beliefs an attractive possibility, even supposing that it is a live possibility in these circumstances. In sum, my thesis is simply that a person may have good reason overall for accepting a religious belief, given a state of epistemic parity (or perhaps moderate epistemic disadvantage), if the belief is received from someone to whom she is related in trust and if the adoption of the belief will help to sustain this relationship.

I note briefly one further objection to this argument. It might be said: contrary to what you have maintained, we have particular reason to be sceptical about what we are told by people to whom we are related in trust. For in such relationships, there is a risk that we will allow our emotional involvement to distort our reading of the relevant evidence. This is not a state of affairs to be commended, but deplored; it reflects a weakness, albeit an understandable one. I agree that in cases of this kind, we do need to be careful in our assessment of the evidence, for the risks of self-deception here are greater than they would normally be. However, it is one thing to decide what the evidence really is, and another (in cases where the will has some role) to determine what belief to adopt in response. My suggestion is not that trust-relationship considerations should shape our reading of the evidence, only that these considerations may have a legitimate role to play when we determine which belief to hold in light of the evidence. Such an approach need not imply self-deception, or any shrinking from established facts.

In the discussion so far, I have presented an alternative route to something like the conclusion which William James endorsed in his essay 'The Will to Believe'. Like James, I have proposed that a person may be justified in holding a religious belief in a state of evidential (and more generally of epistemic) parity. I have made this case with particular reference to the moral justification of beliefs which arises in the context of trust relationships. This discussion could be seen as an elaboration of James's argument, in so far as it spells out just which benefits may follow on from the adoption of a religious belief; in this way it gives some content to his claim that the religious option is 'momentous'. But the case I have presented seems not to depend upon the particular apparatus which James invokes, and in my view, is more clearly stated without that apparatus. It is simply a matter of generalising from the role we accord trust-relationship considerations in other contexts.

We began with the question: what burden of proof is reasonably placed on the natural theologian? I conclude that for some people, those raised in theistic communities, this burden is at any rate not as onerous as in other spheres (such as natural science). If someone has good trust-relationship reasons for holding theistic beliefs (or religious beliefs of some other kind), then those beliefs are sufficiently justified, I suggest, providing that epistemic considerations do not tell against them (or tell against them only moderately). This is a burden of proof which, I suggest, the natural theologian can meet, in the way we have discussed in Chapters 1 to 4. So here is one way of inserting our theoretical discussion from the first part of this book into a broader context, in such a way as to bring that theoretical approach to the question of whether theistic belief is rational to some sort of pragmatic resolution. In the remainder of this chapter, I shall examine the relevance of trust-relationship considerations for religious belief from a rather different perspective. This time, the considerations I cite will be relevant to people generally, regardless of their upbringing or community setting.

Relationship to God as a trust relationship

So far I have been concerned with the relevance of trust-relationship considerations to the justification of religious belief in so far as religious beliefs contribute towards our trust relations with other human beings. I shall now seek to apply the trust-relationship example in a new way. This time, I shall argue not by reference to relationships between human beings, but by reference to the trust relationship which is said to obtain potentially between human beings and God. I shall begin by making some remarks about Christian theism in particular, before examining whether similar considerations can be introduced in relation to a more general theism of the kind that might be justified on natural theological grounds.

In the Christian context it is clear enough that the relationship between the human person and God may be understood by analogy with the trust relationships which hold between human beings. This is especially true because Christians regard their relationship to God not only in interpersonal terms, but more precisely by analogy with the trust relationship between a small child and its parent. In consequence, Christian faith is often said to involve not merely *fides*, the belief that there is a God with certain purposes, but also *fiducia*, a commitment of the person to God in trust. As John Hick notes, *fiducia* is 'a religious trust which may be compared with trust or confidence in another person'.[21] We might add that *fiducia* may be compared more exactly to the trust which arises in the context of close, for instance familial, relationships, rather than to the trust we may wish to show human beings in general.

The natural theologian who subscribes to the argument from design has good reason to adopt this same sort of framework, I suggest. According to the argument from design, the world's source is personal, where the meaning of 'personal' is related to its meaning in human contexts, at least to the extent that human persons can discern in some measure the purposes, or design, of the divine person. Moreover, according to the design argument, the personal source of the world is actively concerned for the well-being of creatures. If the designer is indeed properly characterised as a personal source of being, interested in creaturely flourishing, then we have a sound foundation, surely, for comparing the relationship of designer and human beings to that of parent and children in the human context. In short, if there is a designer, we have reason to conceive of our relationship to him or her by analogy with trust relationships in the human context.

Now it might seem that this fact (that our relationship to God, if there is a God, is properly one of trust) can make no difference to the justification of the belief that there is a God. Certainly, my trust relationship to someone can supply me with reasons for holding various beliefs about her (beliefs which are presupposed in the trust commitment); but my trust relationship with someone surely cannot give me reasons for supposing that she exists in the first place. That would be hopelessly circular. As Hick comments, *fiducia* surely presupposes *fides*.[22] (Trust in God surely presupposes the belief that there is a God.) All the same, I suggest, the thought that our relationship to God is properly a trust relationship can make a difference to the justification of religious belief.[23]

To see why this is so, we might begin with an analogy. Suppose I receive a letter which purports to be from my wife. And suppose that this letter makes some claim whose truth matters for the persistence of our relationship as a trust relationship. In this case, we might say, I should give some weight to the fact that if the author is who she professes to be, then I have particular reason to believe what she says. Of course, my trust-relationship reason for believing the contents of the letter will be strongest when I know that the letter has been written by my wife. However, this reason will still have some force, I suggest, even if there is some uncertainty about the identity of the author of the letter.

This sort of example suggests a parallel with the case which interests the natural theologian. The natural theologian who attaches some weight to the design argument supposes that there is some reason to consider the world as a kind of communication, one which reveals the providential purposes of its source. Now in this case too, we may suppose, the real identity of the source of the communication is uncertain (indeed, we may be uncertain about whether we are dealing with a communication at all). Nonetheless, by analogy with the example of the letter, it may be urged that we have a distinctive, moral reason to believe the apparent communication, assuming that there is at least some prospect that it is genuine, and assuming that if genuine, then it will bear vitally upon the relationship between ourselves and its source. For if the source of the communication is indeed God, or a benevolent personal source of our being, then we have a trust-relationship reason for believing it to be true. To put the matter more concretely, I might reason as follows: I see there is some reason to suppose that, for example, the natural beauty of the world is best interpreted as evidence of God's providential care for the world; at the same time, I see that this interpretation is (let us say) no more probable than not; in that case, while epistemic considerations alone may leave me undecided on the question, I still have good reason overall to subscribe to the idea of design, because in doing so I have some prospect of fulfilling a fundamental moral ideal: the ideal of responding in trust to someone to whom I ought to be related in trust.

This might sound rather involved, but I think such considerations do in fact play a part in the religious commitment of many people. William James hints at such a view in 'The Will To Believe'. There he observes that we sometimes feel that in believing we perform the universe the greatest service we can, and he intimates that this feeling may be relevant to our determination to hold religious beliefs.[24] One possible gloss on his remark would be this: if the universe were personal, then prima facie our relationship to it would properly be one of trust, just as our relationship to our parents (our biological rather than our metaphysical source) is prima facie properly one of trust; but we can best show such trust by holding religious beliefs, that is, by believing the ultimate reality to be good and trustworthy. To put the matter in James's terms, if the holding of religious beliefs is a way of rendering service to God, then we may have a moral reason for holding such beliefs, given that our relationship to God, if there is a God, is properly one of service.

There are two spirits in which this sort of reasoning could be rehearsed. Someone might adopt theistic belief on a purely pragmatic basis, supposing that in all likelihood there is no God, but choosing to act as if there were for the sake of the good which would result if there should be a God. (Compare the case of someone who believes that a certain commission almost certainly does not come from his beloved, but who undertakes to fulfil it anyway, just in case it should do so.) On the other hand, someone might suppose that the bearing of epistemic considerations on religious questions is broadly neutral or somewhat favourable. Trust-relationship considerations might move such a person to hold religious beliefs in the sense of committing herself to their truth (and not merely in the sense of acting as if they should be true). If the conclusions of Chapters 1 to 4 can be sustained, then we have some reason to suppose that we find ourselves in the second of these situations, one which makes belief in the full sense possible, and not merely belief in the 'acting as if' sense.

So here is one way in which trust-relationship considerations may make a difference to the moral justification of theistic belief. To put the matter briefly, someone might suppose that by being a theist, she may well be performing a service to God, and that she has a moral reason for performing such a service, if indeed there is a God. If the belief which arises in this case is to be more than the 'acting as if' kind of belief, this moral argument will still depend upon epistemic considerations, but again it may be enough to show that these considerations are equally balanced on either side of the question. Note that this sort of justification will only apply to forms of religious belief which conceive of the ultimate reality in personal terms. And the case will apply most forcefully to those faiths which model our relation to this reality on, for instance, the child-parent relation. By contrast, the first sort of argument I presented, which took the trust relationships between human beings as its starting point, will be equally relevant to all forms of religious belief. Indeed, it will also apply to morally rich forms of atheism.

This sort of argument clearly has some relevance to the justification of revealed religion. In general, natural theology can provide a kind of prolegomenon to revealed theology. For instance, if there is an epistemic argument of some weight for the idea that there is a God, then that argument should make a difference to our assessment of the plausibility of miracle claims, which in turn may make a difference to our understanding of the plausibility of various other notions propounded by a revealed religion.[25] The moral considerations which we have been examining can supplement this sort of epistemic argument if a revealed tradition represents itself as a disclosure given in trust by one to whom we are properly related in trust. In this case, we will have a distinctively moral reason for adopting the claims advanced in the revelation; and this reason may give us good grounds for endorsing these claims rather than simply suspending judgement, in the case where epistemic considerations alone are indecisive.

I have been arguing that trust-relationship considerations may supply a moral case which can 'top up' the epistemic case for *fides* so making *fides* overall reasonable. Next I want to look just briefly at a particular example of this sort of justification. Suppose there are epistemic grounds for thinking that the world derives from a transcendent, personal source. And suppose that epistemic considerations are neutral on whether or not this source is good. Now, once more, we might suppose that prima facie our relationship to our metaphysical source is properly one of trust. If that is so, then in the case we are considering, epistemic considerations may carry someone as far as the idea that the world has a transcendent personal source, and trust-relationship considerations may then bring her to the further thought that this source is properly regarded as trustworthy, assuming again that epistemic considerations do not provide positive reason for thinking otherwise.[26]

It is worth noting this possibility since some natural theological arguments purport to show that the world's source is personal, without seeking to establish at the same time the goodness and trustworthiness of this source.[27] However, the natural theological argument I have used cannot proceed in this way so readily. For the design argument tends to conflate the questions of whether the world has a personal source and whether that source is good: it is the goodness of the world which leads us to think that its source is both personal and good. So if the design argument is to make use of trust-relationship considerations, this is most obviously done by supposing that the argument's task is to make an epistemic case for the thought that the world's source is both personal and good; given an epistemic case of this kind, trust-relationship considerations may then provide a further, moral justification of belief in the way we have discussed.

This emphasis on the role of trust-relationship considerations reflects, I would argue, the lived character of religious belief. For instance, it is often noted that religious beliefs seem to be impervious to empirical refutation: it seems the faithful do not treat their beliefs as mere hypotheses, to be held tentatively, depending on the outcome of our empirical enquiries. There are various explanations of this. Following our discussion, we might offer this explanation: the tenacity with which religious beliefs are held, by comparison with empirical beliefs, reflects the believer's sense that for moral (and not merely empirical) reasons, trust constitutes a proper response to the source of the world. In the same way, in relationships of trust in the human context, once we have entered a trust relationship, we will have good reason to refrain from subjecting the trustworthiness of the other person to evidential examination (for to do so would be to place oneself outside the relationship as a trust relationship). Moreover, we may have a good reason to enter into a trust relationship in the first place for non-epistemic reasons, for instance if the person in question is properly related to us in trust in virtue of being the source of our being. In this way, trust-relationship considerations may help to explain the paradoxical willingness of believers to commit themselves with relative certainty in matters of religion in spite of the relative absence of compelling epistemic grounds for religious belief. Again, Wittgenstein notes this sort of difference between religious and empirical belief. Thus he remarks that if someone asks me whether I believe that there is a German aeroplane overhead, I could quite sensibly reply: 'Possibly, I'm not sure.' But such a reply would make no sense, he suggests, in response to the question: 'Do you believe in the Last Judgement?' It would make no sense because in the nature of the case to believe at all here is to believe with a conviction which does not admit of such doubts.[28]

It is worth noting that some commentators have objected to the argument from design, and natural theology more generally, on the grounds that it represents religious belief as akin to a scientific hypothesis: as though it should be held in a provisional sort of way, in deference to developments in our empirical enquiries.[29] I hope I have shown how the design argument may be embedded within a larger framework which appeals to moral as well as epistemic considerations, and which thereby gives due acknowledgement to the deeply rooted and emotionally resonant character of religious commitments.[30]

I noted in Chapter 3 how the parent-child relationship may prove important for the construction of a theodicy. In the context of theodicy, the relevant feature of the analogy is the child's inability to comprehend its parents' purposes. In this chapter I have again appealed to the analogy between God and a parent. And again, I have suggested that the analogy may be relevant to our willingness to consider the world's source as good and trustworthy. But in this case, another feature of the analogy is relevant, namely the fact that the relationship between parents and children is properly one of trust. Clearly, this consideration is logically independent of the first: our relationship to our parents is properly one of trust even if there should be no disparity of understanding between us. Given that the imagery of the parent-child relationship is so deeply inscribed in the piety of theistic religions, it is interesting to note the multi-faceted relevance of this analogy for natural theology.

Conclusions

I have been arguing that a person's religious beliefs may contribute towards her participation in trust relationships, both in relation to other human beings and in relation to God. To this extent, I have proposed, there is a moral case for religious belief, just as there is in general a moral case for upholding beliefs which are integral to one's trust relationships with other human beings. Where this case appeals to our trust relationships with other human beings, it is I think relatively straightforward. Establishing the relevance of a prospective trust relationship to God to the belief that there is a God is somewhat more difficult, since there must be a suspicion that any such venture will be circular. However, I have tried to show how this concern may be addressed.

Apart from its intrinsic interest, I have broached this topic for two reasons. First, I have wanted to bring out the significance of our survey, in Chapters 1 to 4, of the evidential case for and against the claim that the goodness of the world is its *raison d'être*. That discussion issued in the conclusion that there is a reasonably robust evidential case for the hypothesis of design. The discussion of this chapter suggests that this reading of the epistemic case is enough to make belief in design (of the kind which involves commitment to truth) overall reasonable once allowance has been made for trust-relationship considerations. This moral case allows us to offer an overarching argument for design which does not depend upon any precise consensus concerning the strength of evidential considerations. Typical exchanges on these matters suggest that disagreement concerning the strength of any such evidential case is likely to be deeply entrenched. (Again, I suggest that this outcome is also somewhat predictable on natural theological grounds.) In these circumstances, it is clearly important that a natural theology should offer a way of building constructively upon the evidential case without presupposing that everyone ought in good conscience to find it entirely persuasive. The central concern of this chapter has been to provide some such way of drawing out the significance of evidential considerations.

My second, related purpose has been to give due acknowledgement to the place of non-evidential factors in the justification of religious belief. I have done this, first of all, by commenting on the role of communities in the handing on of religious beliefs, and secondly by noting that relationship to God, if there is a God, is properly one of trust. It would generally be recognised, I think, that these features of religious commitment must have a certain primacy in any *psychological* account of the formation of religious belief, in so far as there is a high correlation between people's religious beliefs and the beliefs of their community of origin, and in so far as a person's religious belief is grounded in her sense that belief is a precondition of showing trust in the ultimate nature of things. I have tried to indicate how these characteristics of religious belief are also germane to its justification (and not merely its psychological origins), for moral rather than epistemic reasons. Clearly, this approach offers a further contribution to our study of the role of evaluative commitments in shaping the nature and rationality of religious belief.

This completes my discussion of the justification of the belief that the goodness of the world is its *raison d'être*. I have tried to show that there is overall (when epistemic and moral considerations are given due weight) a sufficient justification for theistic belief (or more exactly, belief in design), though the strength of this case will vary from person to person, and is unlikely to be absolutely compelling for many people, if anyone. If all of this is so, then the remaining chapters of this book will retain some interest, I hope. Allowing the reasonableness of theistic belief, how should we conceive of God? The approach I have taken is committed to thinking of God as personal and providential. But there are a number of ways of developing these ideas within an overarching theory of the nature of God and God's relation to the world. This conceptual issue, of how we should conceive of God, has a particular contemporary importance, in so far as the decline of religious belief in recent times reflects, I suggest, not so much a sense that the claims of religion are unreasonable (not properly grounded in the evidence for instance), but rather a sense that they don't really matter. It is, I suggest, indifference towards religious belief, rather than perplexity about its justification, which constitutes the principal contemporary challenge to religion. In these first five chapters, I have tried to show how religious beliefs may be grounded in various evaluatively rich evidential and moral considerations; and to this extent I have already broached the question of why religious beliefs should matter. But further discussion of this question will call for an examination of what we should understand by 'God'; for contemporary alienation from religion is often rooted in a disenchantment with conventional representations of God. In the concluding section of this book, I shall seek to forge a connection between the goodness of the world and the concept of God.

Part IV

The goodness of the world and the concept of God

6 Worship and the concept of God

Introduction

In Parts I and II of this book, I have argued that there are grounds for thinking of the world's goodness as its reason for existence. In Part III, I argued that even if the evidential case in support of this claim is less than conclusive, trust in the fundamental goodness of reality remains legitimate in the light of trust-relationship considerations. The argument so far has given more attention to the world and its goodness than to the inherent nature of God. This seems appropriate: in the nature of the case, we should not expect to have much insight into the inner dynamics or constitution of God on the basis of reason alone. The case of Part III presupposes that God is at least a personal source of being.[1] And the argument of Parts I and II presupposes that God is beneficent. But beyond these minimal claims, I have said little about the nature of God.

In this final part, I shall try and expand on the minimal theism of Parts I–III. There are a number of reasons for doing this. First of all, I suggest the principal challenge to theism in the contemporary world is not so much the feeling that religious belief is not adequately supported evidentially, but more a sense that it is lacking in any existential consequence. And in turn, this sense is rooted in a failure to find God as conventionally portrayed a focus of attraction.[2] The earlier sections of this book offer an initial engagement with this difficulty. For instance, I have tried to ground the argument from design in an evaluatively rich appreciation of the world. And I have tried to understand the point of religious commitment, in part, in communitarian and trust-relationship terms. But in this final part of the book, I want to take this case further by saying something about the ways in which the divine nature may echo the attractiveness of the world. Clearly, this represents an extension of the basic theme of this study: the goodness of the world as a foundation for natural theology.

There is a further reason for appending a discussion of the concept of God to our earlier discussion. It is often supposed that the principal difficulty for the argument from design is its tendency to issue in an anthropomorphic conception of God, on account of its willingness to compare God's activity in making the world to the activity of human beings when they act purposefully and benevolently. In this Part, I shall try to show how the argument from design may be married to a religiously adequate conception of God. For instance, I shall align the argument with a conception of God which in certain respects owes more to Aquinas's understanding of God as subsistent existence than to modern individualistic accounts of the divine nature. In keeping with the attempt of earlier chapters to take the lived character of religious belief as a starting point for natural theology, the discussion in this concluding section of the book will take worship and the notion of salvation as a first point of reference for our understanding of the divine nature.

In this chapter, I shall consider how an examination of the nature of worship may furnish an understanding of the concept of God.[3] I begin by looking at some standard models of divinity in traditional and recent writing. Discussion of the concept of God can be represented as a debate between two schools (each of which comprises a number of approaches), where one party maintains that God is immutable and impassible, and the other that God is changing and capable of being affected by the world. I shall take Aquinas as a paradigmatic representative of the first, 'classical' approach. According to Aquinas, God cannot, strictly speaking, be reckoned as an individual thing of this or that kind; rather, God is being itself, or subsistent existence. In effect, this approach treats particularity as in need of explanation. Thus we are invited to look for an explanation of the fact that a thing changes in this way rather than that, or is affected in this way rather than that, or has a finite nature which includes these capacities but not others. In turn, if an explanation of mutability, passibility and existence by kind is to be free from ultimate circularity, then we will need to suppose that there is a reality which is immutable, impassible, and free from the constraints of a finite nature. This general approach offers a striking example of epistemological concerns driving a concept of God. However, for present purposes, I am concerned not with the epistemological underpinnings of this rendering of the concept of God, but simply with the concept itself.[4]

In contemporary philosophy of religion, the classical account, according to which God is 'simple', has largely been displaced by a range of models which prefer to think of God as an individual person, who is changing (and therefore temporal), and related to things in the world not only as their cause but also in various respects as their effect.[5] Two kinds of consideration lie behind this development. First of all, this modern approach reflects a philosophical concern regarding the internal consistency of the classical view. For instance, some commentators have urged that the notion of pure being is nonsensical: the idea of being without particularity makes no more sense, it has been claimed, than the idea of pure history (as though one could have history in abstraction from particular events).[6] Or again, it has been said that it makes no sense to suppose both that the world makes no difference to God and that God has knowledge of the world.[7] A second kind of concern is more religious than philosophical in flavour. Here it is said that the classical view fails to provide for the interpersonal dimension of the believer's relation to God. Above all, this is because interpersonal relations, so it is said, require reciprocity: they demand that each party should be able to affect the other.[8] But, of course, an impassible God cannot partake of such a relationship.

It is not my intention to adjudicate between these two approaches. Instead I want to chart a sort of middle ground between them. More exactly, I shall argue that establishing the religious relevance of a God conceived individualistically may require some use of notions which are more commonly associated with the rival view. It is worth noting that the minimal theism I have outlined so far, which postulates a transcendent source of value who relates to the world providentially, is neutral between these two views, both of which endorse this core conception of God. As I shall explain, the concept of God which emerges from the following discussion will provide a further contribution to our project of grounding theistic belief in evaluative commitments, by showing how the goodness of mundane things provides a kind of fragmentary image of the goodness which God has whole and entire.

The religious adequacy of the individualistic model

I shall take Richard Swinburne's works *The Coherence of Theism* and *The Existence of God* as a benchmark for my presentation of 'the' individualistic approach, although of course a great variety of views may be brought under this general heading.[9] The God depicted in these works has duration, and changes over time as he learns of new developments in the world. (I shall keep to the masculine pronoun here, following Swinburne's usage.) This reflects the fact that, in at least some cases, creaturely choices logically precede God's knowledge of those choices.[10] Moreover, this God acts in the world for reasons which are broadly, if not in all their detail, intelligible to human beings.[11] Lastly, the God Swinburne portrays is logically contingent. In so far as his powers and knowledge are unbounded, such a God is more likely to exist than relatively 'complex' things like ourselves.[12] So to this extent, there is a connection between God's nature and his existence. But this connection is probabilistic: while God's existence is more likely than that of other things, it is not logically necessary. Indeed, Swinburne shows some sympathy with the view that the existence of anything at all is a priori 'vastly improbable, or at least not very probable'.[13]

Writers in the classical tradition are likely to take exception to this picture on metaphysical grounds, arguing that an allegedly divine agent of this kind must be causally dependent. But I wish to examine Swinburne's approach from another perspective, by considering its religious adequacy. So for the sake of argument, I shall take Swinburne's account of the divine nature for granted, and ask what religious significance, if any, attaches to a being of the kind he has described. More exactly, I shall ask: why should we suppose that the God Swinburne portrays would be worthy of worship? Our first recourse in addressing this question must be Swinburne's own account of the rationale for worship. He writes that to worship is:

> to show respect towards a person acknowledged as *de facto* and *de jure* lord of all. Such a person deserves a peculiar kind of respect for two reasons. Firstly, whatever our dependence on other beings, they depend on him. He is our ultimate benefactor, and has the right to be such. Secondly, he has incomparable greatness; if greatness deserves respect, he deserves a peculiar respect.[14]

Here the entitlement of God to receive worship is grounded in a similarity between human beings and God. More exactly, worship is represented as a limiting case of the sort of respect we owe to other human beings, in so far as we depend on them, and in so far as they have achieved greatness. What should we make of this account?

On Swinburne's view, worship can be understood by extrapolation from attitudes (such as respect) which are appropriate in our dealings with other human beings. To this it may be objected that in worship, the believer is engaging in an activity which finds no real parallel in our relations with created things. This is the first difficulty for Swinburne's approach which I would like to advance for consideration. Does his account represent relationship to God in worship and relationship to human beings as too closely alike?

A related issue is this. Swinburne holds that worship is a paying of respect to one who is owed service, in so far as he is our benefactor. But unless it is complemented by other images, this model may encourage the sense that relationship to God is a wearisome business. Analogously, if we were required to offer repeated acknowledgement of our dependence upon some human benefactor, then we might well find this relationship restricting, if not (in the case where our benefactor wields genuine power) oppressive. Of course, in reply it might be said that this only goes to show the inappropriateness of extrapolating from what obtains in our relationships to human beings to what should obtain in relationship to God. But this reply is not, I suggest, so readily available to Swinburne, since he positively invites extrapolation from the human case to the divine. Sometimes theistic belief is rejected for moral reasons, on the grounds that the dependence on God which believers profess is incompatible with human flourishing, in rather the way that excessive dependence on, for instance, a parent figure is incompatible with a person's full development. (Don Cupitt's writings offer a good example of this sort of approach.)[15] Such criticisms tend, I think, to overlook significant differences between our relationship to any divine reality and our relationship to human beings. But Swinburne's approach may leave itself open to this sort of charge, in so far as it models relationship to God on our relationship to human beings, and in so far as it stresses the importance of professing dependence on God.

In sum, I am putting two questions to Swinburne's account. First of all, I wonder about the suggestion that worship can be adequately understood by extrapolation from any aspect of our relationships with human beings. And secondly, I fear that if we choose in particular the debtor-benefactor relationship as our model, then we will find relationship to God oppressive. I do not wish to deny that respect is in part what is involved in worship, or that relationship to God is in part properly conceived as relationship to a benefactor. My suggestion is just that this sort of account is misleading in so far as it lays too much emphasis on analogies drawn from interpersonal relations in the human context, and in so far as it singles out the relationship of debtor to benefactor as particularly relevant.

It will be evident from my earlier summary of Swinburne's

approach that on his view there are many striking points of resemblance between human beings and God. Thus both are temporal, changing, have limited knowledge of the future, are affected by others, and so on. None of these parallels holds on the classical account. This deep-seated similarity between God and human beings on Swinburne's view suggests that he needs to place particular emphasis on the distinctiveness of the divine nature when explaining the rationale of worship. For clearly, worship is not an appropriate response to human beings (excepting complications to do with the idea of incarnation). In other words, if we are to find Swinburne's approach religiously adequate, we will want some reassurance that the God he portrays remains sufficiently different from human beings to ensure that he is worthy of worship, although they are not. But rather than identifying such distinguishing features, Swinburne's understanding of worship directs our attention to similarities between our relationships to God and to human beings, in so far as both human beings and God can be our benefactors, and so on. Of course, Swinburne notes that God is our 'ultimate' benefactor and that his greatness is 'incomparable'. Even so, I am left feeling that this account of the rationale for worship, bearing in mind the relatively anthropomorphic conception of God with which it is allied, fails to accord sufficient weight to the difference between our relationship to God and our relationship to creatures.

The classical theologian may well find in all of this confirmation of her own understanding. She may suppose that the fundamental difficulty with Swinburne's approach is precisely its anthropomorphic conception of God. Given such a conception, it may be said, it is hardly surprising that Swinburne proves unable to articulate what is distinctive about worship. This suggestion invites us to take our discussion so far as a kind of *reductio ad absurdum* on religious grounds of any approach which represents God in the style of Swinburne's model (as an individual, existing in time, and so on). But before drawing this conclusion we need to think about whether we can supply some other rationale for the worthiness of worship of a Swinburnean kind of God.

In the passage I cited just now, Swinburne writes that God is worthy of the respect we show in worship as the '*de facto* and *de jure* lord of all'. In this section, I shall argue briefly that a God such as Swinburne describes would not conceive his relationship to other beings primarily, if at all, in terms of lordship, where lordship implies that others are beholden to you, on account of their dependence upon you. I shall try to substantiate this claim by exploring first of all the way in which a human being's ontological status should condition her attitudes towards other people. Suppose we draw a distinction between basic and derived abilities. My ability to ride a bicycle is a derivative ability: it is one I have acquired by the exercise of other abilities, such as the ability to move various parts of my body. But evidently not all of my abilities can be of this derivative kind. In particular, since I am not self-caused, the most fundamental of my abilities, those which are implied in my very existence, cannot derive from my own activity. Even if we suppose that all the abilities I possess at present are derivative, my existence in the first place as an agent with the capacity to generate derivative abilities will need to be presupposed. This capacity must be basic.

Granted that some of our abilities are basic, our capacity for activity is ultimately a 'given'. This suggests that whatever benefits we may have conferred upon others, our relation to them is never properly one of 'lordship'. While others may depend upon us, in engendering that dependence, we are ourselves dependent upon our initial endowment of basic abilities. So we might say: when others are dependent upon us, we are merely sharing with them the possibilities which are inherent in our basic powers. And since these powers are a 'gift' (that is, are not of our making), it cannot be right to make this sharing the basis of a relationship of subservience. Of course, not everyone has acknowledged the force of considerations of this kind. But the validity of such an association of ideas seems to be recognised in, for instance, the traditional Christian teaching that human beings should relate to one another in humility. At least in part, this teaching rests on the idea that since we are indebted ourselves to a beneficent God, it would be a mark of ingratitude to consider our relationship to people who in turn depend upon us in terms of power or domination. (Compare the Gospel parable of the servant who is shown mercy by his benefactor but fails to follow this example in his treatment of his fellow servant: Matthew 18: 23-35.) This teaching retains its relevance, I suggest, even if a person does not believe in God. For whether or not there is a God, it is clear that I am not (and cannot be) the ground of my existence. And so long as I am not the ground of my existence, then I will have reason to consider that existence as a 'gift', to be received in gratitude and humility.

Now by parity of argument, it is clear that Swinburne's God must also have certain powers which are basic. But if his existence, like ours, is ultimately a 'given', then surely his existence, like ours, is to be received in gratitude and humility. In turn, this suggests that just as power and subordination are the wrong categories for understanding inter-personal relations in the human case, so 'lordship' (understood in this sense) is not the most helpful notion for understanding the relationship of Swinburne's God to his creatures.

A further distinction is useful here. Clearly, the most basic powers of Swinburne's God are indeed a part of him. But these powers do not exhaust what he is. For instance, on Swinburne's account God's decision to create is free in the libertarian sense.[16] It follows that God's knowledge of the world does not follow directly from his initial stock of basic powers. Hence we must distinguish between the basic reality which is ultimately presupposed in the existence of such a God and the particular pattern of world-dependent thoughts and world-sustaining intentions and activities which make up his reality more 'concretely'.[17] So we might express the point that Swinburne's God will not think of his relationship to other beings in terms of 'lordship' more precisely by saying that *qua* a mind with world-dependent thoughts, this God has good reason not to understand his relationship to others in terms of subordination, in so far as he is himself dependent upon his basic powers.

These thoughts provide a further way of articulating our reservations about Swinburne's rationale for worship, as it applies to the God he describes. I am suggesting that *qua* a mind who has knowledge of the world, this God is a dependent being; and we should doubt whether such a God would relate to the world as its 'lord', where lordship implies a hierarchical relationship, which is grounded in an asymmetrical relationship of dependence. Interestingly, these considerations do not apply (or at least, do not apply so straightforwardly) to the God of classical theism. For on the classical view, there is no possibility of drawing a distinction in God between a core reality of basic powers and the actualisation of that reality in particular choices and activities. So there is no question on this approach of God *qua* individual mind with knowledge of the world exhibiting dependence on God *qua* core reality. It is true that such a God will have powers which are basic, and some may feel that this fact alone is enough to exclude the idea of 'lordship' in the sense we are considering. However, on the classical view, these powers will be identical with God, so the notion of dependence will not have the same application here. So in this respect too, there is some reason to suppose that the classical account is free from the difficulties which seem to beset Swinburne's approach.

Developing the individualistic model

In the *Summa Theologiae,* Aquinas remarks that God created a great diversity of creatures so that the deficiencies in one kind of thing would be remedied by the positive characteristics of others. In this discussion, we find him drawing out the implications of his conception of God as pure being. As pure being, God expresses the nature of existence in general. By contrast, individual things, like ourselves, express the nature of being in a limited way, as our existence is circumscribed by a finite nature. However, if you put together a sufficiently diverse set of individual things, Aquinas suggests, then a representation of the nature of being itself will after all be achieved, albeit a partial and fragmentary one. According to Aquinas, this is what God has done in the creation. Thus he writes that:

> God planned to create many distinct things, in order to share with them and reproduce in them his goodness. Because no one creature could do this, he produced many diverse creatures, so that what was lacking in one could be made up by another; for the goodness which God has whole and together, creatures share in many different ways. And the whole universe shares and expresses that goodness better than any individual creature.[18]

These remarks might suggest that if Thomas had been convinced that his doctrine of God as pure being was untenable, then he would have chosen the cosmos as a whole as the proper object of religious regard in preference to a Swinburnean kind of God. For the thought expressed here is that no individual thing (not even an individual of the kind described by Swinburne, we might suppose) can capture the nature of being as fully as the totality of individuals of diverse kinds. However, rather than pursuing this thought, I shall argue instead that this passage in fact furnishes a way of bringing out the religious significance of Swinburne's God, even allowing for the differences between his model of God and Aquinas's.

The text I have just cited implies, among other things, that anything which is divine should offer a unitary summation of the nature of existence in general. On this understanding there is good reason after all, I suggest, to regard Swinburne's God as a proper recipient of religious concern. For as the source of the world, and one who has perfect knowledge of the world, Swinburne's God does express in an integrated way the nature of existence in general. I do not wish to suggest that the claim to divinity of Swinburne's God might rest solely on his ability to play this summative role. (Suppose we were able to record every fact, in some integral way, within a book; even so, the book would have no claim to be considered divine.) Rather, we may suppose that Swinburne's God is properly considered divine in so far as he expresses the nature of existence in an integrated *and causally effective* way: his role as the source of the world allows us to say not merely that he sums up the nature of created things, but more exactly that he contains them within himself as their cause.

While this account might offer some sort of parallel with Aquinas's proposal that a divine reality will provide a unitary expression of the nature of existence in general, we might wonder how it helps to further the view that Swinburne's God is a fitting object of worship. We might make a start on this question by noting that by adopting this general approach, we will be able to draw upon a range of human responses to the world which are religiously richer than those which provide the basis of Swinburne's account. (Recall that in his discussion, Swinburne appeals to the notion of respect, along with the debtor–benefactor relationship.)

For instance, human beings often express wonder and awe at the very existence of things. Now if there is a God of the kind Swinburne describes, he is ultimately, I suggest, the proper object of this wonder and awe. For our sense of wonder before the existence of the world is properly a sense of wonder before the primordial existent, in whom the existence of all other things is contained. If we allow that God is rightly the object of wonder and awe, in so far as he contains the totality of existence within himself, then we might offer this understanding of worship: in worship, we might say, the believer acknowledges in wonder and reverence a reality which is supremely valuable, because it contains within itself, from a causal point of view, the existence of all other things. On this view, it is God's role as a causally effective summation of the nature of existence which provides the basis for his worthiness of worship. In turn this suggests that it is the ability of Swinburne's God to offer some analogue to the Thomistic conception of God as pure being which underwrites his claim to be worthy of worship.

Of course, on Swinburne's account, divine existence, as well as creaturely existence, is logically contingent. This may suggest that within the framework of Swinburne's approach, we should think of God as an object of wonder not only in so far as he contains within himself the existence of all other things, but also in so far as he exists at all. It seems to me that the contingency of Swinburne's God poses no difficulty for the rationale for worship which I am offering. On this account, in worship the believer celebrates the very existence of things, by fixing her attention on the reality in which the marvel of existence is primordially expressed. And that reality will be God, whether or not the existence of God is treated as logically contingent. With Swinburne therefore, I disagree with those philosophers who have thought that no being who is logically contingent could be a fitting object of worship.

I do not claim that considerations of this kind provide an exhaustive account of the nature of worship. No doubt other considerations are also relevant (I shall mention one shortly); and no doubt, the considerations we are discussing themselves invite elaboration. My claim is only that this approach provides a more promising starting point than Swinburne's. In particular, it seems to come closer to the profundity of the believer's experience in worship. In worship, I suggest, the believer does not take herself fundamentally to be giving thanks to a benefactor, or praising the remarkable greatness of a particular individual. Rather, in worship the believer relates herself to the marvel of existence, by placing herself in wonder and adoration before the one in whom all existence is contained.

I have suggested that one basic challenge for any account of worship is to point to some respect in which human beings and God differ, in order to sustain the thought that worship is a proper response to one but not the other. The account I have just outlined seems able to meet this challenge. It suggests that Swinburne's God is worthy of worship not fundamentally as an individual, subject to change, affected by the world, and so on. These properties of Swinburne's God (properties he shares with human beings) prove to be of no religious consequence. What matters, from the religious point of view, is the fact that Swinburne's God is the primordial expression of the wonder of existence in general. This understanding of what it is that makes the agent Swinburne describes worthy of worship seems to respect our sense that the appropriateness of worship rests on some fundamental difference between human beings and God. For it seems that human beings cannot play this role of summing up in a unitary and causally effective way the totality of things, though certainly they may command our respect, and be related to us as our benefactors. Notice that this account also seems able to rebut the charge that relationship to God in worship is oppressive. On this view, worship is not fundamentally a matter of expressing subservience before a particular individual who is our benefactor (though this is not to say that such images have no place). It is rather a way of celebrating, in wonder and reverence, the very existence of things.

I have suggested that worship is connected with the attitudes of wonder and reverence before the existence of things. The appropriateness of this sort of response to the world is, I think, quite widely acknowledged, and not only by people who consider themselves religious. It is worth noting some examples of such attitudes, as part of our ongoing attempt to show how the arguments of natural theology may be rooted in familiar evaluative responses to the world. John Muir, a founding figure of the American conservation movement, writes of an occasion when he was wandering in a remote Canadian swamp, and came across two white flowers of a rare orchid, *Calypso borealis,* standing apart from the surrounding plants. Muir tells us that he was overwhelmed by the sight of the flowers, and sat down beside them and wept for joy.[19] This response might seem merely sentimental; but it is not difficult to understand Muir's reaction more sympathetically. In part he seems to have been impressed by the contrast between the flowers and their drab surroundings in the swamp. More importantly for our purposes, he seems to have been moved by the thought that given their location, the beauty of the flowers cannot have been intended for human benefit. Albert Schweitzer seems to have reached a similar conclusion about the inherent value of things in nature when watching a herd of hippopotami on an African river. Like Muir, Schweitzer found in this experience a touchstone for his evolving sense of the limits which must be placed upon human exploitation of the natural world.[20] More recently, Rachel Carson, another inspirational figure for the environmental movement, has described various experiences which, in her view, carry the same sort of significance as Schweitzer's:

> From my own store of memories, I think of the sight of a small crab alone on a dark beach at night, a small and fragile being waiting at the edge of the roaring surf, yet so perfectly at home in its world. To me it seemed a symbol of life, and of the way life has adjusted to the forces of its physical environment. Or I think of a morning when I stood in a North Carolina marsh at sunrise, watching flock after flock of Canada geese rise from resting places at the edge of a lake and pass low overhead. In that orange light, their plumage was like brown velvet.[21]

The experiences reported by these writers all seem to involve, first, a sense of wonder, and also a powerful feeling that the value of various features of the natural world is not reducible to any contribution they might make towards the meeting of human needs or wants. Thus Muir's experience is set in a swamp far removed from human habitation. Similarly, Carson's experiences have as their setting times or places (in the early morning light, or on a dark beach) which seem unlikely to suit the needs of human observers. And Schweitzer appears to value the hippos not as a potential food source, nor as objects of aesthetic contemplation, but simply as a perspective on the world which is worthy of respect in its own right. In a way then all three writers are pleading for an extension of Kant's principle that persons are to be treated as ends and never merely as means, so that the principle comes to apply in at least some contexts to non-human forms of life.[22]

Experiences of this kind point to the possibility of an ecstatic appreciation of the existence of things. I speak here of valuing the very existence of things because the goodness of the flowers, and so on, is seen to consist in their merely existing, and does not depend on the thought that their existing might make possible some further state of affairs. This sort of response to the world echoes, I suggest, Aquinas's thought that the many diverse forms of existence which we encounter in the cosmos, when taken together, provide our clearest image of God who is existence itself. Thus these experiences locate the goodness of things in their *very existence*, and not in the thought that they might have some use.[23] And they invite us to look to the *cosmos as a whole* (to crabs and hippos, as well as human beings) as a proper object of ecstatic wonder.[24]

This sort of marvelling at things need not be tied to any sense that their existence is improbable, or likely to be transient, although it can be deepened in these ways. (These sentiments seem to be involved in Carson's response to the crabs, for instance, and they are implicit in Muir's appreciation of the orchid flowers.) If this sort of wondering at the existence of things can be separated from any sense that their existence is improbable, then it need not carry any implication of design: it need not lead us to think that there must be a transcendent contriver who is responsible for the world's existence. However, granted that there is some other reason to believe in design, then an ecstatic response to the existence of things is rightly extended to that reality in which the nature of all existence is primordially expressed. If I wonder at the goodness of the crab's existing, and marvel at the goodness of the hippopotamus's existing, how much more should I wonder at that reality in which the existence of all crabs and all hippopotami, and the cosmos itself, is contained.

This ecological perspective has a further relevance for this broadly Thomistic understanding of the rationale for worship. For alongside the notion that the natural world has an intrinsic value, there is a further idea which is central to the perspective of 'environmentalists', as we saw in Chapter 4; namely, the idea that things exist not as isolated individuals, but within a complex web of other things, animate and inanimate. Holmes Rolston gives concise expression to this fundamental principle of ecological thinking when he writes that:

> A species is what it is inseparably from its environment. The species defends its kind against the world, but at the same time interacts with its environment, functions in the ecosystem, and is supported and shaped by it . . . Neither the individual nor the species stands alone; both are embedded in a system.[25]

This holistic appreciation of things in nature has an obvious affinity with Thomas's thought that the cosmos constitutes an integrated whole; and in turn that idea is essential for his claim that the cosmos offers a representation of God, whose reality is supremely unitary.

For reasons such as these, it may be that ecology represents the obvious conversation partner for contemporary natural theology, just as mathematical physics was the preferred conversation partner during the Enlightenment. A natural theology which is grounded in a dialogue with this new discipline would differ in various ways from its earlier counterparts. Notably, it would be more willing to draw upon evaluative premises, more willing to see wonder at the existence of things as a clue to the religious meaning of the world, and less inclined to understand the divine purposes in narrowly anthropocentric terms. This last claim impinges directly on the argument from design, of course. Although I have not drawn attention to the issue in my earlier presentation of the argument, I suggest that the versions of the design argument I have presented are compatible with this perspective. For instance, an argument in Tennant's style need not imply that natural beauty is to be valued merely because of its contribution in enriching human life. On the contrary, we may, and I think we should, affirm that natural beauty has, in some measure, an intrinsic value, as Schweitzer and others have intimated.

The account I have offered so far fails to capture one important idea which is clearly articulated in Aquinas's notion of God as subsistent existence. On Aquinas's view, God does not only sum up the nature of existence, as its source; he also contains every 'pure' perfection (every perfection which can be freed from a limited form of existence) within himself in a uniquely concentrated, or 'simple' and undifferentiated, way. Swinburne's account of the divine nature makes only limited use of this idea. Indeed it is somewhat difficult to see how the notion could be sustained independently of Aquinas's thought that God is not so much an individual being, as subsistent existence. Despite the obvious difficulties in expressing this sort of idea, some such understanding of the nature of God's perfection does seem to be presupposed in ordinary religious thinking. In particular, it seems that an adequate account of God's goodness must hold that this goodness is not reducible to God's role as the source of the world, and must maintain more exactly that God's goodness involves somehow a rich integration of the goodness we encounter in the world.

We can make some progress with this question, while retaining the basic assumptions of Swinburne's ontology, by noting that on Swinburne's view something can be causally dependent on God and yet part of God. For instance, God's intention to create is dependent upon the divine mind, and yet part of God. We might go on to speculate that a Swinburnean God would have the power not only to create a world such as ours, but also to make a radiantly attractive synthesis of the goodness which is evident in created things. Suppose next that this synthesis is fully dependent on God, just as the divine intentions are fully dependent on God. In that case, we would have reason to say that it is part of God, and not a created thing. Suppose furthermore that this synthesis fully expresses what God is. In that case, we would have reason to say not merely that it is part of God, but that it is fully God. Of course, this account offers no illumination concerning what such a synthesis of the world's perfections might involve; nor does it indicate how this synthesis might fully express what God is. However, these remarks do indicate how the Swinburnean kind of model might in principle be extended so as to accommodate the Thomistic insight that God's goodness involves an integration of the goodness of creatures. (And besides, it is no proper ambition of a natural theological concept of God to render the inherent nature of the divine fully transparent!)[26]

This understanding of God's goodness calls for an extension of our account of worship. Given this understanding, worship will not be simply a matter of relating oneself in wonder to a reality which contains all existence within itself. It will also be a matter of marvelling at the radiant attractiveness of God in himself or herself. So this understanding allows us to think of worship as a fitting response to God not only in virtue of God's metaphysical ultimacy, but also in virtue of his or her inherent goodness. (Of course, on Thomas's view, these two things cannot be prised apart.) The view which is beginning to emerge here does something, I think, to bridge the gap between the idea of a designer and the idea of God. I have offered an account of what worship consists in which is intended to bring out the worthiness of worship of Swinburne's God considered as a transcendent mind. Since the argument from design also represents the world's source as a transcendent mind, there is some reason to suppose that we can draw upon the notions I have just expounded in order to explain how a designer would be worthy of worship. In particular, a designer would be capable of playing the dual role of providing a causally effective summation of the nature of existence, and comprising a synthesis of the perfections which are manifest in creation.[27]

In developing this account of the nature of worship, I have emphasised the difference between God and things in the world. Nonetheless, these thoughts are capable of being developed in an incarnational direction. For instance, it seems in principle possible that something within the world should sum up the nature of existence in general. If we suppose, following Christian tradition, that the basic purpose and tendency of the world has to do with the creation of love in community, then we might infer that only a consciously relational being could play such a role in full. If such a being were to express unreservedly (and proleptically) the communitarian character of the world, then it would to that extent have some claim to be related to the sum of what exists in the way that Swinburne's God is. Of course, this understanding omits the thought that the summation in question is a causally effective one; and it omits the thought that this individual should not only sum up the nature of the world, but also provide a radiantly attractive synthesis of its goodness. Nonetheless, there is enough here I think to provide one starting point for an account of the possibility of incarnation.

I have been arguing that a God of the kind Swinburne describes may be considered supremely good in so far as he presents a radiantly attractive synthesis of the perfections evident in created things. However, there is another issue to be considered when approaching the question of divine goodness, one which has to do with God's activity in creation. It is this sort of goodness, rather than the goodness which relates to the inherent character of the divine being, which is often the focus of contemporary discussions of divine goodness. This is especially so in so far as these discussions treat the question of divine goodness in relation to the problem of evil. In this section I shall offer some brief comment on how we might understand the goodness of God in relation to God's activity.

Some philosophers have supposed that a world will be consistent with the goodness of God no matter what its character. One recent writer who seems to come close to this view is Brian Davies. At any rate, Davies is clear that God is subject to no obligations in his dealings with creation, and that in general his goodness is not an instance of moral goodness.[28] It seems to me that Davies is right to downplay the idea of moral goodness when we speak of God, in favour of a more ontological understanding of divine perfection. However, even granted the primacy of the ontological approach, some connections must still be drawn, surely, between the goodness and activity of God: only some creations, we want to say, would properly express the nature of this goodness. In my earlier discussion of the problem of evil, I advanced one understanding of the sort of connection which might be made here, suggesting that if there is a God, then the created order will contain no integral whole which is overall bad. We need not say that this sort of connection between the divine goodness and what God does is a matter of God being bound by obligations. (This is the claim to which Davies takes particular exception.) But we should say that the making of certain worlds (those which contain integral wholes which are overall bad) does not lie within God's compatibilist power.

So on my account the goodness of God, where God's activity is concerned, is in part a matter of God not creating any world which contains integral wholes which are overall bad. Following Aquinas, we might suppose that another mark of a divinely made world would be the diversity of creatures it contains. For on Aquinas's view, such a world will image God more effectively than one which contains creatures which are relatively few in number and kind. (Its ability to image God is, we might suppose, one central index of the goodness of creation.)[29] Our earlier discussion of the nature of God's 'lordship' suggests a further connection between God's goodness and activity, at any rate where a Swinburnean kind of God is concerned. I have argued that *qua* a mind with world-dependent thoughts, Swinburne's God is dependent upon his basic powers; and that this dependence should condition his attitudes towards other beings, so that he sees his relationship to them in terms other than those of power and hierarchy. So in turn we might suppose that such a God would understand his activity not as a matter of rendering others beholden to him, as their benefactor, but as a matter of sharing with them the possibilities which are latent within his own endowment of basic powers. Given the existential challenge to religious belief we noted earlier, it seems there are also sound pastoral reasons for favouring such an account over the view that it is simply God's power over the world which establishes the appropriateness of religious attitudes.[30]

This approach offers a parallel with Charles Hartshorne's well-known distinction between the abstract and the concrete poles of the divine nature.[31] In particular, these Hartshornean notions recall respectively the idea of God as basic power and as an individual mind with knowledge of the world. Thus the basic power or powers of a Swinburnean God will be immutable, impassible, and necessary; for these powers are implied in the very existence of such a God, and will therefore be marked by the same persistence over time and immunity from destruction as the divine existence itself. By contrast, considered as a world-dependent mind, Swinburne's God is (like the world) changing, passible, and contingent. However, Hartshorne treats the abstract pole of the divine nature as merely a simplification of the fullness of the divine reality. On his view, while this simplification may have a certain point philosophically, it is devoid of any religious significance.[32] By contrast, on the account I have given, reference to the basic power is needed for an appreciation of the self-understanding of a God conceived individualistically (whether in the style of Swinburne or in the style of Hartshorne), and is therefore essential for an appreciation of the relationship of such a God to other beings. More generally, the approach I have followed is consistent with various Hartshornean moves concerning the superiority of change over changelessness, and so on, but does not require them. It identifies divinity in the first instance not by reference to some such theory of the nature of perfection, but by reference to the idea that a thing is divine in so far as it discloses the nature of being. Such an approach is, clearly, closer in spirit to the Thomistic account in its understanding of the rationale for ascriptions of divinity.

I have been considering the question: is Swinburne's ontology rich enough to sustain religious attitudes? In brief, the answer to this question which is beginning to emerge is 'yes', but not perhaps for the reasons Swinburne gives. A God conceived as Swinburne proposes is worthy of worship, I suggest, not fundamentally as our benefactor, but as an integrated and causally effective expression of the nature of existence, who presents a radiantly attractive synthesis of the perfections we encounter in the world. As promised, this account offers I think a kind of middle ground in the debate between classical theologians and their modern counterparts. For while it grants that a God such as the God Swinburne describes is properly considered divine, it grounds this claim to divinity in notions which are drawn from the classical tradition. In particular, on this view, it is the ability of Swinburne's God to offer an analogue to the notion of God as subsistent existence which provides the basis of his claim to be worthy of worship. This proposal invites us to move away to some extent from the familiar debate between classical theologians and their opponents, in search of a shared sense of what it is that makes God God.

If the approach I have outlined is basically correct, then issues of immutability and impassibility are of no religious consequence (except in so far as they have to be invoked to enable God to play the role of providing, for example, a causally effective summation of the nature of existence). At a time when many have abandoned the classical approach, claiming to detect within it some sort of incoherence, the general strategy I have been exploring has some value, I think, as a way of preserving certain religious insights which are clearly enshrined within the classical view, by showing how these insights may be articulated independently of their original metaphysical context.

The anthropological basis of the proposal

So far I have argued that a God conceived individualistically can satisfy the Thomistic understanding of what it is to be divine, in so far as such a being sums up in an integral, causally effective and supremely attractive way the nature of existence. I now want to support my claim that this approach is faithful to the basic tendency of religious practice by drawing upon some anthropological material. This discussion will be focused in particular upon the idea of God as a causally effective summation of the nature of existence.

Philosophers of religion rarely make use of anthropological considerations, and one can see why this should be so. Philosophy of religion, it may be said, is the study of religion in so far as it is intelligible to human reason, whereas anthropology studies religion from a practical rather than a conceptual point of view. Moreover, where anthropology is concerned with religious beliefs, these beliefs are often enough not developed with any conceptual sophistication, and are unlikely therefore to hold much philosophical interest. Regardless of the truth or otherwise of this assessment of the relevance of anthropological considerations, in one respect at least the anthropological data surely do have an important role to play in the philosophy of religion. Whatever the logical adequacy of a particular system of religious ideas, it will hold no real relevance for religious life if it fails to engage the affective and imaginative dimensions of human understanding. So in determining the overall adequacy of a religious viewpoint, it is not enough to make reference to its logical properties; it is also necessary to consider whether it can be embedded from the point of view of feeling and imagination within a religious practice. And in turn, the anthropological data offer a rich source for understanding the kinds of idea which are capable of animating human life from a religious point of view.

Clearly, I am returning here to a theme from earlier chapters – in particular, the idea that the existential dimension of religious belief should be taken seriously in philosophical accounts of its nature and rationality. I am not proposing, or denying, that the anthropological data provide much insight into, for instance, the nature of God's goodness, or any substantive issue of that kind. My object is rather to isolate certain recurring structural features of religious thought, with a view to throwing some light on the way in which religious ideas manage to gain some purchase on the human imagination.

I shall note two examples from anthropology which bear out the thought that the conception of God as a concentrated expression of the nature of existence is capable of infusing a religious life. First of all, I turn to Daniel Merkur's survey of Inuit religious belief.[33] According to Merkur, Inuit religion contains a class of powers which play a role precisely parallel to the role of the Forms in Platonic metaphysics.[34] Merkur calls these entities 'indwellers', here translating the Inuit expression *inue*. More exactly, an indweller corresponds typically not to a single species or some other narrowly defined kind, but to a whole field of human experience. Among the most significant examples are the indwellers of the wind, the earth, and the sea. Merkur notes furthermore that indwellers are conceived in personal terms, and that the personality attributed to each reflects the range of experience with which it is associated. For instance, the Wind Indweller is said to have a stern personality, in view of the severity of arctic weather conditions.[35] (Of course, in ascribing personal qualities to the indwellers, the Inuit tradition departs from Plato's understanding of the Forms.)

The most interesting of the *inue* from a conceptual point of view is the Sea Mother, known by some groups as Sedna.[36] As an indweller, the Sea Mother is 'the personified idea of the sea and all its animals'.[37] But among some Inuit, she has come to function as a supreme reality, absorbing the roles of other metaphysical entities.[38] For these groups, the Sea Mother plays the part of an ultimate Form, expressing the character of Inuit experience not merely in relation to the sea, but in general. According to shamans in this tradition, 'the

Sea Mother is the Wind Indweller is the Caribou Mother is the Earth Indweller is the Moon Man'.[39] Merkur shows some sympathy for the idea that this development discloses the basic tendency of Inuit practice more generally, in so far as he understands it as a natural outgrowth of Inuit spirituality, rather than needing to be explained in terms of the influence of Christian missionaries.[40]

The relevance of Merkur's study for our question is clear. The Inuit seem to conceive of their divinities not fundamentally as particular individuals, though Sedna and the other indwellers are represented as individuals, but rather as compressed and causally effective images of whole regions of experience. At any rate, it is the ability of indwellers to play this latter role which establishes their religious significance. Thus to be related to the Sea Mother, for example, is not to be related simply to an individual, but to the basic powers of existence as these are expressed in relation to the sea. Hence Keith Ward can write as follows about the meaning of one story in the Sedna tradition:

> Perhaps there may be those who take literally the story of the girl who began to eat her giant parents and was cast by them beneath the sea – the fundamentalists of Inuit religion. But just as it is clear [to the Ainu of the northern Japanese islands] that spirits do not really eat the food offered to them, so it is quite clear that there is no such person beneath the waves who controls the movements of whales and seals . . . What is here represented in an image is the character of the sea itself, as a power for good and harm. What the shaman meets in the dream-quest is this internalised image of the powers which bound Inuit life.[41]

Similarly, Ward writes that the Sea Mother offers 'an eidetic representation of the harsh, often arbitrary-seeming and yet life-supporting conditions of the Arctic world'.[42] We may say therefore that Sedna is not so much an individual entity living in the sea (though she is pictured in these terms), as the sea itself (considered eidetically).[43] And in so far as she can assume a role of even greater generality, in the way we have noted, she could even be regarded as Being Itself. Notice too that Sedna does not represent the nature of Being Itself in a book-like fashion (by means of some purely conventional system of denotation), or in a merely causal way. Rather, there is, it seems, a real analogy between the character of the world and what she is like in herself, in so far as there is a correspondence between her personality (which is not reducible to its effects) and the character of the world. (For instance, the bad weather is correlated with her bad temper.) Here we find a kind of analogue of Aquinas's idea that the perfections of the world are expressed in pre-eminent form in God.

It is rather remarkable, I think, to discover Thomas's highly abstract account of the nature of divinity as Being Itself being echoed in this way in the anthropological literature. If nothing more, the anthropological literature throws into new relief the religious significance of Thomas's teaching. The doctrine of pure being, we might infer, is not merely a metaphysical abstraction, but apparently reflects a basic tendency of the human imagination in its dealings with the world. Again, my suggestion here is not that figures such as Sedna provide an adequate focus of religious concerns: the content of such figures may (or may not) involve all sorts of practical and theoretical confusions. I only wish to stress the character of these figures as integral expressions of the character of whole regions of experience, and hence as summations of the nature of being.

In further support of this thesis, I shall offer one more example from the anthropological literature. Clearly, the general suggestion which is evident in Merkur's approach has parallels in more familiar traditions. Think for instance of the way in which the Greco-Roman gods seem to epitomise whole regions of human experience. Thus by analogy with the case of the Sea Mother, we might regard Poseidon (or Neptune) as an eidetic representation of the sea. However, rather than looking further at these familiar cases, I shall discuss just briefly Godfrey Lienhardt's survey of the religion of the Dinka of the southern Sudan.[44] Lienhardt is another reflective commentator, who shares with Merkur a sensitivity to the philosophical nuances of the material he is considering.

Like the Inuit, the Dinka think of their world as shaped by powers which correspond to various ranges of experience. Thus Lienhardt writes that:

> the free-divinities DENG, ABUK, and GARANG correspond to fields of experience which are special aspects of the total to which Divinity corresponds. We have indicated what these fields are in general – that imaged by DENG includes the phenomena of the sky associated with rain, that imaged by ABUK is the life of the gardens and the crops, and that imaged by GARANG . . . includes the heat of the sun and certain heated conditions of the human body.[45]

Here again we find that the powers image different regions of experience. Moreover, again in keeping with some tendencies of Inuit thought, the Dinka apparently suppose that the powers lack clear criteria of individuation, and that ultimately they are not to be distinguished from one another. Lienhardt offers an explanation for this state of affairs:

> If the Powers image different ranges of experience, we should not expect the several accounts of them given by the Dinka to agree in details, nor their assertions about them severally, when pieced together by us, to have the connectedness and logical consistency of reflective thought . . . Divinity is manifold as human experience is manifold and of a manifold world. Divinity is one as the self's manifold experience of it is united and brought into relationship in the experiencing self.[46]

This account suggests an a priori understanding of why the powers of Dinka religion must ultimately be conceived as a unity. The powers of the Dinka (and equally of the Inuit) will be distinct in so far as they image different ranges of experience. But this distinction will at the same time point towards an underlying unity, in so far as these various ranges of experience are unified (or 'synthesised', as we might say, in a Kantian vein) by the one subject of experience. So in Dinka thought too, we find a movement towards the idea that the diversity of the powers is compatible with an underlying unity, which in turn suggests the possibility of a power which offers a compressed image of the nature of being in general. It is worth noting also that the powers of Dinka religion are also treated as personal, and that human beings' relationship to them is conceived in moral terms, as in Inuit thought.

The writings of anthropologists such as Merkur and Lienhardt are particularly eloquent on these points of comparison, since they are not philosophers or theologians, and apparently do not appreciate the closeness of the connection between the picture they offer and the Thomistic account. For instance, Merkur notes that the Inuit view resembles a familiar western view in so far as it represents the indwellers as Forms in Plato's sense, but he then qualifies this by remarking that: 'Western philosophic analogies fail to be precise, however, because *inue* are not impersonal ideas but personal beings'.[47] But of course, this combination of ideas is present in western philosophy. In particular, the tradition of Christian Platonism has combined precisely these emphases; and in Aquinas too, we find the view that God is both personal and Goodness itself, and so on. Similarly, Lienhardt discusses the power named Nhialic in these terms:

> Nhialic is figured sometimes as a Being, a supreme personal Being even, and sometimes as a *kind* of being and activity which sums up the activity of a multiplicity of beings, while the word 'God' has no such extended meaning in our common speech. So the word Divinity, thus written with the capital letter and without definite or indefinite article, is here used to translate *nhialic.* 'Divinity', like *nhialic,* can be used to convey to the mind at once *a* being, a *kind* of nature or existence, and a quality of that kind of being.[48]

Again, the writer does not note that a central strand of the western tradition offers a close parallel to this way of thinking. For the term 'God' bears precisely this extended meaning in Thomism (and Christian Platonism), where God is said to be both loving and Love, both wise and Wisdom, and so on, since God is his nature.

These examples from the anthropological literature are enough to demonstrate, I hope, that the notion of divinity as a personal, integrated and causally effective summation of the nature of existence is not merely a philosophical construct. Far from being an alien intrusion of philosophy into the sphere of religious understanding, the notion appears to have independent origins deep within the religious imagination. These examples are particularly significant for our purposes because they seem to suggest that the synthesis of an individualistic account of God and the Thomistic idea of God as pure being, which I outlined earlier, is practically speaking a possibility. Thus both the Inuit and the Dinka direct their religious concerns to particular individuals, but it appears that these individuals have a claim to be considered divine only in so far as they express in an integrated and causally effective way the nature of existence in general.

So far I have argued that the Thomistic notion of God as a supra-individual reality finds various parallels in the writings of anthropologists. Now God's transcendence of individuality on the Thomistic view is bound up with the thought that the causal relationship between God and the world is uni-directional. It is the uni-directionality of this relationship which ensures that God does not become simply another example of an individual thing acting upon and reacting to the various things which stand in its environment. So it would be interesting to learn whether the primal religions share not only an idea of divinity which transcends individuality but also a sense of the uni-directionality of the relationship between the powers and the realm of human existence. There is perhaps some reason to suppose that this is so, though the view under discussion may be too theoretical to be clearly formulated within any primal tradition. For instance, it has been suggested that in these religions, 'there is a deep sense that man is finite, weak, and impure and stands in need of a power not his own'.[49] This sort of notion can also be supported by reference to our case studies. Thus Merkur observes that the indwellers are:

> completely autonomous and disinterested in people. Inuit can hurt themselves by abusing *inue* or derive benefits by being in accord with them. In both cases, the *inue* are what they are, with neither positive or negative ambitions toward human beings . . . Neither the basic temperaments of the indwellers nor the consequent characteristics of the phenomena in which they indwell are determined by human activity.[50]

Of course, the thought that the indwellers are disinterested in human beings apparently differs from the idea that God acts providentially. But in terms of what it says about the agency of indwellers, this account recalls the Thomistic idea of divine impassibility, rather than the view that God's relation to creatures is one of reciprocal dependence.[51] In a similar vein, Lienhardt writes that 'if the word "passions", "*passiones*", were still normally current as the opposite of "actions", it would be possible to say that the Dinka Powers were the images of human *passiones* seen as the active source of those *passiones*.'[52] Here too the emphasis is upon the powers as sources of activity, with no reference to the idea that they might themselves be affected. This emphasis on the powers as agents presumably has its life-setting in a sense of human dependence on nature. This connection is well expressed in Richard Nelson's discussion of the religion of the Koyukon of Alaska:

> Underlying their closeness to nature is the need to subsist on resources that are often elusive and difficult to obtain. Thus for the Koyukon, life has always been fraught with insecurity, in a land that can bless with abundance or curse with scarcity as the ebb and flow of nature dictates. Confronted with these uncertainties, and depending so completely on the beneficence of the land, the Koyukon protect their livelihood by augmenting practical skills and knowledge with an understanding of the supernatural.[53]

Here too, the believer's relation to the spiritual realm is tied to a sense of human dependence upon the natural world. I conclude that, to some extent, the link between a unilateral conception of divine agency and a non-individual conception of God which we find in the Thomistic tradition is also evident in the beliefs of the primal faiths.

Before concluding I note two qualifications which need to be appended to this account. I have concentrated on the points of similarity between the Thomistic tradition in particular and the approach of various primal religions. But of course there are also striking differences between the primal religions and the faiths standardly studied by philosophers and theologians, and a full account of the relationship between the primal and more familiar traditions would need to give due weight to these differences.[54] Moreover, in certain respects the primal traditions seem to present a closer parallel to the views of process theists, rather than Thomists, above all in so far as they consider the natural world as conscious or en-spirited.[55] However, if we keep our attention fixed on the model of divinity (and divine agency) which is evident in the primal religions, then the conclusion to be drawn, I suggest, is that this conception recalls the Thomistic scheme in the various ways I have discussed. It is worth noting too that while Aquinas does not subscribe to the panpsychism of process theists, his thought contains a parallel to this view, in so far as he thinks of nature as pervasively teleological, and thinks that this teleology points to the organising presence of a mind. Thus in the Fifth Way he writes:

> Goal-directed behaviour is observed in all bodies obeying natural laws, even when they lack awareness. Their behaviour hardly ever varies and practically always turns out well, showing that they tend to goals and do not hit them merely by accident. But nothing lacking awareness can tend to a goal except it be directed by someone with awareness and understanding . . . Everything in nature, therefore, is directed towards its goal by someone with understanding, and this we call *God*.[56]

Of course, the Fifth Way is a version of the argument from design. And it is true more generally that this argument is naturally aligned with a conception of the world as en-spirited.

Conclusions

In Chapters 1 to 5, I considered the reasonableness of religious belief. More exactly, in Chapters 1 to 4, I examined the availability of evidence for and against the thesis that the world's goodness is its reason for existence; and in Chapter 5, I addressed the further issue of how strong the evidential case must be if our thesis is to be the object of reasonable belief. In the present chapter, I have tried to show how the rudimentary concept of God emerging from this earlier discussion (the idea of a personal, transcendent source of value) may be developed in a religiously sensitive way.

To summarise, I have defended the thesis that a thing is divine in so far as it discloses the nature of existence, in a causally effective way, and offers a radiantly attractive synthesis of the goodness evident in created things. Again, this notion marks a sort of middle ground between the Thomistic and individualistic models of God – it is broadly Thomistic in its understanding of what qualifies something as divine, but consistent with the individualistic model, in so far as an individual thing can satisfy this conception of divinity. In my view, this approach saves the believer from having to commit herself on the question of whether the Thomistic notion of pure being is really coherent. Since there is some dispute on this question, that is a significant advantage. In general, this line of reflection invites us to suppose that the issues in dispute between classical theists and their modern adversaries are fundamentally a matter of religious indifference; it invites us to move away from these disagreements towards a shared sense of what qualifies something as divine, regardless of its particular character in terms of whether or not it is immutable, impassible, and so on.

This way of viewing the issues, I have suggested, offers a more secure basis for defending the religious adequacy of the individualistic model than does Swinburne's account. For instance, it allows us to understand worship by reference to the wonder and reverence we feel before the existence of things, rather than starting from the religiously impoverished notion of respect. Moreover, such an understanding of what it is to be divine is broadly consonant, I have argued, with the anthropological literature. This gives us further reason for thinking that a conception of God of this kind is religiously relevant; for the anthropological data apparently imply that the religious imagination has an inherent propensity to think in these terms. In the present context, the significance of this fusion of the individualistic and Thomistic conceptions of God is that it offers a way of turning aside the charge that the design argument must issue in a religiously deficient conception of God. On the contrary, I have argued, the conception of God as an individual mind (the conception which emerges from the design argument) can be wedded with certain significant elements from the conception of God as pure being, so as to provide a clear rationale for the worthiness of worship of a God conceived individualistically.

At the outset of my discussion, I noted that alienation from religion in its modern guise often involves a rejection of religious belief on existential grounds, rather than an evidential objection to the claims of religion. I have tried to develop an understanding of the divine nature which takes into account this estrangement from the conceptual framework of theism, by showing how the idea of God can play a role in human life which is both affirming and profound. In particular, I have represented God as worthy of worship not so much as a particularly powerful benefactor, who requires in exchange for the benefits he has conferred a repeated acknowledgement of our dependence upon him. Rather, I have talked of God as the primordial expression of existence, and pointed to familiar human responses to the world (responses of wondering and marvelling at the existence of things) which invite extrapolation in the direction of worship.

I have also offered an account of God's goodness which does not turn fundamentally upon representing God as a moral agent. While I have affirmed the partial appropriateness of this model, I have tried to broaden it, by portraying God's goodness as a rich and integrated expression of the many perfections which we encounter in the world. This conception of God represents a further contribution to our ongoing consideration of the nature and significance of the goodness of the world. I have been arguing that God's reality is made known most clearly at the limiting point of our encounter with the attractiveness of the world. The existential point of religious belief and practice ultimately relates, we might suppose, to our deep-seated need to relate ourselves to the basic conditions of our existence in their totality, and to respond to these conditions in trust. The account I have offered in this chapter, together with our earlier discussion of the goodness of the world, seeks to show how the concept of God can contribute constructively to this most fundamental of human projects.

In the next chapter, I want to set out one further understanding of the concept of God. This further account will be logically independent of the approach I have taken in this chapter, but will have clear affinities with it. My main concern will be to show how aesthetic experience may be important for natural theology not only evidentially, as I argued in Chapter 1, but also in helping to shape our conception of what God is.

7 Salvation and the concept of God

Introduction

In Chapter 6, I explored the concept of divinity by reference to the concept of worship. In this chapter, I shall relate the concept of God to another concept of central importance to the religious life, namely the concept of salvation. This discussion also represents an extension of the discussion of Chapter 1. There, aesthetic experience was treated evidentially, as relevant epistemically to the thesis that the world's goodness is its reason for existence. In the present chapter, I shall consider the relevance of aesthetic experience for the concept of God, and in particular for an account of the sense in which the world points towards or represents God.

This chapter (again like Chapter 6) is also intended to address a fundamental logical challenge to the natural theologian, namely the challenge of showing how it is possible to talk meaningfully about God. Given that our words are fitted for the description of finite things, it behoves the natural theologian to explain how we are able to keep track of their meaning when they are used in relation to God. In turn, this seems to require some sort of understanding of the sense in which the world points towards or represents God. Given some such understanding, we can then see how the perfection terms we use in relation to creatures need to be stretched when they are used of God. Standard accounts of the relation between God and the world maintain that the world represents God by virtue of resembling God. In this chapter, I shall set out another approach, one which is consistent with the thought that the world resembles God, but which starts from the idea that God is the necessary complement of the world's perfections. The meaning of this proposal will become clear as I proceed.

I begin by reviewing various ways of developing the thought that the world represents divinity by imaging or resembling it. I shall assess these accounts against certain insights concerning the relationship of God and the world which are implicit, so I shall argue, in the concept of salvation. I shall argue that these insights are recorded in the Thomistic understanding of God's relation to the world, but not so clearly recognised in individualistic accounts of God's nature. In the concluding part of the chapter, I shall sketch out an understanding of the sense in which the world represents God which builds on the notion of salvation, but does not simply recapitulate the Thomistic view. The key concept in this account will be drawn from aesthetic experience.[1]

The world's resemblance to God

Aquinas gives two arguments in support of the idea that the world resembles God.[2] First of all, he suggests that the world must resemble God since it is caused by God. This idea seems to rest on the thought that there must be some sort of correspondence between God's intentions and the character of the world, given that God created the world intentionally.[3] And more exactly, the idea seems to be that if there is no distinction between God's being and God's intentions, then any correspondence between the world and God's intentions must imply a correspondence between the world and God *simpliciter*.[4] Aquinas's second argument maintains that 'God is self-subsistent existence and must therefore contain the full perfection of existence'.[5] From this it follows that the world resembles God in so far as it bodies forth, in a limited way, the nature of existence.

These two ways of grounding the idea that the world resembles God both depend upon the doctrine of divine simplicity. Thus the identity of divine intentions and divine being will hold only if the doctrine of divine simplicity is true. And to say, with Aquinas's second argument, that God is self-subsistent existence is just to say that God is simple. Now the simplicity doctrine, as Aquinas formulates it, has proved to be controversial; and the natural theologian has at least an *ad hominem* reason therefore to find an account of the sense in which the world represents God which is free from any detailed dependence on this doctrine. One way of proceeding here would be in the way suggested in Chapter 6: we might suppose that a God conceived individualistically will present a unitary synthesis of the perfections evident in the world. If this idea is granted, then we can keep hold of the thought that the world resembles God in so far as it provides an image, albeit a fragmentary one, of the nature of existence. However, for the purposes of this chapter, I shall assume that this model is not available. After all, the notion of a synthesis of mundane perfections is not obviously coherent, and some may find it unacceptable.

There have been a number of attempts in the philosophy of religion literature to reformulate the doctrine of divine simplicity so as to meet modern objections to it. We might wonder whether these newer versions of the doctrine will license the inference from simplicity to resemblance in the way that Aquinas envisages. For instance, Thomas Morris has argued that the simplicity doctrine may be upheld in a more modest form, by restricting its scope to those properties which belong to God necessarily and uniquely.[6] But if God's intention to create is contingent, as orthodox Christians have traditionally supposed, then this formulation of the doctrine will not permit the equation between the being of God and the divine intentions which is required by the first of Aquinas's arguments for resemblance. Moreover, this restricted version of the doctrine is incompatible with the idea of self-subsistent existence, for that idea does not admit the possibility of various divine properties, some contingent and some not.[7] In general, Morris's approach seems to issue in an individualistic conception of God, albeit that God's knowledge and power, for example, unlike the knowledge and power of creatures, are one and the same property.[8]

In sum, Aquinas's account of the sense in which the world resembles God is not open to us, unless we are willing to adopt the doctrine of subsistent existence or some close analogue of that doctrine. Assuming (if only for *ad hominem* reasons) that this doctrine, or some close analogue, is not available, we need next to consider whether an individualistic conception of the divine can provide some foundation for the idea that the world resembles God. The modern treatment of God as an individual being offers a straightforward understanding of the sense in which the world resembles its creator, especially if we suppose that God shares with creatures such properties as passibility, mutability, embodiment, and so on. However, this approach seems to overlook certain notions of religious importance which are enshrined within the Thomistic account.

For example, without further elaboration, the individualistic view invites the thought that God is merely another example of a good thing; and that view seems difficult to reconcile with the belief, essential to theism, that God is good in some special or pre-eminent sense. William Alston has suggested one way of addressing this difficulty. He argues that we may consider God as the individual exemplar who establishes paradigmatically what it is to be good.[9] But even when developed in this fashion, the individualistic approach still seems to offer a rather attenuated understanding of the divine goodness when compared to the conception which is advanced in the Thomistic scheme. One point of difference in particular stands out.

On the individualistic view, we seem to have lost the thought that God's perfection involves an integration of the many perfections which are manifest in the created order as a whole. Instead, this perfection represents simply the limiting case of the perfections of individual creatures.[10] By contrast, on Aquinas's view, we can say that the world as a whole offers an image, extended in space and time, of the unitary reality which is God. Thus (to revert to a text we have discussed already) Aquinas remarks that:

> God planned to create many distinct things, in order to share with them and reproduce in them his goodness. Because no one creature could do this, he produced many diverse creatures, so that what was lacking in one expression of his goodness could be made up by another; for the goodness which God has whole and together, creatures share in many different ways. And the whole universe shares and expresses that goodness better than any individual creature.[11]

So the Thomistic view differs from the individualistic approach in affirming a 'holistic' understanding of the divine goodness, according to which it is the world as a whole, rather than individual creatures, which offers our clearest image of God.

Moreover, the claim that God's goodness has this holistic character is religiously important, I suggest, whatever difficulties there may be in Thomas's particular formulation of the doctrine; for it can be related to a number of ideas of fundamental importance which are implicit in the concept of salvation. First of all, we must surely say that the believer should seek not simply her own salvation (her own ultimate fulfilment), but fulfilment in relation to other human beings and, I would add, fulfilment in relation to the wider community of the cosmos. After all, so much of ourselves is bound up with our relations to other human beings and the natural world that it makes little sense to talk of the ultimate happiness of the individual person in isolation from her social and cosmological context.[12] In turn, if we do understand salvation in this communitarian way, and if we also suppose that it is the individual as saved, or perfected, who offers the clearest representation of the divine nature, then it seems to follow that God's reality must be revealed most clearly in the corporate perfection of creatures, rather than in their perfections considered individually. For if it is the perfected individual who best images God, and if the perfected individual cannot be conceived apart from her community, then it is the community, rather than the individual considered in isolation, which offers the richest image of the divine nature. In sum, the idea that it is the world as a whole which most clearly echoes the perfection of God can be related to two persuasive claims concerning the nature of salvation:

- The saved (rather than the imperfect) individual offers the best image of the divine nature.
- The nature of the saved individual can only be conceptualised in relation to the wider social and cosmological community.

These claims together support the idea that God's perfection is *holistic*, in the sense that it is the world as a whole which best represents the nature of the divine perfection. We might suppose more exactly that the divine perfection will involve an *integration* of the perfections of creatures. After all, God is a unity. The idea that God's reality has this integral character can also be supported from the side of creatures rather than from the side of God, as it were. For the perfection of the individual will presumably require her to be related to her community in a closer, more integral way. This suggests again that if God's reality is best understood by reference to the perfected individual, then this reality must be understood more exactly by reference to the created order in its unity.

So here is one claim that the Thomistic account of the relation between God and the world seems to articulate more clearly than the individualistic approach, a claim which seems furthermore to have a certain religious importance in so far as it follows from various plausible notions concerning the nature of salvation. There is a further thought which any satisfactory account of the sense in which the world represents God must surely capture. For the believer does not wish to say merely that the world as a perfected whole represents God, but also that its perfection, or salvation, is to be found in God. In other words, the believer will want to say that it is through relationship to God that the world as a whole will find fulfilment, and not merely that on achieving fulfilment the world will (as a whole) resemble God. I suggest that this idea too is not clearly enough inscribed within standard individualistic accounts of God's nature.

These accounts do of course suppose that God is implicated in the perfection of the world in so far as God's activity is a causal precondition of that perfection. But we should surely say that God's presence to creatures is not simply a causal precondition of their fulfilment, but also constitutive of that fulfilment. On this view, the creature's enjoyment of God is, to say no more, a central part of what salvation consists in. Of course, individualistic accounts may also say that it is through the enjoyment of God that the believer will find genuine happiness. But while God continues to be conceived as an individual, there is a risk that relationship to God will remain one relationship among others, and accordingly a risk that the believer's happiness will be tied in part to relationship to God, but also *and independently* to relationship to other individuals. Such an account seems to admit the possibility of a conflict between commitment to God and commitment to creatures; and that possibility is surely excluded by the traditional claim that there is an internal relation between love of God and love of creatures. The possibility of such conflict can be removed by supposing that in so far as my fulfilment depends upon my relationship to other creatures (and surely it does so depend, at least in part), this relationship in turn depends upon relationship to God, not merely causally, but constitutively.

The Thomistic approach may be able to address these concerns more effectively. At any rate, if God is not an individual being, but Being Itself, then it is easier to suppose that we encounter God in all things in so far as they exist. In this way, it may be relatively simple to establish a logical link between commitment to creatures and commitment to God, so as to ensure that the fulfilment which consists in the first kind of relationship is integrally tied to the fulfilment which consists in relationship to God. I shall not pursue this thought further, but note simply that there is some initial reason to suppose that the Thomistic account may be more receptive to the concerns we are discussing.

I conclude then that an adequate account of the relationship between creatures and their source should capture the following ideas:

- The world as a whole, rather than particular individuals, offers the best image of the divine nature.
- More exactly, it is the world as an integrated whole which offers the clearest representation of God's reality.
- Relationship to God is, at least in part, constitutive of an individual's ultimate happiness.
- More exactly, in so far as a creature's ultimate happiness depends upon her relationship to creatures, that relationship depends

upon relationship to God not only causally but constitutively, with the consequence that commitment to God cannot be relativised by reference to commitment to creatures.

These ideas all depend upon certain plausible notions concerning the nature of salvation or an individual's ultimate fulfilment in the way I have shown. We could summarise their import by saying that the relationship of God and the world should be understood *integrally* and *non-relativistically*.

These thoughts suggest a question: is it possible to develop an account of the relationship between God and the world which will satisfy these various requirements without simply recapitulating the doctrine of divine simplicity? I shall consider two responses to this question. In the next section, I shall introduce Teilhard de Chardin's account of the sense in which the world resembles God. After noting some difficulties which this approach raises, I shall then present a further model, which starts from the notion of complementarity, and seeks to interpret the resemblance relation in terms of this more fundamental notion.

A Teilhardian account

I have suggested that standard individualistic accounts of the divine nature fail to respect in full certain plausible notions concerning the nature of salvation; and I have proposed that the doctrine of divine simplicity shows more promise of meeting these concerns. However, the theist has good *ad hominem* reasons, I have noted, for trying to develop an account of these matters which does not depend on the doctrine of divine simplicity. In this section, I shall consider whether the writings of Pierre Teilhard de Chardin provide a way out of this impasse. His approach has an obvious appeal in this context, because it does not depend upon conceiving of God as an individual, but shares various affinities with Aquinas's doctrine of God, without merely recapitulating that doctrine.

The general outline of Teilhard's approach to the nature of God and God's relation to the world is well known. On Teilhard's view, the evolutionary history of the world represents the earlier phases of a gradual process of transformation which will culminate in a perfect centring of individual things on a transcendent focus. We might pause briefly to note more exactly the sense of this claim. In general, the process of evolution involves, clearly, a transformation of simpler forms of matter into more complex and at the same time more integrated structures. Thus over time, so we are told, atoms have formed into molecules, molecules into cells, cells into organisms, and simple organisms into complex, thinking organisms. According to Teilhard, each of these transformations provides an example of how individual things may enter into closer relationship with one another, and in this sense converge upon a common focus, while at the same time preserving their identity and indeed enhancing their capacity for individual self-expression. This process is set to continue, Teilhard hypothesises. In particular, we should expect radical changes in travel and communications to open up new possibilities for human life. At its limit, this process of development will result in a state which involves at once a perfected integration and differentiation of individual things. At this point, the world will be drawn into the being of God, and God will be 'all in all'.[13]

This account, when conjoined with various other Teilhardian claims, seems to meet the various requirements we have listed for an understanding of the relationship of God and the world which keeps in view the nature of salvation. First of all, Teilhard proposes that there is a likeness between the world considered as a perfected whole and God. Of course, on this view, the world's perfection is to be realised at some future time, as the culmination of the evolutionary process, and we cannot grasp the nature of this perfection in any detail from our present vantage point. However, we can understand what is involved in general terms by analogy with the transformations which are evident in earlier phases of evolution. Thus we can see that this final state of the world will be one of integration. So Teilhard's proposal is more exactly that the world as an integral whole will present a likeness to God. So the first of our two conditions is satisfied: Teilhard's account of the relationship between the world and God allows for the integral character of this relationship.

Moreover, according to Teilhard, in this integrated state, the world will not merely image God, but will be drawn into the being of God: the relationship between the two will be an organic one, he suggests. Thus he writes that: 'As early as in St. Paul and St. John we read that to create, to fulfil and to purify the world is, for God, to unify it by uniting it organically with himself.'[14] On this view, the world's perfection is related *constitutively* to relationship to God, in so far as that perfection depends upon the world being united organically to the reality of God. By the same token, it seems that creatures' relationship to God *cannot be relativised,* since the perfection of our relationship to one another depends constitutively upon our relationship to God. Thus Teilhard's model also satisfies the second of our conditions.

Moreover, Teilhard's account seems to meet these conditions while keeping clear of the controversies surrounding the doctrine of divine simplicity. In particular, on Teilhard's view, the notion of integrated perfection can be understood by analogy with the process of evolution. Thus there is no need to expound this notion in its limiting case by reference to the Thomistic thought that God is Being Itself. On this view, the integrated perfection which is God is imaged, albeit imperfectly, by the material structures which we encounter in the world, in so far as these structures are already integrated in some measure, and point towards further stages of integration, which will bring the world into an organic relation to God.

So Teilhard's view, like the traditional Thomistic account, sponsors, at least implicitly, a doctrine of analogy. The state of the world at present (above all in so far as it has achieved a state of integrated differentiation) offers an imperfect representation of the world in its perfected state at the close of evolution. And the world in its perfected state offers a representation of God, in so far as it resembles the integrated perfection of God, and bears an organic relationship to the divine reality. Thus at one remove, the world in its present state images God, imperfectly. Again, although the nature of this relationship cannot be grasped at all precisely, the general character of what is envisaged can be illustrated by reference to earlier stages of the evolutionary process. It follows that the words we use to describe mundane things can also be used of God, providing that their sense is stretched in a way which is faithful to the stretching of the world's perfections which is evident in the process of evolution.

So Teilhard's approach seems to offer a way of meeting certain religious concerns which are addressed in Thomas's account, and arguably overlooked in modern, individualistic accounts, while avoiding the contentious metaphysics of the doctrine of divine simplicity. However, Teilhard's view poses problems in its turn. In particular, the evolutionary analogy, which lies at the heart of his account, may not be able to play the role which he appears to assign to it. Suppose we take as an example the evolution of the human brain. This development, we might suppose, should provide a clear example of what is to be expected, in general terms, in future phases of evolutionary transformation; for a central contention of Teilhard's writings (and notably of *The Phenomenon of Man*) is that the human person, and more exactly the human brain, provides the pinnacle of evolutionary achievement so far, and thus the clearest example of the ultimate direction of the whole evolutionary process. I shall talk more exactly of human consciousness, since it is the brain's ability to sustain consciousness that marks it out as the summit of evolutionary development. (I am not presupposing a particular theory of the relationship between brain and mental states; my suggestion is just that whatever the nature of this relationship, it is the brain's connection with consciousness, and thought, which must be of interest to Teilhard when he accords the brain this pre-eminent status.)

Now consciousness is, on most accounts, a radically emergent phenomenon: its character cannot be read off from the character of earlier phases of evolutionary history. If that is so, then these earlier phases will not provide an image of the nature of consciousness: the things which exist at earlier stages of the evolutionary process (or things of their type) may supply the raw materials from which brains are made; but the inherent character of these earlier things will provide no substantive clue to the nature of consciousness. In turn, this suggests that the relationship between the earlier and later phases of evolution cannot play the role Teilhard ascribes to it: the earlier phases do not after all adequately represent the later; and we therefore have no guarantee that the world as currently constituted offers an image of the world in its final state, and thereby an image of God.

However, there are other aspects of Teilhard's thinking which suggest that he would contest the basic assumption of this line of criticism. For Teilhard believes that all material things are mental in some degree, providing they have an appropriate degree of internal organisation. For instance, on his view even atoms have an interior life. If that is so, then we may say that the nature of the human mind is after all pre-figured in earlier phases of evolution, since it is pre-figured in the interior life of atoms. And by extension, we may then say that the present state of the world pre-figures the divine reality.

However, panpsychism is not a widely held view. And Teilhard's own arguments for it seem unconvincing. In brief, he supposes that we can only make sense of the appearance of consciousness at later stages of evolution on the assumption that some sort of proto-consciousness was present from the beginning.[15] But human consciousness is presumably radically different from the sort of consciousness we may attribute to an atom. And in that case, we are still left with a significant ontological leap, which in turn calls into question the explanatory power of the hypothesis of proto-consciousness. Teilhard seems to invite this sort of objection when he writes that 'modern thought . . . is beginning to see that there is definitely *more* in the molecule than in the atom, *more* in the cell than in the molecule, *more* in society than in the individual'.[16] We want to ask: if we can allow this sort of ontological transition, why think it necessary to postulate a kind of proto-consciousness to render intelligible the emergence of human consciousness?

In fact, even if we grant the idea of panpsychism, Teilhard's approach may still be unable to provide a satisfactory account of the sense in which creatures resemble God. For instance, if we suppose that atoms are conscious, then we should surely say that it is atoms considered individually (not collectively) which provide the clearest image of the human mind; for the human mind is not a compound of a number of individual consciousnesses. But in turn, this suggests that on Teilhard's approach, it is individual things, rather than the world as a whole, which best image God. And that claim violates the requirement that the world's relationship to God should be understood holistically.

So while it is initially suggestive, Teilhard's evolutionary model seems to present certain difficulties if it is taken as an account of the sense in which the world represents God. This is first of all because it requires the assumption of panpsychism, for it is only on this assumption that the earlier phases of evolution will clearly represent the later. And secondly, while Teilhard's account can articulate the notion of resemblance if we admit the truth of panpsychism, it fails at this point to safeguard the thought that the resemblance relation should be understood holistically. So we are still searching for an account of the relationship between God and the world which will fully respect certain insights which are embedded in the concept of salvation. I shall now set out a further approach which comes closer, I think, to meeting these requirements.

A final approach: the relation of necessary complement

The various models we have considered so far offer rather different accounts of the sense in which the world may point towards or represent divinity, depending on whether God is understood as Being Itself, or as a paradigmatic exemplar, or as an integrated whole by analogy with examples of integration drawn from evolution. However, these accounts have this much in common: they all draw upon the notion of resemblance in order to spell out the sense in which the world represents God. I shall now consider another way of formulating the idea that the world represents God. This time the core notion will be complementarity rather than resemblance. I begin by explaining what I mean by the notion of complementarity in this context.

We sometimes sense that the parts of a great work of art constitute an integral whole. And accordingly we may suppose that if one part (not too large a part) of such a work were to be removed, then the character of that part could in principle be inferred from a knowledge of the remainder of the work. For instance, we may feel that the various elements of a great painting belong together as an integral whole, and that the removal of one of these elements, and its replacement by something else, or its non-replacement, would detract from the work as a whole. Thus we sometimes suppose that there is one thing and one thing only which is able to complete a work of art. Let us call the relationship which binds one part of a work of art to the thing which is able uniquely to complete that part the relationship of complementarity.

Drawing on examples of this kind, we may say that one part of an aesthetic object may represent the rest of the object. Notice that in such cases, the representation does not turn upon resemblance: there is no necessity that the complementary element should mirror (or be mirrored by) the element which is already in place. Nor is the representation like the merely conventional representation which is characteristic of linguistic denotation. Nor yet is it like the relation of symptom to cause.[17] Instead, it has to do with the way in which one object may uniquely identify another by virtue of the aesthetic relationship which unites it to this further object. Clearly, if this sort of example is to throw any light on the sense in which the world represents God, then we will need to envisage, more exactly, the case where the object which is signified in this fashion is itself aesthetically perfect, quite apart from its relation to the signifier, and can be related aesthetically to the signifier without its own perfection being marred.

Suppose then that the relationship between the world and God is like the relationship between a thing which calls for completion aesthetically and the thing which uniquely provides for that completion, where this model is interpreted in such a way as to safeguard the divine perfection. It is worth emphasising that although this proposal sounds rather abstract and speculative, it has a clear affinity with familiar religious responses to the world. For those responses often involve the sense that the beauty and goodness of the world cannot be finally satisfying in themselves, but call for completion through their relationship to some transcendent reality. Allowing that our proposal has some interest in so far as it is faithful to a central strand of religious thought and feeling, we need to ask: does this understanding of the relationship between God and the world give due acknowledgement to the insights which are implicit in the concept of salvation? Recall that according to our earlier discussion, a satisfactory theory should respect the following claims:

1 It is the world as a whole, rather than particular individuals, which offers the best image of the divine nature.
2 More exactly, it is the world as an integrated whole which offers the clearest representation of the divine nature.
3 Relationship to God is constitutive of an individual's ultimate happiness.
4 More exactly, in so far as a creature's ultimate happiness depends upon her relationship to other creatures, that relationship in turn depends upon relationship to God not only causally but constitutively, with the consequence that commitment to God cannot be relativised.

The necessary complement model certainly allows us to say that it is the world as a whole rather than individual things within it which provides the clearest representation of God. Analogously, that part of the work of art which we already have (let us call this part the 'initial element') must be considered as a whole if it is to point to the character of the remainder of the work (let us call this part the 'complementary element'): while a part of the initial element might in principle be enough to infer the character of the complementary element, in general it is clearly the initial element *as a whole* which offers the best representation of the complementary element. After all, there may well be several ways of completing a mere fragment of the initial element; and any such fragment will therefore fail to represent the complementary element to the extent of uniquely identifying it.

The necessary complement model also seems to imply that the complementary element must contribute to the integration of the various parts of the initial element. For example, we might suppose that if the final movement of a symphony is to complement its earlier movements, then it must bring those earlier movements into a new and closer relationship, so that their unity is displayed. The final movement may for example repeat themes from earlier movements, while elaborating upon them and relating them to one another in new ways. Similarly, the final chapter of a novel may help to bring out latent connections in earlier parts of the story, so ensuring that the work as a whole constitutes a satisfying aesthetic unity. Of course, some aesthetic theories may wish to downplay the role of unity as a criterion of aesthetic merit. But at any rate, a work of art must surely comprise more than a jumble of uncoordinated elements; and this suggests that there is a close connection between aesthetic completion and integration. Given that connection, we may say that the relationship of the initial to the complementary element is not only holistic, but also such that it is the initial element considered as an integrated whole which offers the clearest clue to the nature of the complementary element.

So the necessary complement model is able to meet, I suggest, criteria (1) and (2). Again, this is significant in so far as these criteria flow from an understanding of salvation which acknowledges its communitarian character, and recognises more exactly that salvation implies participation in an integral community. I turn now to criteria (3) and (4). Criterion (3) proposes that relationship to God is constitutive of an individual's ultimate happiness; and (4) adds that the individual's happiness in relation to other creatures is constitutively dependent upon relationship to God. Suppose we concentrate on criterion (4) here. Correspondingly, we might say that it is only with the introduction of the complementary element that the parts of the initial element can be fulfilled in relation to one another. Moreover, this dependence upon the complementary element is not merely causal (indeed in the ordinary case, it will not be causal at all). It is, rather, constitutive, in so far as the parts of the initial element depend for their fulfilment in relation to one another upon an organic, and more exactly an aesthetic, relation to the complementary element.[18]

In this way, the necessary complement model of God's relationship to the world also satisfies criterion (4); and in turn this indicates that it satisfies criterion (3), since four amounts to a more detailed specification of (3). Hence the model respects the thought that there is an internal relation between the love of God and the love of creatures. This suggests that the necessary complement model may play a part in meeting the existential challenge to religious belief which we noted earlier. If our fulfilment in relation to other creatures is constitutively dependent upon relationship to God, then there can be no question of divinity 'not mattering'.

In these various ways, the necessary complement model arguably marks an improvement on the approaches we have considered so far. It improves on standard individualistic approaches by clearly articulating the thought that relationship to God is integral and non-relativistic. It improves on the Thomistic approach to the extent that it keeps clear of the controversies surrounding the doctrine of subsistent existence. And it improves on Teilhard's scheme by avoiding the epistemic problems implicit in his use of the emergence relation; for as the example of artistic inspiration indicates, there is in principle no difficulty in supposing that a person may grasp the character of an aesthetic whole granted an initial knowledge of only part of the whole. Thus one agreeable feature of the necessary complement model is its implication that it is as it were the creative artists of the religious life (the saints we might say, rather than the philosophers) who will have the clearest insight into the divine nature.

Although the necessary complement model differs from these other approaches in these various respects, it does not imply that the notion of resemblance should play no part in our understanding of the relationship between the world and God. On the contrary, it invites the thought that there must be some sort of resemblance between the world and God, corresponding to the affinity which there must be between a number of parts which together comprise a single aesthetic whole. So to this extent, the necessary complement model also endorses the thought that the world resembles God. However, it sets limits to the implications which are to be drawn from this idea, by placing it within a larger interpretive context. In other words, the necessary complement approach suggests that the notion of resemblance should not play a foundational role in our understanding of the relationship between the world and God, but should be interpreted in a way which conforms to the implications of the necessary complement model, above all in so far as this model implies that the world is related to God integrally and non-relativistically.

So far I have not offered a general critique of the idea that the resemblance relation might serve as a *starting point* for our understanding of the relationship between God and the world; instead I have concentrated on some of the difficulties which are posed by several applications of this approach. However, there is one difficulty to which such approaches may be prone in general. For an account which works primarily in terms of the idea of resemblance seems likely to suggest that mundane things constitute a kind of inferior imitation of God, and such a view seems, potentially, unhelpful from a spiritual point of view.

For instance, it might encourage the thought that we should love God *rather than* creatures. (Similarly, given the opportunity of viewing an original Van Gogh, we might not wish to give any attention to copies of it.) Or at any rate, this model might encourage us to think of creatures disparagingly, as gods *manqués*. By contrast, the necessary complement approach encourages us to suppose that creatures are good not simply in so far as they image God, but in themselves, although their goodness is not ultimately separable from the goodness of God in so far as it depends for its fulfilment upon relationship to God. Such an approach seems likely to foster an appreciation of creatures on account of their own distinct character, rather than simply as distant approximations to what God is.

Of course, while it offers these various advantages over other accounts, the necessary complement model is not without difficulties of its own. Notably, the notion of a necessary complement remains so far no more than a postulate. We may know what the relation of necessary complement amounts to in the case of works of art, but what would it be for something to bear this relationship to the world as a whole? And why suppose that anything in fact plays this role? To address these concerns, I shall offer a brief elaboration of the necessary complement model.

In thinking further about how God could play the role of necessary complement, we might return to some of the examples we considered earlier. For instance, when we suppose that the earlier parts of a great piece of music call for completion in precisely the way indicated by the composer, we are supposing that these earlier parts can only be brought into proper relation with one another by virtue of their relationship to the remainder of the piece. The remainder of the piece may achieve this effect in various ways, for example by repeating earlier themes, so establishing new relationships between them. If we follow this analogy, then we might say that God is able to complete the beauty of the world because there is within the being of God some sort of composition which corresponds to the various component parts of the world. In that case, the divine reality might in some fashion recapitulate the being of the world, and thereby bring its elements into a new and deeper relationship to one another.

This suggestion presents a structural parallel to what happens when the later parts of a musical composition take up themes from the earlier parts and thereby bring those earlier parts to completion. But we may still be left wondering what such a relationship might amount to in the case of God and the world. It might help at this point to develop the aesthetic model in a social idiom.

For instance, a man might say that his relationship to his wife was in some measure fulfilled or brought to completion when he came to know her parents. More exactly, he might say that certain elements from his relationship to his wife were repeated in the context of his relationship to her parents, and thereby set in a new and richer context. (Compare the musical analogy again.) For example, he may have found that his relationship to them enabled him to learn more about some of her formative experiences; or again, he may have come to a better understanding of her by discovering various aspects of her personality in them. By means of such examples, we can give some content to the thought that my relationship to another person may depend for its completeness upon my relationship to a further individual, a parent in particular. And by extension we might think that our relationship to other human beings may depend for its completeness upon our relationship to their metaphysical, and not merely their biological, source. Given such a metaphysical source, our relationship to others could in principle be completed not merely in one or two cases, but in a more general and thoroughgoing fashion.

In terms of this sort of analogy, we can make some sense of the idea that the human community as a whole represents God in so far as it points towards the divine reality as the necessary complement of its inter-personal perfection. Of course, since it rests on a parental analogy, this approach invites the thought that God may be conceived as an individual. But again, it qualifies the individualistic model by suggesting that we relate to God not so much as to another individual, but through the community. God's reality is revealed at the limit of our relationships with other human beings, as the constitutive condition of the fulfilment of those relationships.

Of course, by analogy, there will be other, similar ways of further specifying the necessary complement model. For instance, we might suppose that God is the necessary complement of the world considered as a narrative. On this view, the many individual stories which make up the world are completed in God. Analogously, the final chapter of a book may bring to completion the various episodes related in earlier parts of the book. Again, to play this role, the final chapter must include some reference to earlier episodes, and must somehow bring out the full significance of their relations to one another. This view does not push us so readily in the direction of an individualistic conception of God, though it is not evidently inconsistent with such a view. Again, such an approach points towards a spirituality which does not aim to encounter God directly, any more than one might hope to understand the last chapter of a book without reference to its earlier chapters. Instead, the way to God lies through the world, and through a deep immersion in the structures of meaning which are evident in the world.

However, while we may be able to cast some light on the necessary complement relation in these various ways, it may be to some extent unanalysable. Similarly, we may sense that a certain element in a painting is essential to the completeness of the picture, without being able to point to any mechanism whereby this element contributes to the integration of the remainder of the picture. Indeed, a person may sense that the world needs some complement to bring its goodness to fulfilment and may sense that something in fact plays this role, without being able to specify what such a reality could be like. In this case, not only can the mechanism not be specified, but the necessary complement itself cannot be identified at all precisely. This suggests that the necessary complement proposal may hold some interest even if we cannot spell out the relation in any detail, whether in the ways I have indicated or in some other way. However, if any of these analogies do work, then naturally they have a useful role to play, by giving the necessary complement idea a clearer form, so preparing the way for a closer examination of the proposal.

So far I have concentrated on what content we might give to the necessary complement model as applied to the relationship between God and the world. But we should also say something about its epistemic basis; and in this connection, the argument from design proves to be important. If the design argument is viable, in the ways we have discussed, then the theist can represent the necessary complement model of God as a natural extension of what we know about the world as designed. For instance, if the world was made for aesthetic (among other) reasons, then we may reasonably infer that its aesthetic properties will be brought to completion. We may then hold that God is that reality, whatever its precise nature, upon which the world depends for its aesthetic fulfilment, constitutively and not merely causally. Similarly, if we allow that the designer is a moral agent, then we may suppose that the world will be brought to fulfilment in social or inter-personal terms; and again we may point to the reality which plays the role of necessary complement in this connection, and remark: this is what we call God.

So the design argument provides an evidential basis for the conception of God which is advanced by the necessary complement model. In general, in so far as the design argument succeeds in grounding the idea that reality is ultimately governed by a moral, aesthetic and narrative purpose, then we may suppose that the world is to be brought to completion in all of these respects; and we may then speak of God as whatever plays that role constitutively (as well as causally). Notice that this account provides a ready sense in which divinity is not only the 'efficient' cause of the world, but also its 'final' cause, in so far as the world's perfection depends constitutively, and not only causally, upon its relationship to God. Moreover, this approach, like the approach of Chapter 6, allows us to speak of God not merely as an individual mind, but as Beauty and Meaning and Love. For on this view, our best clue to the goodness of God is supplied not by individuals, but by the community or the cosmos itself considered as an integrated whole, aesthetically, narratively, and inter-personally.

Conclusions

The debate concerning the sense in which the world represents God admits of no single, simple solution. In this chapter, I have surveyed three familiar approaches, and taken note of one alternative. I conclude that the idea of God as necessary complement, while it calls for further development, offers certain advantages over more standard approaches, which in one way or another prefer to understand the relationship of the world to God primarily in terms of resemblance. In particular, the necessary complement model manages to capture certain notions of genuine religious importance which are, arguably, better represented in the Thomistic model than in standard individualistic accounts of the divine nature: namely, the idea that it is the world as an integral whole which offers the clearest representation of God, and the idea that the fulfilment of creatures in their relations to one another depends constitutively upon their relationship to God. In turn, these ideas seem to flow from certain plausible claims concerning the nature of salvation, in particular the idea that salvation is in community, and the idea that the world's perfection is to be found in God and not merely through God. As well as improving upon the individualistic approach in these ways, the necessary complement model also escapes some of the philosophical perplexities which are commonly said to beset Thomistic metaphysics; and it offers a clearer account of our epistemic access to God than is possible on Teilhard's evolutionary understanding of the relationship between God and the world.

In this chapter I have sought to reply to two challenges to theistic belief: a logical challenge concerning the meaning of the terms we use in relation to God, and an existential challenge, concerning the possibility of representing God as an object of attraction. In concluding I return to these two issues.

Of course, each of these various theories of the relationship between God and the world will generate its own perspective on the meaning of religious language. For instance, the necessary complement model suggests that perfection terms can be used of God in so far as there is in principle a discernible (and complementary) connection between the goodness of the world, considered as a perfected aesthetic whole, and the goodness of God. It is not clear that the meaning of our terms is to be stretched any more or less on the necessary complement approach, as compared with approaches which are grounded in the idea of resemblance.[19] However, on such an approach our terms will signify the divine reality in a different way, corresponding to the different line of projection which points from creaturely perfection towards the divine perfection. Analogously, an inferior copy of a great Shakespearean play and the first four acts of such a play may both point in rather different ways towards the character of the final act.

Each of these various theories will also generate its own 'spirituality'. On the account provided by the necessary complement model, the world is not fundamentally an imitation of God, even if it does represent God by pointing towards the divine reality as the constitutive condition of its completion in aesthetic and other terms. So on this view, there can be no question of forsaking the world on the grounds that it is merely an inferior imitation of the original perfection which is God. Moreover, on the necessary complement approach our fulfilment in relation to creatures is tied to our fulfilment in relation to God. The implication of this approach is that we encounter God's reality at the limit of our appreciation of what is most attractive in the world, since the world's attractiveness depends constitutively for its completion upon God. So such an approach invites the thought that to understand God is to understand the structures of meaning which we encounter in our mundane experience. This is to say that the deepest understanding of God is reserved for those who value and love the world most deeply.

For the purposes of this chapter, I have assumed that the model of Chapter 6 is not available. I have tried to show how, even without this model, or some other close analogue to the notion of subsistent existence, it is still possible to develop an understanding of God which captures certain religiously important features of Aquinas's account. The approach of this chapter and that of Chapter 6 are logically distinct: one could think of divinity as a radiant synthesis of the world's perfections without thinking of it as the necessary complement of those perfections, and vice versa. However, the two models are easily united into a single account. This is in part because both favour an understanding of God as supra-individual. It is also because there are specific points of correspondence between the two theories. In particular, the synthesis idea provides one way of articulating the thought that the being of God somehow recapitulates the being of the world; and that thought is one which the necessary complement model can put to use, in spelling out the sense in which God's perfection completes the perfection of the world. More exactly, we might suppose that divinity completes the world by bringing its elements into closer relation with one another, and that its ability to do this is connected with the fact that the counterparts of those elements already exist in a perfectly integrated way within the divine being. (Compare the case where the last chapter of a story takes up some of its earlier themes, and sets them in an integrated relation to one another, thereby giving those earlier themes their full meaning.) If the synthesis model can fill out the necessary complement model in this way, that would confirm my suggestion that Thomas's account of the resemblance relation already contains the insights which the model of God as necessary complement is intended to preserve.

The necessary complement model also shares with the synthesis model a concern to ground the concept of God in familiar religious responses to the world. The idea of God as necessary complement reflects, I have suggested, the familiar religious sense that the beauty of the world cannot be finally satisfying in itself, but calls for completion in some way. Thus both approaches point towards a spirituality which starts from a sensitivity towards the goodness of created things, and both invite us to move towards a sense of God's reality in this way, through the world, rather than by means of some immediate encounter with God as a particular object of experience.

In these ways, I hope the models of Chapters 6 and 7 help to address the question we posed at the beginning of Part IV: how might the argument from design generate a religiously satisfactory account of the divine nature? In response to this question, I have been arguing that the design argument can provide an epistemic foundation for a conception of God which respects various insights to do with the nature of worship and salvation. If that is so, then there is a strong presumption that the argument is capable of upholding a religiously sensitive account of the divine nature.

Lastly, this chapter provides a further contribution to our ongoing discussion of the goodness of the world. I have argued that the goodness of the world may give us some intimation of the goodness of God in so far as it depends (integrally and non-relativistically) on God for its fulfilment. Hence the goodness of the world is relevant to theistic belief not only evidentially, but also in so far as it provides our clearest clue to the nature of divinity in itself.

Conclusion

Conclusion

Between Cleanthes and Demea

There is a longstanding and deep-seated tension within theistic thought. Some theists rejoice in the world. Others find it depressing, and hold to religion as a refuge from the wretchedness of human life. This second group tend of course to emphasise the difference between God and the world, supposing that God is sublimely perfect and the world radically corrupt. By contrast, believers of the first school maintain that there is some sort of affinity between creatures and God. There is apparently a fundamental opposition here on two related issues, concerning the goodness or otherwise of the world, and its ability to represent the divine nature. Despite their seeming incompatibility, both these perspectives are deeply rooted in theistic tradition.

Of course, the design argument belongs naturally within the first of these schools, in so far as it is grounded in an appreciation of the goodness of the world. Moreover, as traditionally formulated, it depends on drawing an analogy between God and human beings, in respect of their purposes, and in respect of what they produce. Members of the second school are likely to complain that in these ways, the design argument compromises the sovereignty of God. Accordingly, they will favour other kinds of argument for the existence of God; or they may maintain that human reason necessarily falls so far short of any truth pertaining to God that we should rely upon faith in defiance of reason, or revelation in defiance of natural theology.

These tensions are wonderfully evoked in Hume's *Dialogues,* where they are played out in the disagreement between Cleanthes and Demea. Of course, Cleanthes is impressed by the goodness and order of the world, and on this basis he propounds an argument from design. On the other side, Demea is persuaded of the misery of human life, and finds Cleanthes's conception of God repugnant, on the grounds that it assimilates the majestic God to sinful human beings. In place of the design argument, Demea commends the use of a priori arguments for the existence of God. Watching this disagreement unfold (and provoking it) is Philo, whose own position, if it is not to be interpreted as merely sceptical, points perhaps to the view that religious belief must rest upon faith, and not upon reason. Each of these various approaches represents an integrated complex of ideas, to do with the nature of the world, of human beings, and of God. Epistemologically and spiritually, Demea recommends an escape from the world of sense experience, in favour of reliance upon pure reason, and a turning towards a further, better world, which is our true home. By contrast, on Cleanthes's view, sense experience offers a route (perhaps our only route) to knowledge of God, and accordingly immersion in the world of sense experience carries a spiritual significance.

In this work, I have tried to address this strain in a way which upholds the partial validity of both these perspectives. Like Cleanthes, I have defended the argument from design; and like Cleanthes, I have argued that the world's goodness provides an intimation of the goodness of God. But at the same time, I have tried to show how the design argument can be married to a conception of God which draws its inspiration from the doctrine of divine simplicity, a doctrine which has Demea's support, and which gives due recognition to the radical difference between God's reality (which is not merely individual) and the reality of creatures. The case I have made seeks to accommodate Demea's critique of Cleanthes in other ways too. Notably, it does not claim that the goodness of God is evident in every detail of the world's working, and to this extent it accepts Demea's protest that the world is often enough a place of trial and not of fulfilment.

I have developed this last theme in two ways. First of all, I have conceded, in some degree, the Demean claim that, in the nature of the case, we cannot hope from our finite perspective to fathom the purposes of God. Thus any design argument which represents God's purposes in creation as altogether transparent must be rejected on a priori grounds. Furthermore, I have argued that in order to be a fitting object of divine creation, it is not necessary that this world should be the best possible world, nor that it should be manifestly superior to other types of world, nor even that it should be overall very much better than not. It is enough that it (or each of the integral wholes of which it is comprised) should be worth something overall. On this understanding, the thought that the world is designed in no way implies that human life should be free from tribulation. So the approach I have offered provides a sort of middle ground between Cleanthes and Demea by defending a version of the argument from design which places limits on our ability to discern the divine purposes, which does not endorse a facile optimism about the working of the world, and which is allied to an account of the divine nature which affirms central parts of Demea's conception of God.

Re-enchanting the world

Over recent centuries, the argument from design has commanded a wider popular following than any of the other traditional arguments for the existence of God; and accordingly, there is good reason to suppose that the demise of theistic belief from a sociological point of view reflects a general sense that the design argument has failed to make its case. In part, the argument's difficulties can be attributed to the decision of Paley and others to ground their reasoning in features of the world which later proved susceptible of a rival, scientific kind of explanation. But these difficulties derive still more fundamentally from two deficiencies in standard formulations of the argument.

First of all, arguments from design have tended to rely upon a broadly scientific, evaluatively neutral conception of the world. Notably, they have been impressed by the world's regularity over space and time, and have taken this sort of merely empirical datum as their starting point. But unless it is supplemented by other images, this understanding of the import of human experience is ultimately inimical to religious belief, because it diminishes the world, by representing it in merely mechanical (or at any rate in regular and value-free) terms; and hence it diminishes God, who comes to be understood merely as a kind of celestial engineer. Thus the argument from design, as formulated in recent centuries, has had the effect of undermining the very conception of the world which is the soil for a religiously rich sense of the attractiveness of God.

Moreover, standard formulations of the argument from design have tended to picture God as, fundamentally, an individual mind. On this view, the world is a disclosure of the divine in so far as it reveals God's purposes. But this conception of the sense in which the world reveals God appears religiously impoverished, when contrasted with the mediaeval conception of God as subsistent existence. On this older view, God is not simply a powerful individual whose purposes are good, but a uniquely concentrated expression of what it is to be. On this view, the goodness and beauty of the world provide a clue not just to God's benevolent intentions in relation to the world, but to the goodness and beauty of the divine being in itself. Again, this understanding of God and God's relation to the world is crucial if the existential point of religious belief is to be preserved. Otherwise, divinity becomes merely a kind of computing device, of extraordinary powers, and not a reality whose inherent character is made known at the limiting point of our encounter with the attractiveness of the world.

I suggest then that the argument from design as defended in recent times has often represented both the world and God in ways which are ultimately damaging to religious belief. In this book, I have tried to develop a version of the design argument which is free from these difficulties. Hence I have grounded the argument in a lively appreciation of the goodness of the world. And I have sought to align the argument with a religiously sensitive, non-individual understanding of the divine nature, which respects both the anthropological data, and the conception of God which is implicit in the notions of worship and salvation.

All versions of the design argument lend support to the view that the world is enchanted, in the sense of being informed by the activity of a mind. But in its historical guise the design argument has played a central part in the disenchantment of the world, to the extent that it has viewed the world as lifeless and machine-like, and to the extent that it has severed the bond, which was characteristic of earlier ventures in philosophical theology, between the goodness of the world and the inherent nature of divinity. In this book, I have tried to reclaim this older sense of the world's enchantment, by showing how the design argument may be grounded in an evaluatively rich conception of the world, and how it may issue in a conception of God which sees divinity as echoed in our deepest encounters with the world considered as good and as beautiful.

Taken as a whole, the book constitutes a plea to value the world. In Chapters 1 to 4, I have argued that the goodness of the world is the most fundamental fact about it: it is its reason for existence. So if asked what the world basically is, our reply should not be, 'a machine', or 'a chance collocation of atoms', but rather 'a locus of value'. In Chapter 5, I argued that the world's goodness also carries a moral significance: it stands as an invitation to respond in trust to the basic conditions of our existence. Lastly, in Chapters 6 and 7, I have represented the world's goodness as a revelation of the inherent character of the primordial source of existence. Hence the goodness of the world provides our surest clue to our origins and our destiny: it tells us why the world should exist, and offers a glimpse into what its final consummation will involve.

Notes

Introduction

1 Kant 1933: A623/B651: 520.
2 I shall make further connections with ecological themes in setting out a rationale for worship in Chapter 6, and again in my discussion of the problem of evil in Chapter 4.
3 However, there have been recent book-length discussions which bear comparison with the present volume in terms of their subject matter. It may be wondered how these discussions differ from this work. The most recent such discussion is Peter Forrest, *God Without the Supernatural* (1996). I find myself in agreement with much of Forrest's book. However, the present work is more clearly founded on the perception of value in the world and differs in its approach to natural beauty in so far as it aims to rebut the biophilia hypothesis (see Chapter 1). Moreover, my approach to the role of moral considerations in the justification of religious belief is different from Forrest's, as is my treatment of the concept of God. However, my arguments on these points are not clearly incompatible with Forrest's discussion. The present work will also differ from Richard Swinburne's defence of natural theology in *The Existence of God* (1991) and *The Coherence of Theism* (1993). Again, I am sympathetic to a great deal of Swinburne's discussion, but in Chapter 2, it will be clear that my approach to consciousness as evidence for theism is different from his. Similarly, the discussion of Part IV offers a sustained engagement with, and at points dissent from, Swinburne's understanding of the concept of God.
4 For classic treatment of the basic belief proposal, see A. Plantinga and N. Wolterstorff (eds) *Faith and Rationality* (1983). Important recent formulations of the argument from religious experience include W. Alston, *Perceiving God* (1991) and K. Yandell, *The Epistemology of Religious Experience* (1993).
5 For instance, Anthony O'Hear argues that religious experience can contribute nothing to the rationality of religious beliefs, because of its uncheckability: O'Hear 1984, ch. 2.
6 For instance, speaking of religious experience in particular, Richard Swinburne writes:

> one would not expect too evident and public a manifestation . . . If God's existence, justice, and intentions became items of evident

> common knowledge, then man's freedom would in effect be vastly curtailed. However, one might expect certain private and occasional manifestations by God to certain men.
>
> (Swinburne 1991: 244)

Of course, this claim carries rather radical implications for the earlier phases of Swinburne's argument, since it suggests that natural theology is also likely to fall short of providing 'evident common knowledge' of God's existence and nature. I return to this matter in my concluding remarks below.

7 As Plantinga notes, people will disagree on the examples which are relevant in establishing criteria for proper basicality. He infers that: 'criteria for proper basicality arrived at in this particularistic way may not be polemically useful': Plantinga 1983: 77. Even if I have a basic disposition to hold a given religious belief, I may still have to reckon with a further basic disposition which inclines me to hold some other belief which is incompatible with that first belief, and in this connection I may again need to have recourse to evidence. See Wykstra 1989, especially pp. 435–7.

8 As Plantinga notes, a properly basic belief is only *prima facie* justified: Plantinga 1983: 83–4.

9 I am drawing here upon Wykstra (1989). Anthony Kenny also makes a case for the enduring importance of natural theology, if religious belief is to be properly basic for at least some people: *What is Faith?* (1992) ch. 3.

10 Of course, it may be said that religious experience, treated non-evidentially, provides an adequate stopping point for justification in the case of religious beliefs, while there is no direct perceptual experience of electrons. This position leads us back to the considerations noted above.

11 For an argument of this form, see John Schellenberg, *Divine Hiddenness and Human Reason* (1993).

1 Providence and beauty

1 See M. J. Buckley, *At the Origins of Modern Atheism* (1987).

2 The following summary is drawn from my essay 'Design arguments' (Wynn 1998).

3 See Anaxagoras, in J. Barnes (ed.) *Early Greek Philosophy* (1987) ch. 18.

4 Aquinas 1989: I 2 art. 3, pp. 13–14.

5 R. H. Hurlbutt describes these developments in *Hume, Newton, and the Design Argument* (1965). P. Byrne offers a description of the resulting deism in *Natural Religion and the Nature of Religion: the Legacy of Deism* (1989).

6 Hume 1990: 53. The text was first published, posthumously, in 1779.

7 See the opening of his *Natural Theology: or, Evidences of the Existence and Nature of the Deity, Collected from the Appearances of Nature* (Paley 1802).

8 See for instance Gaskin 1988 and Doore 1980.

9 Hume 1990: 58, 86–91, 60, 77–8, 72–3.

10 Ibid.: 92–5.

11 Ibid.: 121.

12 For a modern statement of the Darwinian view, and its implications for the design argument, see R. Dawkins, *The Blind Watchmaker* (1986).

13 See Tennant 1930, ch. iv; Hambourger 1979; Swinburne 1991, chs 8–10

and appendices; and Walker 1978, ch. xii.

14 Thus he remarks that the argument 'enlivens the study of nature, just as it itself derives its existence from and gains ever new vigour from that source': Kant 1933, A 623/B 651.

15 See J. D. Barrow and F. J. Tipler, *The Anthropic Cosmological Principle* (1986); I. Barbour, *Religion in an Age of Science* (1990) ch. 5; and J. Leslie, *Universes* (1989).

16 For contrasting interpretations of this fact see see Barrow and Tipler as reviewed by W. L. Craig (1988).

17 For different approaches here, see Swinburne 1991: 314–22 and W. Drees, *Beyond the Big Bang. Quantum Cosmologies and God* (1990: 87).

18 Some commentators have distinguished between 'teleological' and 'eutaxiological' versions of the design argument. Only the first of these is said to depend on the identification of purpose in the world; the second rests simply on the observation of order, and the thought that such order is unlikely to have arisen by chance. Plainly, my approach will be more oriented towards the first version of the design argument, although as we have seen, the arguments from regularity and purpose are often difficult to distinguish. For the eutaxiological/teleological distinction, see Barrow and Tipler 1986: 29. A similar distinction can be found in T. McPherson, *The Argument from Design* (1972: 8).

19 See Tennant 1930, volume ii, *The World, the Soul and God.* The following discussion of Tennant's argument draws on my paper 'Beauty, Providence and the Biophilia Hypothesis' (Wynn 1997c).

20 Tennant 1930: 90.

21 Compare Robert Hambourger's discussion of the way design would have to be woven into the natural order, in Diamond and Teichman (1979).

22 Mackie 1977: 43.

23 Taylor 1989: 59. See his defence of the 'best account principle' in this volume.

24 Forrest 1996: 135.

25 Mackie notes this point: Mackie 1977: 43.

26 Peter Forrest in his recent formulation of the argument from beauty takes an interest in both kinds of beauty: Forrest 1996: 134. I return to Forrest's discussion later.

27 Their usage is based more or less precisely on Kant who writes:

> in what we are wont to call sublime in nature there is such an absence of anything leading to particular objective principles and corresponding forms of nature, that it is rather in its chaos, or in its wildest and most irregular distortion and desolation, provided it gives signs of magnitude and power, that nature chiefly excites ideas of the sublime.
>
> (Kant 1911: 92)

28 Tennant 1930: 91.

29 Ibid.: 91–2.

30 Tennant does not draw attention to the distinction between aesthetic value and the value of beauty. But evidently there is such a distinction. For instance, many contemporary works of art have renounced any interest in beauty, but without surrendering all concern for aesthetic values.

31 Hume 1990: 53.
32 Ibid.: 86–91.
33 The difference of scale between the two does not obviously provide a relevant point of distinction, in so far as beauty is not in any simple way a function of size. However, the case of the sublime may be different.
34 Patrick Sherry has discussed some of the ways in which we might make sense of the idea that mundane beauty offers a clue to the nature of divine beauty. See his *Spirit and Beauty. An Introduction to Theological Aesthetics* (1992) for instance p. 152.
35 Compare John Wisdom on the 'connecting technique' in his essay 'Gods' (Wisdom 1953: 158–63).
36 Ulrich 1993: 94.
37 Compare T. J. Diffey's remark that:

> In virtually all instances of natural beauty, certainly in Britain and perhaps in most of the world, it is false to take 'natural' as meaning the absence or exclusion of human agency. It has often been noted that particularly in small, heavily populated countries such as Britain today it is very difficult to find 'unspoiled' tracts of nature.
> (Diffey 1993: 48)

38 Moreover, our tendency to find some life forms attractive may well be connected with their fitness for their environment, just as we find symptoms of health in human beings attractive. At the same time, we need to recognise that the presence of living things can inform our appreciation of landscapes, in ways which are out of all proportion to their size. Thus Aldo Leopold remarks:

> Everybody knows, for example, that the autumn landscape in the north woods is the land plus a red maple, plus a ruffed grouse. In terms of conventional physics, the grouse represents only a millionth of either the mass or the energy of an acre. Yet subtract the grouse and the whole thing is dead. An enormous amount of some motive power has been lost.
> (Leopold 1987: 137)

39 Wilson 1984. Interestingly, Wilson also thinks that the biophilia hypothesis can be extended to the case of religion. Thus he writes that given the hypothesis 'the necessary conditions are in place to cut the historical channels of art and religious belief' : in Kellert and Wilson 1993: 33. This offers an understanding of religious beliefs which is rather different from Wilson's better known proposal that such beliefs are important for the cohesion of a society. For the latter view see his *On Human Nature* (1978) ch. 8.
40 A useful collection of such work is contained in Kellert and Wilson 1993. The following discussion is particularly indebted to this text.
41 In fact, the evidence proves to be somewhat complicated. In particular, there is more evidence to show that we are biologically predisposed to retain such self-protective responses rather than to acquire them in the first place. For a summary of such research, see Ulrich 1993: 76–86.
42 Ulrich 1993: 89–92.
43 Appleton 1990: 15.
44 Ulrich 1993: 103.

45 Ulrich offers an overview of this research: ibid.: 98–106.
46 Tennant 1930: 90.
47 In place of proof, Tennant offers 'alogical probability', meaning that the argument does not provide a precisely quantifiable measure of probability. See his discussion of probability in ch. xi of vol. i.
48 Tennant 1930: 92.
49 Forrest 1996: 135.
50 Denis Cosgrove, cited by Appleton (1990: 10).
51 For some indication of the diversity of approaches, see Simon Schama, *Landscape and Memory* (1996).
52 Ulrich 1993: 126.
53 John D. Barrow, *The Artful Universe* (1995: 95–6).
54 Yi-Fu Tuan offers some thought-provoking remarks on this topic and related issues in 'Desert and ice: ambivalent aesthetics' (Tuan 1993, for instance p. 114).
55 Ibid.: 155.
56 Here I have adapted an example from Forrest 1996: 133.
57 This point could be related to Peter Forrest's proposal that naturalistic explanations of natural beauty fail to recognise that we have a 'resilient sense of the transcendent character of beautiful things' (Forrest 1996: 135). In other words, we have a sense that they point beyond themselves to some supremely beautiful reality, which is not itself an object within the world.
58 Haldane 1994: 98.
59 Ibid.: 99.
60 Soper 1995: 227.
61 Tennant addresses this issue in Tennant 1930: 88–9. I shall say more on the question of prior probability in Chapter 2.

2 The world as a source of value

1 Some of the material in this chapter has been drawn from my paper 'Emergent phenomena and theistic explanation'(Wynn 1999a). I am grateful to a reader for *International Philosophical Quarterly* for helpful comments on an earlier draft of this discussion, and to members of the Philosophy Department at the University of Glasgow for further useful suggestions.
2 Interestingly, the best-known theological proponent of an evolutionary argument from consciousness supposes that consciousness is not a novel phenomenon, arguing instead that the universe had a psychic dimension from its inception. See Pierre Teilhard de Chardin, *The Phenomenon of Man* (1959), for instance pp. 268–71. Although I and the writers I discuss take a different view of this matter, much of the argument of this chapter could be transposed into a Teilhardian idiom. See especially the discussion of Rolston's argument from complexity below.
3 Swinburne 1991, ch. 9. As well as propounding the argument I consider, Swinburne has also urged that naturalism fails to explain consciousness in so far as it fails to explain which soul is connected with which brain. This argument is less interesting, to the extent that it depends upon Swinburne's substance dualism, a view which is not widely held among philosophers. See his *Is There a God?* (1996: 89). Unless otherwise indi-

cated, further references to Swinburne's work will concern *The Existence of God* (Swinburne 1991).

4 In fact, Swinburne's argument also makes reference to various other mental items, including beliefs and intentions. Confining our attention to phenomenal qualia will help to simplify the discussion. Where these other mental items are concerned, the notion of psycho-physical correlations raises broader issues concerning the holism of the mental. Compare J. L. Mackie, *The Miracle of Theism. Arguments For and Against the Existence of God* (1982: 123–4).

5 Swinburne 1991: 171.

6 Ibid.: 171–2. The original quotation speaks of intentions rather than experiences.

7 Locke 1975, book iv, ch.iii, section 29, quoted in Adams 1987b: 249.

8 Locke 1975: iv, iii, 6. On the impossibility of thought arising from matter, see iv, x, 10.

9 This is made clear in Swinburne's reply to Mackie: 'Mackie, induction and God' (Swinburne 1983: 389). This material is reprinted in Appendix A of the revised edition of *The Existence of God* (Swinburne 1991). By contrast, Swinburne thinks that no brain could account for the fact that one soul rather than another is connected with it: see note 3.

10 Swinburne 1991: 173.

11 Ibid.: 171.

12 I take it that God does have reason for ensuring that there are regular, type–type correlations between brain states and qualia, so that his creatures are not simply bewildered by their environment. But on Swinburne's account, there is no explanation of why God prefers one set of regular correlations over others. Contrast Leibniz's approach, which is discussed in Adams 1987b: 253–4. See also Forrest's discussion of the ways in which the functional roles of brain states may constrain the ways in which they appear: *God Without the Supernatural* (1996: 191–2).

13 Swinburne 1983: 390. Compare Swinburne 1991: 103. Of course, Swinburne's approach here is reminiscent of the kalam cosmological argument.

14 Mackie's criticism can be found in Mackie 1982: 100, 129–30. Swinburne replies in Swinburne 1983: 387–9.

15 Of course, these two claims may be related: our sense that the naturalistic account of emergent phenomena is inadequate may trade on the sense that theism would provide a superior explanation.

16 Swinburne 1991: 173-4.

17 Ibid.: 174.

18 Ibid.: 173.

19 Thus Swinburne writes: 'from the very nature of science it cannot explain the highest laws of all; for they are that by which it explains all other phenomena' (Swinburne 1991: 139). Thus naturalism ultimately fails to explain the particular character of natural laws. As I have noted, in Swinburne's view, it also fails to explain the fact that there are any physical regularities. Thus he writes: 'The universe might so naturally have been chaotic' (ibid.: 136).

20 Compare Swinburne's remark that: 'the powers and liabilities of large-scale objects are determined by those of their fundamental constituents' (ibid.: 140). A natural extension of this idea would be the

thought that the powers and liabilities of the most basic constituents of the material universe are inexplicable from a naturalistic point of view, since their behaviour cannot be explained by reference to their component parts.

21 The naturalist might be tempted to offer an evolutionary explanation of the regularity of these correlations, for such regularity will ensure that a creature's experience is more easily ordered. However, naturalists are more likely, I suggest, to suppose that such regularities are (at least) physically necessary.

22 The second and third questions are posed in Adams 1987b: 243; the first is raised on p. 259, and the fourth on p. 245.

23 Ibid.: 245.

24 Ibid.: 256.

25 Incidentally, this question seems to be the issue which concerns Locke, though his approach also differs from the argument I outline in my concluding section. He maintains that materialist accounts of thought are simply absurd: it is no more possible to get thought from matter in motion than to get something from nothing. See again Locke 1975: iv x 10.

26 Smart and Haldane, *Atheism and Theism* (1996).

27 These questions and others are listed in Smart and Haldane 1996: 113.

28 Smart and Haldane 1996: 113. Haldane attributes this line of argument to Peter Geach in *Mental Acts* (1958). See Geach 1958 especially ch. 10.

29 Smart and Haldane 1996: 114. I take it that there are counterexamples to this claim. For instance, if I were raised in a community which lacked cats and the concept *cat*, but encountered a cat one day, then I could presumably form the concept of cat under those circumstances even without the presence of others who already had the concept. But Haldane's argument is tersely stated; its intention, I suggest, is to direct our attention to the most basic features of our conceptual scheme, or to our ability to use language in the first place.

30 Smart and Haldane 1996: 115, 133–4.

31 Ibid.: 116.

32 Ibid.: 117.

33 In other words, how was his second-order power to acquire this first-order power actualised? Haldane draws this distinction in Smart and Haldane 1996: 115.

34 Perhaps it will be said that Adam's power of concept use was actualised through the agency of an angel; but this makes no difference to the fundamental issue here, since the agency of the angel will in turn be miraculous.

35 In his original exposition of innatism, Haldane remarks:

> I am pretty sure that Smart and I agree that to defend this view you have to be willing to make large claims - such as that our ideas were given us by God who implanted the right number, of the right sort, at the right time.
>
> (Smart and Haldane 1996: 113)

His own account seems ultimately to drive him in the direction of this same hypothesis.

36 Smart and Haldane 1996: 99–106.
37 Ibid.: 169. Smart adds that this would be a rare event. I presume he says this for empirical reasons; I do not see why he should be committed a priori to the view that such events must be rare.
38 Ibid.: 198.
39 Ibid.: 102.
40 Ibid.: 198. Haldane discusses this issue at greater length in 'The mystery of emergence' (Haldane 1996). Here, drawing on Richard Spencer-Smith's account, he defines novelty so: A property P is novel in x if x has P, and there are no determinates P' of the same determinable as P, such that any constituents of x have P'. Further references to Haldane's work will concern Smart and Haldane 1996 unless otherwise indicated.
41 Smart and Haldane 1996: 102. The first of these claims corresponds to Haldane's rejection of 'fading conceptuality'.
42 This seems to be the sort of explanation that is envisaged by Spencer-Smith in his paper to which Haldane's 'Mystery of emergence' paper (Haldane 1996) is a reply. See his notion of interactional emergence in 'Reductionism and emergent properties' (1995). In his discussion with Smart, Haldane appears to exclude this possibility a priori by invoking a more ambitious notion of explanation, according to which a scientific explanation must involve reference to an intelligible mechanism, or show how descriptions of emergent phenomena follow deductively from the laws of physics and descriptions of the kind which feature in physics: see for instance Smart and Haldane 1996: 101.
43 Rolston 1987: 107.
44 Ibid.: 108.
45 Ibid.: 113, my emphasis.
46 Similarly he suggests that naturalism fails to explain 'why the life process never really runs downhill': Rolston 1987: 122.
47 Ibid.: 122.
48 This tendency of the natural world is evident not least in the aftermath of evolutionary 'crashes', as for example at the close of the Permian and Cretaceous periods. As Rolston notes, 'these crashes were followed by swift resurrections, both with more diversity in species and with more complex uppermost forms' (Rolston 1987: 118).
49 See for example his classic work *The Phenomenon of Man* (Teilhard de Chardin 1959). I return to Teilhard's work in Part IV, where I voice some reservations about his approach. But as my discussion of Rolston indicates, I am sympathetic to his vision, even if not to all the details of his argumentation.
50 In the summary which follows, I shall draw on John Leslie's *Universes* (1989). A more technical discussion can be found in Barrow and Tipler 1986.
51 Leslie 1989: 34.
52 Ibid.: 36–7.
53 Ibid.: 38–9.
54 Ibid.: 3.
55 Ibid.: 39–40.
56 Forrest 1996: 50.
57 Compare Leslie 1989: 17–18.
58 There has been an extended debate on the possibility of making use

of a priori judgements of probability in this connection. The focus of this discussion has been Swinburne's proposal that simplicity can serve as an overriding measure of a priori probability: Swinburne 1991, for instance pp. 52–6. Sceptical treatments of the question can be found in R. Prevost, *Probability and Theistic Explanation* (1990), ch. v, and D. H. Mellor, 'God and probability' (1969). See also Mackie 1982: 146–9 and O'Hear 1984: 131–43. I have ventured some observations on Swinburne's approach in Wynn 1993.

59 I have borrowed the example from H. E. Kyburg, *Probability and Inductive Logic* (1970: 36).

60 Of course, more or less general understandings of what constitutes 'this cosmos' are possible. But the central idea is that the data of fine-tuning suggest that we need to expand our ontology beyond the cosmos which we observe. Leslie distinguishes various forms of the many-worlds hypothesis in Leslie 1989: 66–8.

61 For contrasting approaches, see Swinburne 1991: 314–22, and Drees 1990: 87.

62 Peter Forrest sets out the challenge from inductive reasoning with admirable clarity: Forrest 1996: 146–8.

63 Bayes' Theorem holds that:

$$P(h/e.k) = \frac{P(h/k)\ .\ P(e/h.k)}{P(e/k)}$$

where e is the evidence, h the hypothesis, and k background knowledge, and where $P(h/k)$ is read as 'the probability of the hypothesis on the evidence'. The theorem is explained in Swinburne 1991: 64–7. If we are interested in the relative probability of two hypotheses on certain evidence, then $P(e/k)$ will cancel out, of course. For contrasting understandings of the possibility of estimating the value of $P(h/k)$, see G. Priest, 'The argument from design' (1981: 422–3) and G. Schlesinger, *New Perspectives on Old-Time Religion* (1988) ch. 5.

64 Forrest 1996: 28.

65 See the references above for Swinburne's discussion of simplicity and its relevance to theism.

66 I present a similar line of argument, rather unclearly as it seems to me now, in my paper 'A priori judgments and the argument from design' (Wynn 1996a).

67 See for example, W. Alston, 'Some suggestions for divine command theorists' (1989b) and R. Swinburne, *The Coherence of Theism* (1993) ch. 11.

68 Compare Swinburne 1991: 261–2.

69 Leslie 1989: 167.

70 Leslie shows some sympathy for this view: Leslie 1989: 168.

71 Of course, there are other theistic arguments which seek to build on a sense of the explanatory poverty of evolutionary naturalism, in addition to those I have reviewed in this chapter. See for example Alvin Plantinga, *Warrant and Proper Function* (1993) ch. 12.

3 Providence and evil

1 There is an asymmetry in this formulation. I take it that a good must be more than compensating, because if only as good as the evil is bad, then

the question of why God should permit the evil when nothing on balance is gained remains to be answered. I take it that an evil which is avoided need only be as bad as the evil which is tolerated (not worse) because in this case evil will result either way.

2 An omnipotent God may also be unable to realise certain goods without tolerating certain evils even if the evils in question are not the logically necessary preconditions of those goods, if the pattern of human choice (where those choices are free in the libertarian sense) so dictates: see Plantinga 1975: 53.

3 In Chisholm's terminology, the goods in question must not merely 'balance off' the evils, but 'defeat' them: that is, the evils must be logically tied to the corresponding goods. More exactly, the theodicist should think in terms of 'total defeat': Chisholm 1990, for instance p. 62.

4 An argument of this kind is advanced in Stephen Wykstra's paper 'The Humean obstacle to evidential arguments from suffering: on avoiding the evils of "appearance"' (1990). I shall return to Wykstra's discussion below.

5 Compare P .T. Geach, *Providence and Evil* (1977), ch. 1.

6 A fuller version of parts of the following discussion can be found in my paper 'Evil and opportunity cost' (Wynn 1996c).

7 Alvin Plantinga may make such an assumption about what the theist needs to establish in relation to moral evil when he writes that: 'a world containing creatures who are sometimes significantly free (and freely perform more good than evil actions) is *more valuable*, all else being equal, than a world containing no free creatures at all' (Plantinga 1990: 85, my emphasis). Contrast the view of J. L. Mackie in *The Miracle of Theism* (1982), for instance p. 172. The debate between Mackie and Plantinga is complicated by the fact that neither seems willing to see the other's understanding of freedom as a case of genuine freedom.

8 Hick 1981: 44, my emphasis. Of course, Hick's views on these matters must now be interpreted in the light of his suggestion that the personal God of Christian theism has a merely phenomenal status. See his *An Interpretation of Religion. Human Responses to the Transcendent* (1989), ch. 14.

9 This seems to be the implication of, for instance, this remark: 'In order to be a person, exercising some measure of genuine freedom, the creature must be brought into existence, not in the immediate divine presence, but at a "distance" from God': Hick 1981: 43.

10 Hume 1990, part xi, p. 118.

11 Schlesinger 1988: 55.

12 Compare Plantinga 1975: 91.

13 Rawls 1972, ch. iii.

14 Surprisingly perhaps, there is not much evidence of philosophers trying to generalise Rawls's discussion in this sort of way. The only example known to me is Marilyn McCord Adams' passing reference in 'Horrendous evils and the goodness of God' (1990: 215).

15 I noted in Chapter 1 that versions of the design argument which take as their premise some feature of the world which is not a necessary condition of human life are better able to resist the 'many worlds' objection to the design argument. But here we find that such arguments are not so effective as their alternative in meeting another kind of objection. This brings out again the importance of a cumulative-case approach to the argument from design.

16 Adams 1987a: 66. Adams is quoting Leibniz at this point.

17 Adams takes a different line on this point. He writes:

> It seems to me implausible to suppose that the required identities could have been maintained through generations in which the historical context differed radically from the actual world by the omission of many, or important evils. Even if the identity of the parents be presupposed, could it be the same individual sperm cell, and not just one like it, originating in such a different context?
>
> (Adams 1987a: 68)

18 Yandell 1994: 12. The notion of a 'virtue circumstance' is introduced as follows: 'X is a virtue circumstance only if a moral agent is in X, and how that agent acts in X contributes to her becoming virtuous or to her becoming vicious' (ibid.: 9).

19 Yandell 1994: 13.

20 Adams 1987a: 73.

21 See for instance Marilyn Adams' emphasis on the role of eschatological considerations in sustaining the claim that God will grant to each individual a life that is overall a great good to him or her: Adams 1990, especially pp. 218–20. See also Mark T. Nelson, 'Temporal wholes and the problem of evil' (1993). Nelson comments: 'if my life leads to heaven, then earlier parts of my life, even moments of pain and loss, turn out to have been parts of a "saved life" and become good' (ibid.: 317).

22 The point of this line of argument is partly to counter the claim that God could and should have made a better world which in turn would make possible another set of concrete individuals. That may be so, but we seem understandably committed to the goodness of God creating (perhaps in addition) a world in which the concrete individuals we cherish can exist. Of course, someone may say that while my concrete existence is justifiable in these terms, the existence of others (Hitler perhaps) is not, on account of the great evils they have caused or suffered. I am not challenging this thought here. As I go on to note, I am not proposing that the integral wholes approach provides a fully persuasive theodicy in isolation from other considerations.

23 Rowe 1990a: 130.

24 Alternatively, if human beings do not recognise this lack of unity, then their science must remain in a relatively primitive state, which in turn carries implications for their lives considered concretely*. Or again, we might assume that their science progresses in other spheres while they remain ignorant in this matter, but this invites the thought that God deceives them in this matter.

25 See Anthony Kenny (ed.) *The Wittgenstein Reader* (1994: 290). The source is Wittgenstein's Lecture on Ethics, Culture and Value.

26 Addressing the evidential form of the problem of evil, we might also ask: should we suppose that these integral wholes are in at least many cases significantly better than not?

27 William Hasker offers another way of supplementing the integral whole approach. He argues that the apparent existence of genuinely gratuitous evils poses no threat to theism, in so far as this is necessary for significant moral choice. (A genuinely gratuitous evil is defined as an evil which God could prevent without the loss of a more than

compensating good.) The basic idea here is that if we have reason to believe that there are never any genuinely gratuitous evils, then we have reason to believe that we cannot inflict significant harm by our actions, and accordingly reason to believe that our choices carry no deep moral import. This seems to me an insightful line of reflection, which provides a further way of understanding the failure of the integral wholes approach to offer a complete understanding of evil. See 'The necessity of gratuitous evil' (1992).

28 I disagree here with William Rowe. He writes that:

> The mere assumption that [an omnipotent, omniscient, omnigood being] exists gives us no reason whatever to suppose either that the greater goods in virtue of which he permits most sufferings are goods that come into existence far in the future of the sufferings we are aware of, or that once they do obtain we continue to be ignorant of them and their relation to the sufferings.
>
> (Rowe 1990b: 164–5)

Given chaos theory, we surely do have reason to doubt our ability to identify connections of this kind, even when the goods in question have arisen.

29 Compare Peter Van Inwagen on the metaphysical possibility of worlds different from our own, and the implications of this for the problem of evil: *God, Knowledge, and Mystery. Essays in Philosophical Theology* (1995: 79–81).

30 Although he is generally hostile to natural theology, Alan Olding notes this sort of point: see his remarks on Bugs Bunny in his *Modern Biology and Natural Theology* (1991: 156–8). He comments on the implications for the problem of evil on pp. 162–4.

31 It is worth noting in passing that the distinction between 'merely logical' and real possibilities also carries implications for the idea of an original position. But providing we are willing to admit a reasonably extended set of real possibilities, the earlier discussion will retain its relevance.

32 Wykstra 1990: 155–6.

33 For a contrary view, see John Schellenberg's proposal that the lack of compelling evidence for the existence of God is itself good evidence against the existence of God, since we would expect a God of love to make himself clearly known to human beings: *Divine Hiddenness and Human Reason* (1993).

34 However, I do feel some sympathy with Peter Forrest's approach to this question. He comments: 'Now it is fairly plausible that many people do have the opportunity for a life worth living even if there is no life after death. But I find it quite implausible that everyone does' (Forrest 1996: 56).

4 Theodicy in an ecological mode

1 I am grateful to *Faith and Philosophy* for permission to use material from my paper 'Natural theology in an ecological mode' (Wynn 1999b).

2 By the 'natural world' I mean this planet excluding human beings and their artefacts. Of course, there is not much in our world that is 'natural' in the sense of being in no way affected by human beings; in my usage,

the natural world will include things which are affected by human beings, without merely being human artefacts.

3 Stephen Clark notes some of the difficulties in this association of Christian belief and environmental depredation: 'Global religion' (1994: 113–18).

4 The point is noted by Francisco Benzoni in 'Rolston's theological ethic' (1996: 339).

5 However evaluative notions quickly arise here; after all, the point of developing an ecological understanding is to be clear about the conditions of flourishing of ecosystems. See also the quotation from Rolston which follows.

6 Rolston 1989: 20.

7 Hume 1990: 121-2. The second passage is quoted in Rolston 1995: 104.

8 'Nature', in Mill 1963–77, vol. 10: 398. The text is quoted in Rolston 1995: 87. Similarly Mill remarks that: 'In sober truth, nearly all the things which men are hanged or imprisoned for doing to one another, are nature's everyday performances' (ibid.: 385). The passage is quoted in Rolston 1989: 39.

9 'Is life worth living?', in James 1896: 43–4. Rolston cites the passage in Rolston 1989: 30.

10 See his letter to Joseph Dalton Hooker, quoted in Rolston 1995: 87. As Rolston notes, Darwin's assessment of the process is not always so bleak.

11 Gould 1980: 20–1. The passage is cited in Rolston 1987: 128.

12 Crick 1988: 6, cited in Rolston 1995: 96.

13 It is significant that even Demea takes issue with Philo's judgement here (and not only Cleanthes, whose theism is grounded in the design argument): Hume 1990: 122–3.

14 See Rolston's *Environmental Ethics. Duties to and Values in the Natural World* (1988: 53). In fact, some three hundred sheep, 60 per cent of the herd, died as a result.

15 Rolston 1989: 20.

16 Rolston 1987: 136.

17 Rolston 1995: 106.

18 Ibid.: 109.

19 Rolston 1988: 207.

20 Rolston 1995: 99.

21 Ibid.: 99.

22 Ibid.: 96.

23 Rolston 1989: 261.

24 Ibid.: 261. See also Rolston's 'Does nature need to be redeemed?' (1994b) especially pp. 218–21. I am grateful to Professor R. J. Berry for drawing my attention to this reference.

25 Rowe 1990a: 129–30.

26 Rolston 1988: 242.

27 The same sort of point is made in Olding 1991: 156–8 and 162–4, and in Van Inwagen 1995: 79–81.

28 Rolston distinguishes between intrinsic, instrumental and systemic value. The first is not confined to sentient life forms; for instance, it extends also to plants. The value of the system is not reducible to that of its products; its creativity has an inherent value. Rolston proposes that: 'The objective, systemic process is an overriding value, not

because it is indifferent to individuals but because the process is both prior to and productive of individuality' (Rolston 1988: 191).

29 Ibid.: 240–1.

30 Ibid.: 239. Rolston's remarks here are compatible with Tennant's view of natural beauty, as discussed in Chapter 1, providing we allow that a pictorial sense of the world's beauty is appropriate at least in part. An advocate of Tennant's approach might say that Rolston's account offers a theistic rationale for the partial failure of any purely pictorial understanding of the world's beauty.

31 Wykstra 1990.

32 Rolston 1989: 26.

33 As we have seen, there are other themes in Rolston's work which point in the direction of a design argument. See Chapter 2.

34 Rolston 1989: 133.

35 Ibid.: 43.

36 Ibid.: 249.

37 Of course, the biophilia hypothesis provides a striking example of how this general thesis might be developed. See Stephen Kellert and Edward Wilson (eds) *The Biophilia Hypothesis* (1993). I discuss the hypothesis in Chapter 1.

38 Murdoch 1970: 84.

39 Compare Murdoch's comment that: 'we take a self-forgetful pleasure in the sheer alien pointless independent existence of animals, birds, stones and trees' (ibid.: 85).

40 Rolston 1989: 43.

41 Ibid.: 24. Rolston also has interesting things to say about how the solitariness of encounters with nature is a precondition of genuine community (ibid.: 228).

42 Ibid.: 88. He goes on to compare this sort of respect to love of enemies in the human sphere.

43 Rolston does offer this sort of assurance. See his distinction between nature and culture in Rolston 1988: 181–2.

44 Ibid.: 191. See Arne Naess's reference to ethicists who refuse 'to acknowledge that some life forms have greater or less intrinsic value than others': 'The deep ecological movement: some philosophical aspects' (Naess 1995: 166). It is clear from this paper that Naess envisages a more radical restructuring of human relations to the natural world than does Rolston.

45 Compare Stephen Clark's remark that sacramental theism 'declares, almost above all, that although "Nature" is to be respected, it is not now exactly as it should be' (Clark 1998: 127). In fact, I think Rolston does hold that 'wild nature' is open to improvement; he just doubts whether we are capable, in many cases, of contributing to its improvement. Rolston identifies a limited role for 'management' of wilderness in *Conserving Natural Value* (1994a: 187).

46 I would like to thank Professor Rolston for his helpful comments on an earlier draft of this chapter, and for finding time to talk to me about his work during a busy visit to Edinburgh. I am also grateful to members of the King's College, London, philosophy of religion seminar for their comments on this material.

5 A non-epistemic case for trusting in the goodness of the world

1 Some of the material in this chapter has been taken from my paper 'Trust-relationships and the moral case for religious belief' (Wynn 1997d). I am grateful to the journal's reviewers for helpful comments on the paper.
2 James 1979: 13–33.
3 These terms are explained in ibid.: 14–15.
4 The date of publication of this lecture is 1896; presumably the address itself was given in that year or shortly before. As Ludwig Schlecht notes, it is reasonable to suppose that James himself was not an orthodox Christian. Nonetheless, he did think of the divine as a personal, providential force at work in the universe (Schlecht 1997).
5 James 1979: 30.
6 Ibid.: 22.
7 Ibid.: 31–2.
8 Gale 1991: 357.
9 Contrast Richard Swinburne's account of belief, according to which a person believes a given proposition, *p*, 'if and only if he believes that the total evidence available to him makes *p* more probable than any alternative' (Swinburne 1982: 25). On this account, it seems belief will not be directly voluntary. While this understanding of belief may be appropriate in many contexts, there is some reason to suppose that it fails to capture what is involved in religious belief. Compare D. C. Barrett's reply to Swinburne in 'Faith and rationality' (1989), for instance p. 143. Here Barrett argues that the notion of probability is inapplicable in principle to the resurrection of Jesus.
10 Compare Pascal on attending mass and taking holy water: *Pensées* (Pascal 1991), no. 680: 471.
11 See Gale 1991: 361–2.
12 James 1979: 20.
13 Gale himself dismisses this possibility without discussion (Gale 1991: 357).
14 'The ethics of belief' in *Lectures and Essays* (Clifford 1879), reprinted in Pojman 1987: 387.
15 Plantinga 1983.
16 Wykstra 1989.
17 Ibid.: 430. It is worth recalling that on Wykstra's view the belief that there are electrons cannot be properly basic for everyone in a given epistemic community.
18 Some may prefer to think in terms of a state of parity between theism and the disjunction of its alternatives; they may modify the example accordingly. Compare Swinburne 1982: 5-7 and 122–3.
19 Some may suppose that in this case theistic belief would be adequately justified, since in establishing the rationality of the belief, it is enough to show that there is on balance no evidence against it. Whatever view we take on this issue, my point remains that trust-relationship considerations can add something to the epistemic justification of religious belief. For the distinction between 'weak' and 'strong' justification, see Alston 1983: 116.
20 Wittgenstein 1966: 59.
21 Hick 1978: 3. More generally, in the tradition of Saint Thomas, 'formed faith' implies trust in God and not merely knowledge about God, and in the tradition of Luther, genuine Christian faith similarly implies a trust

in God and the holding of good intentions. See Swinburne 1982: ch. 4.

22 Hick 1978: 4.

23 Basil Mitchell raises the same issue when he considers the suggestion that 'the requirement of unconditional faith is one which has its place within the system of theistic belief and cannot properly be interpreted as an obligation to continue to embrace the system itself'. Mitchell notes that while this approach is 'in principle correct' it needs elaboration:

> Just as it is sometimes a duty to believe in a man when appearances are against him, it is a duty to believe in God when the appearances are against him; and the human situation is such that the appearances are often against his existing at all.
>
> (Mitchell 1973: 140–1)

Notwithstanding this elaboration, Mitchell's view seems to be that the belief that there is a God (or commitment to the theistic system) needs to be in place before *fiducia* can be given a role which is somewhat independent of the evidence. Mitchell has raised similar issues in his discussion of the partisan who comes to trust 'the Stranger' after an initial meeting, and persists in this trust in the face of later counter-evidence. In this case, however, the Stranger is clearly known to exist, at least at the time of the initial meeting, and this meeting provides something like evidence for later trust in the Stranger. As Mitchell remarks, 'the partisan has a reason for having in the first instance committed himself, viz. the character of the Stranger': (Mitchell 1971).

24 James implies that we do not know why we should feel this way:

> This feeling, forced on us we know not whence, that by obstinately believing that there are gods (although not to do so would be easy both for our logic and our life) we are doing the universe the deepest service we can, seems part of the living essence of the religious hypothesis.
>
> (James 1979: 31)

25 See for example Joe Houston's defence of the idea that the prior belief that there is a God ensures that Hume's critique of the rationality of belief in miracles fails (Houston 1994, chs 9–10).

26 By contrast, C. S. Lewis seems to suppose that it is only after a person has adopted *fides* that their belief may be subject to 'the logic of personal relations' (Lewis 1960, excerpted in Pojman 1987: 378). Lewis goes on to remark that once a person has made such a commitment, their belief is 'no longer proportioned to every fluctuation of the apparent evidence'. I explore this issue next. Notice that, by analogy with the example of my parents with which I began, if we could be sure that the world has a transcendent, personal source, then there would be a fairly strong moral case for believing that source to be trustworthy, for this belief is properly a precondition of the corresponding trust relationship. By contrast, the holding of theistic beliefs is not properly a precondition of our participation in trust relationships with other human beings.

27 See for example, Swinburne's argument from temporal regularity in *The Existence of God* (1991, ch. 8). Here he argues for the appropriateness of a personal explanation not simply by reference to the goodness of a regular world, but by supposing that in general there are only two kinds

of explanation, personal and scientific, and that the second of these is logically inadmissible in relation to temporal regularity.

28 Wittgenstein 1966: 53.

29 This view is set out clearly in the writings of D. Z. Phillips. See for instance his *Religion Without Explanation* (1976), for example his exposition of Wittgenstein on p. 164.

30 Anthony Kenny notes that in the Roman Catholic tradition, faith is considered both 'free' and 'certain' (Kenny 1983: 71–2). The account I am giving echoes this approach to the extent that it makes belief both voluntary and yet not tentative.

6 Worship and the concept of God

1 It is worth recalling that the argument from design need not issue in this conclusion. See the suggestion of Neoplatonists like Leslie and Clark that God should be understood not as a personal mind but as a creatively efficacious set of ideals. By contrast, the argument of Chapter 5 understands God as potentially the object of an interpersonal relationship. See J. Leslie, *Universes* (1988), ch. 8, and S. R. L. Clark, 'Limited explanations' (1990).

2 Jean-Paul Sartre and Don Cupitt are among the better known exponents of such an existential critique of religious belief. Sartre thinks that human beings are the sole source of values, and that God as traditionally portrayed is incompatible with this central fact about human beings and the possibility of finding (or creating) meaning in human life (Sartre 1969: 626–7). Cupitt takes a similar line when he writes that: 'Religion cannot reach its highest development so long as the divine requirement remains an objective authority external to man which tries to control him from without' (Cupitt 1980: 4).

3 With Ninian Smart, I take it that 'there is an internal connection between the concepts of god and of worship' (Smart 1972: 51). Some of the material in this chapter has been taken from my papers 'Simplicity, personhood and divinity' (Wynn 1997a) and 'Primal religions and the sacred significance of nature' (Wynn 1997b).

4 See Aquinas, *Summa Theologiae* I 3. For sympathetic commentary, see Brian Davies, *The Thought of Thomas Aquinas* (1992), ch. 3.

5 Of course, it will also be said that there is a distinction between creaturely and divine passibility in so far as God's being affected always depends on the divine consent. See for instance Marcel Sarot, *God, Passibility and Corporeality* (1992: 40–1).

6 See for example A. Kenny, *Aquinas* (1980: 59). Contrast B. Miller, *A Most Unlikely God. A Philosophical Enquiry into the Nature of God* (1996: 38–9), and G. Hughes, *The Nature of God* (1995: 34–63).

7 See William Alston, 'Hartshorne and Aquinas: a *via media*' (1989a: 126–7). Contrast *Summa Theologiae* (Aquinas 1989) I 13 art. 7.

8 See Grace Jantzen, *God's World, God's Body* (1984: 55–6).

9 Swinburne 1993, and Swinburne 1991 respectively.

10 These choices are free in the libertarian sense. Of course, some commentators have sought to break the link between libertarian freedom and divine passibility, for instance by reference to the idea of middle knowledge, but this is not Swinburne's approach (Swinburne 1993: 180–1).

11 See Swinburne 1991: 285.
12 Swinburne talks of God's 'simplicity' in this connection, but plainly the term is not intended to carry all the associations which it bears for writers in the classical tradition.
13 Swinburne 1991: 130; see also 283. While thinking of God as logically contingent, Swinburne also allows that God may properly be said to be necessary. See his discussion of ontological and metaphysical necessity, *The Christian God* (Swinburne 1994): 118–21 and ch. 8.
14 Swinburne 1993: 298.
15 See note 2 above.
16 Swinburne thinks that God will do anything which he has overriding reason to do, since he is 'perfectly free': Swinburne 1993: 151–2. But on his account, God does not have overriding reason to create (Swinburne 1991: 130–1).
17 'Concretely' here is used in Hartshorne's sense, to which I return below.
18 I 47 art. 1.
19 At the time, in 1864, Muir was fleeing conscription in the US. The story is recounted in Stephen Fox, *The American Conservation Movement. John Muir and His Legacy* (1981: 43–4). See also Max Oelschlaeger, *The Idea of Wilderness. From Prehistory to the Age of Ecology* (1991: 176).
20 Albert Schweitzer, *My Life and Thought. An Autobiography* (1933: 185–6).
21 Brooks 1973: 315–16. The text is taken from her address on the occasion of her acceptance of the Schweitzer Medal of the Animal Welfare Institute, 7 January 1963. She goes on to write: 'Or I have found that deep awareness of life and its meaning in the eyes of a beloved cat.' I have excerpted this remark since it does not seem so relevant to the generalisation I go on to offer.
22 Kant 1964: 96.
23 It might be asked: isn't the goodness of a thing's existence dependent on what it is? (Is Hitler's existence a good?) I am not claiming that in general things are good merely by virtue of existing. (Compare the discussion of integral wholes in Chapter 3.) I am proposing that very often the goodness of a thing is independent of its usefulness to human beings.
24 Moreover, experiences of this kind also seem to invite the sort of self-transcendence that the religions consider important. See for instance Iris Murdoch's example of watching a kestrel (Murdoch 1970: 84–5). The experience she describes also turns upon a sense that the object of the experience has no human point. Thus she writes: 'we take a self-forgetful pleasure in the sheer alien pointless independent existence of animals, birds, stones and trees. "Not how the world is, but that it is, is the mystical"' (ibid.: 85). The quotation is from Wittgenstein's *Tractatus,* of course.
25 'Duties to endangered species' in Rolston 1989: 215–16.
26 Clearly, this sort of *a priori* argument for the existence of a relational structure within the divine being carries echoes of the Logos doctrine. This understanding of God, as an integration of the perfections evident in the world, offers a further response to the suggestion that any divinity who desired relationship with human beings would be revealed unambiguously. (See Schellenberg's objection to theism as described in the Introduction.) If the world bodies forth, albeit in a fragmentary way,

what God is, then in a significant sense, our relationship to the world is already a relationship to God. Notice too how this understanding of the divine beauty and goodness provides the beginnings of a reply to the Humean objection, noted in Chapter 1, that beauty in God calls for explanation just as much as beauty in the world.

27 At the same time, the design hypothesis has some work to do in showing that the range of the designer's power is compatible with his claim to divinity. The relevant power here seems to be almightiness (reliably holding sway over the destiny of creatures), rather than merely the capacity to do any logically conceivable thing (consistent with being God). Sustaining the idea of almightiness, within the framework of design, will in turn depend, for instance, upon providing a reasonably robust account of evil: one which shows that it is not to be taken as evidence that the world's source is trying but failing to achieve certain ends within the world. Our discussion of earlier chapters provides some indication of how this might be done.

28 Davies 1993: 52–3.

29 See again *Summa Theologiae* (Aquinas 1989) I 47 art. 1.

30 The approach also has obvious christological associations, inviting us to tie the notion of lordship to that of service.

31 See for instance his *Creative Synthesis and Philosophic Method* (Hartshorne 1970: 232).

32 Hartshorne 1969: 152–67.

33 *Powers Which We Do Not Know. The Gods and Spirits of the Inuit* (Merkur 1991).

34 There is one further class of powers in Inuit religion, the spirits. Merkur defines a spirit thus: 'any metaphysical being that does not have a physical correlative and can nonetheless be seen as an apparition or encountered by a shaman in ecstasy may be described by the Inuit as a spirit' (ibid.: 23).

35 Ibid.: 33.

36 In fact, despite its broad currency in the anthropological literature, the term 'Sedna' is limited to some Baffin Islanders: ibid.: 97.

37 Ibid.: 106.

38 For these groups, the Sea Mother comes to function not only as an indweller but as a spirit. In their view, the Sea Mother (or in certain cases, a pictorial representation of her) can be encountered in visionary experience (ibid.: 119). The pictorial representation case provides a clue, according to Merkur, to the roots of shamanic belief in metaphysical idealism (ibid.: 77). He also suggests that in origin the shamanic concept of the Sea Mother was distinct from the notion of the Sea Mother as an indweller (ibid.: 120).

39 Ibid.: 141.

40 Ibid.: 141. At the same time, he notes that the *popular* concept of the Sea Mother, even in those regions where she is given a prominent role in relation to other indwellers, implies only that she is the head of a pantheon, not 'a unified godhead' (ibid.: 110).

41 *Religion and Revelation. A Theology of Revelation in the World's Religions* (Ward 1994: 65).

42 Ibid.: 65.

43 It is worth recalling however that the Inuit interpretation of the Sea Mother can be very concrete, notably when she is encountered as a spirit

in visionary experience: Merkur 1991: 118–19.

44 *Divinity and Experience. The Religion of the Dinka* (Lienhardt 1961).

45 Ibid.: 159–60. Free-divinities are to be distinguished from clan divinities. Only the latter correspond to particular family groupings.

46 Ibid.: 156.

47 Merkur 1991: 32.

48 Lienhardt 1961: 29–30.

49 Harold Turner, 'The primal religions of the world and their study' (1977: 31).

50 Merkur 1991: 33.

51 But note that in visionary experiences, shamans are said to 'assault' and even to 'overpower' the Sea Mother: ibid.: 118. However, the purpose of this exercise is to perform a service to her. (According to the Inuit metaphor, it is to cleanse her hair.) Moreover, restoration of right relations with the Sea Mother depends upon the confession of various faults (ibid.: 137). So even in these cases, she is not merely an object of manipulation. There seems to be some tension here between the conception of the Sea Mother as an indweller and as a spirit. If we follow Ward, we will accord a mythological status to the more colourful descriptions deriving from visionary experience.

52 Lienhardt 1961: 151.

53 *Make Prayers to the Raven. A Koyukon View of the Northern Forest* (Nelson 1983: 226).

54 For instance, Michael Carrithers is impressed by the differences between Dinka religion and conventional western ideas of God, and writes of the extreme difficulty of conveying the meaning of Dinka religion to western audiences: *Why Humans Have Cultures. Explaining Anthropology and Social Diversity* (1992: 187–92).

55 For instance, in the passage I have just cited, Nelson continues: 'They perceive the environment as a conscious, sensate, personified entity, suffused with spiritual powers, whose blessings are given only to the reverent' (Nelson 1983: 226).

56 *Summa Theologiae* I 2 art. 3 (Aquinas 1989: 13–14).

7 Salvation and the concept of God

1 Parts of the discussion which follows have been drawn from my paper 'From world to God: resemblance and complementarity' (Wynn 1996b).

2 *Summa Theologiae*, I 4 art. 2 (Aquinas 1989). Notice that Thomas does not subscribe to the thesis that God resembles creatures: I 4 art. 3.

3 This is the interpretation favoured for instance by T. McDermott in *Summa Theologiae. A Concise Translation* (Aquinas 1989: xxxiii). Note in particular his comment on the Fifth Way.

4 See Davies 1985: 228.

5 I 4 art. 2 (Aquinas 1989), in McDermott's translation.

6 'On God and Mann', in *Anselmian Explorations* (Morris 1987: 121).

7 Even William Mann's restatement of the doctrine, which is intended to respect its original spirit, seems insufficient to underpin Thomas's argument. For on his account, the doctrine relates to property instances. And if God is identical with a property instance (more exactly, a rich property instance), then he is presumably not self-subsistent existence,

but an individual existent. See his paper 'Divine simplicity' (Mann 1982).

8 However, there are defences of the doctrine which remain true to the spirit of Aquinas's account. See for instance Barry Miller, *A Most Unlikely God. A Philosophical Enquiry into the Nature of God* (1996). As I go on to indicate, I am not presupposing the mistakenness of Aquinas's doctrine. My purpose is just to explore, for *ad hominem* reasons, whether there are other ways of articulating certain insights of religious importance which are captured in Aquinas's conception of God.

9 On this view, we are to treat goodness as a 'particularistic' and not a 'platonic' predicate. See Alston's essay 'Some suggestions for divine command theorists' (1989b).

10 See for instance, ibid.: 273. Barry Miller brings out the distinctiveness of Aquinas's teaching on this point by distinguishing between the notions of 'limit simpliciter' and 'limit case' (Miller 1996: 7–10). For instance, the speed of light marks an upper limit to the speed of bodies, and this is a limit simpliciter. But there is no lower limit simpliciter to their speed, but only a limit case (of 0 km/s). If God's perfection is understood as a limit case, then the difference between God and creatures will not be merely one of degree. Using Miller's terminology, we should say that the standard individualistic conception of God understands the divine perfection as a limit simpliciter of the perfection of creatures.

11 I 47 art. 1, in McDermott's translation (Aquinas 1989).

12 Compare the discussion of Chapter 3 on the conditions of our concrete* existence.

13 1 Cor. 15.28; see *The Phenomenon of Man* (Teilhard de Chardin 1959: 322).

14 Ibid.: 322. Teilhard does not infer that God's reality is a matter for the future (since it is organically related to a reality which has yet to exist). Instead, on his view, God exists outside of time (and space). See ibid.: 297.

15 See for instance ibid.: 61.

16 Ibid.: 294.

17 These other approaches are clearly distinguished in Patrick Sherry's work *Spirit and Beauty* (1992: 139–40).

18 Of course, the theist will want to affirm that the creature's fulfilment also depends upon God from a causal point of view. But this claim is quite compatible with the necessary complement model, I suggest: although the initial element of a work of art will not normally be dependent causally upon its complementary element, there is no reason why it could not be so dependent.

19 Some may wish to suppose that it is not so much that the core meaning of our terms needs to be stretched, but rather that certain adventitious associations which they bear in creaturely contexts need to be stripped away when we talk of God; they may read my remark accordingly.

Bibliography

Adams, M. M. (1990) 'Horrendous evils and the goodness of God', in M. M. Adams and R. M. Adams (eds) *The Problem of Evil*, Oxford, Oxford University Press: 209–21.

Adams, R. M. (1987a) 'Existence, self–interest and the problem of evil', in R. M. Adams, *The Virtue of Faith and Other Essays in Philosophical Theology*, New York, Oxford University Press: 65–76.

—— (1987b) 'Flavors, colors, and God', in R. M. Adams, *The Virtue of Faith and Other Essays in Philosophical Theology*, New York, Oxford University Press: 243–62.

Alston, W. (1983) 'Christian experience and Christian belief', in A. Plantinga and N. Wolterstorff (eds) *Faith and Rationality. Reason and Belief in God*, Notre Dame, University of Notre Dame Press: 103–34.

—— (1989a) 'Hartshorne and Aquinas: a *via media*', in W. Alston, *Divine Nature and Human Language. Essays in Philosophical Theology*, Ithaca, Cornell University Press: 121–43.

—— (1989b) 'Some suggestions for divine command theorists', in W. Alston, *Divine Nature and Human Language. Essays in Philosophical Theology*, Ithaca, Cornell University Press: 253–73.

—— (1991) *Perceiving God*, Ithaca, Cornell University Press.

Appleton, J. (1990) *The Symbolism of Habitat. An Interpretation of Landscape in the Arts*, Seattle, University of Washington Press.

Aquinas, T. (1989) in T. McDermott (ed.) *Summa Theologiae. A Concise Translation*, London, Methuen.

Barbour, I. (1990) *Religion in an Age of Science*, London, SCM.

Barnes, J. (ed.) (1987) *Early Greek Philosophy*, Harmondsworth, Penguin.

Barrett, D. C. (1989) 'Faith and rationality', in A. Phillips Griffiths (ed.) *Key Themes in Philosophy*, Cambridge, Royal Institute of Philosophy: 135–43.

Barrow, J. (1995) *The Artful Universe*, Oxford, Clarendon Press.

Barrow, J. D. and Tipler, F. J. (1986) *The Anthropic Cosmological Principle*, Oxford, Clarendon Press.

Benzoni, F. (1996) 'Rolston's theological ethic', *Environmental Ethics* vol. 18: 339–52.

Brennan, A. (ed.) (1995) *The Ethics of the Environment*, Aldershot: Dartmouth.

Brooks, P. (1973) *The House of Life. Rachel Carson at Work. With Selections from her Writings Published and Unpublished,* London, George Allen and Unwin.

Buckley, M. J. (1987) *At the Origins of Modern Atheism,* New Haven, Yale University Press.

Byrne, P. (1989) *Natural Religion and the Nature of Religion: the Legacy of Deism,* London, Routledge.

Carrithers, M. (1992) *Why Humans Have Cultures. Explaining Anthropology and Social Diversity,* Oxford, Oxford University Press.

Chisholm, R. (1990) 'The defeat of good and evil', reproduced in M. M. Adams and R. M. Adams (eds) *The Problem of Evil,* Oxford, Oxford University Press: 53–68.

Clark, S. R. L. (1990) 'Limited explanations', in D. Knowles (ed.) *Explanation and Its Limits,* Cambridge, Cambridge University Press: 195–210.

—— (1994) 'Global religion', in R. Attfield and A. Belsey (eds) *Philosophy and the Natural Environment*, Cambridge, Cambridge University Press: 113–28.

Clifford, W. K. (1879) 'The ethics of belief', in *Lectures and Essays,* London, Macmillan, reproduced in L. P. Pojman (ed.) *Philosophy of Religion. An Anthology,* Belmont, Wadsworth, 1987: 383–7.

Craig, W. L. (1988) 'Barrow and Tipler on the anthropic principle vs divine design', *British Journal for the Philosophy of Science* vol. 38: 389–95.

Crick, F. (1988) *What Mad Pursuit: A Personal View of Scientific Discovery,* New York, Basic Books.

Cupitt, D. (1980) *Taking Leave of God,* London, SCM.

Davies, B. (1985) *Thinking About God,* London, Chapman.

—— (1992) *The Thought of Thomas Aquinas,* Oxford, Clarendon Press.

—— (1993) *An Introduction to the Philosophy of Religion,* new edition, Oxford, Oxford University Press.

—— (ed.) (1998) *Philosophy of Religion. A Guide to the Subject,* London, Cassell.

Dawkins, R. (1986) *The Blind Watchmaker,* Harlow, Longman Scientific and Technical.

Diamond, C. and Teichman, J. (eds) (1979) *Intention and Intentionality. Essays in Honour of G. E. M. Anscombe,* Brighton, Harvester.

Diffey, T. J. (1993) 'Natural beauty without metaphysics', in S. Kemal and I. Gaskell (eds) *Landscape, Natural Beauty and the Arts,* Cambridge, Cambridge University Press: 43–64.

Doore, G. (1980) 'Some better reasons for agreeing with Hume', *Religious Studies* vol. 16: 145–61.

Drees, W. (1990) *Beyond the Big Bang. Quantum Cosmologies and God,* La Salle, Ill., Open Court.

Forrest, P. (1996) *God Without the Supernatural. A Defense of Scientific Theism,* Ithaca, Cornell University Press.

Fox, S. (1981) *The American Conservation Movement. John Muir and His Legacy,* Madison, University of Wisconsin Press.

Gale, R. (1991) *On the Nature and Existence of God,* Cambridge, Cambridge University Press.

Gaskin, J. C. A. (1988) *Hume's Philosophy of Religion,* Atlantic Highlands, N.J., Humanities Press, second edition.

Geach, P. T. (1958) *Mental Acts,* London, Routledge and Kegan Paul.

—— (1977) *Providence and Evil,* Cambridge, Cambridge University Press.

Gould, S. J. (1980) *The Panda's Thumb,* New York, W. W. Norton.

Haldane, J. J. (1994) 'Admiring the high mountains', *Environmental Values* vol. 3: 97–106.

—— (1996a) 'The mystery of emergence', *Proceedings of the Aristotelian Society* vol. xcvi: 261–7.

—— (1996b) *Atheism and Theism,* Oxford, Blackwell.

Hambourger, R. (1979) 'The argument from design', in C. Diamond and J. Teichman (eds) *Intention and Intentionality. Essays in Honour of G. E. M. Anscombe,* Brighton, Harvester Press: ch. 8.

Hartshorne, C. (1969) 'The God of religion and the God of philosophy', in *Talk of God,* London, Royal Institute of Philosophy: 152–67.

—— (1970) *Creative Synthesis and Philosophic Method,* London, SCM.

Hasker, W. (1992) 'The necessity of gratuitous evil', *Faith and Philosophy* vol. 9: 23–44.

Haught, J. (1984) *The Cosmic Adventure,* Ramsey, N.J., Paulist Press.

Hick, J. (1978) *Faith and Knowledge,* Glasgow, Collins, second edition.

—— (1981) 'An Irenaean theodicy', in S. Davis (ed.) *Encountering Evil,* Edinburgh, T. and T. Clark: 39–68.

—— (1989) *An Interpretation of Religion. Human Responses to the Transcendent,* New Haven, Yale University Press.

Houston, J. (1994) *Reported Miracles: A Critique of Hume,* Cambridge, Cambridge University Press.

Hughes, G. J. (1995) *The Nature of God,* London, Routledge.

Hume, D. (1990) *Dialogues Concerning Natural Religion,* ed. Martin Bell, Harmondsworth, Penguin (first published 1779).

Hurlbutt, R. H. (1965) *Hume, Newton, and the Design Argument,* Lincoln, University of Nebraska.

James, W. (1896) 'Is life worth living?' in *The Will to Believe,* New York, Longmans, Green.

—— (1979) *The Will to Believe and Other Essays in Popular Philosophy,* Cambridge, Mass., Harvard University Press.

Jantzen, G. (1984) *God's World, God's Body,* Philadelphia, Westminster Press.

Kant, I. (1911) *Critique of Judgement,* tr. J. C. Meredith, Oxford, Clarendon Press (first published 1790).

—— (1933) *Critique of Pure Reason,* tr. N. Kemp Smith, London, Macmillan, second impression (second edition first published 1787).

—— (1964) *Groundwork of the Metaphysic of Morals,* tr. H. J. Paton, New York, Harper and Row (first published 1785).

Kellert, S. and Wilson, E. O. (eds) (1993) *The Biophilia Hypothesis,* Washington D.C., Island Press.

Kemal, S. and Gaskell, I. (eds) (1993) *Landscape, Natural Beauty and the Arts,* Cambridge, Cambridge University Press.

Kenny, A. (1980) *Aquinas,* Oxford, Oxford University Press.

—— (1983) *Faith and Reason,* New York, Columbia University Press.

—— (1992) *What is Faith? Essays in the Philosophy of Religion,* Oxford, Oxford University Press.

—— (1994) *The Wittgenstein Reader,* Oxford, Blackwell.

Kyburg, H. E. (1970) *Probability and Inductive Logic,* London, Macmillan.

Leopold, A. (1987) *A Sand County Almanac,* Oxford, Oxford University Press (first published 1949).

Leslie, J. (1989) *Universes,* London, Routledge.

Lewis, C. S. (1960) *The World's Last Night,* San Diego, Harcourt Brace Jovanovich, excerpted in L. P. Pojman (1987): 372–8.

Lienhardt, G. (1961) *Divinity and Experience. The Religion of the Dinka,* Oxford, Clarendon Press.

Locke, J. (1975) *An Essay Concerning Human Understanding,* ed. Peter Nidditch, Oxford, Clarendon Press (first published 1689).

Mackie, J. (1977) *Ethics. Inventing Right and Wrong,* Harmondsworth, Penguin.

—— (1982) *The Miracle of Theism. Arguments For and Against the Existence of God,* Oxford, Oxford University Press.

McPherson, T. (1972) *The Argument from Design,* London, Macmillan.

Mann, W. (1982) 'Divine simplicity', *Religious Studies* vol. 18: 451–71.

Mellor, D. H. (1969) 'God and probability', *Religious Studies* vol. 5: 223–34.

Merchant, C. (1980) *The Death of Nature. Women, Ecology, and the Scientific Revolution,* San Francisco, Harper and Row.

Merkur, D. (1991) *Powers Which We Do Not Know. The Gods and Spirits of the Inuit,* Moscow, Idaho, University of Idaho Press.

Mill, J. S. (1963–77) 'Nature', in *Collected Works,* vol. 10, Toronto, University of Toronto Press.

Miller, B. (1996) *A Most Unlikely God. A Philosophical Enquiry into the Nature of God,* Notre Dame, University of Notre Dame Press.

Mitchell, B. (1971) 'Theology and falsification', reprinted in B. Mitchell (ed.) *The Philosophy of Religion,* Oxford, Oxford University Press: 18–20.

—— (1973) *The Justification of Religious Belief,* London, Macmillan.

Morris, T. (1987) *Anselmian Explorations,* Notre Dame, University of Notre Dame Press.

Murdoch, I. (1970) *The Sovereignty of Good,* London, Routledge and Kegan Paul.

Naess, A. (1995) 'The deep ecological movement: some philosophical aspects', in A. Brennan (ed.) (1995) *The Ethics of the Environment,* Aldershot: Dartmouth.

Nelson, M. T. (1993) 'Temporal wholes and the problem of evil', *Religious Studies* vol. 29: 313–24.

Nelson, R. (1983) *Make Prayers to the Raven. A Koyukon View of the Northern Forest,* Chicago, University of Chicago Press.

Oelschlaeger, M. (1991) *The Idea of Wilderness. From Prehistory to the Age of Ecology,* New Haven, Yale University Press.

O'Hear, A. (1984) *Experience, Explanation and Faith. An Introduction to the Philosophy of Religion,* London, Routledge.

Olding, A. (1991) *Modern Biology and Natural Theology,* London, Routledge.

Paley, W. (1802) *Natural Theology: or, Evidences of the Existence and Nature of the Deity, Collected from the Appearances of Nature,* London, Wilks and Taylor..

Pascal, B. (1991) *Pensées,* Paris, Bordas.

Phillips, D. Z. (1976) *Religion Without Explanation,* Oxford, Blackwell.

Plantinga, A. (1975) *God, Freedom and Evil,* London, George Allen and Unwin.

—— (1983) 'Reason and belief in God', in A. Plantinga and N. Wolterstorff (eds) *Faith and Rationality. Reason and Belief in God,* Notre Dame, University of Notre Dame Press: 16–93.

—— (1990) 'God, evil and the metaphysics of freedom', reproduced in M. M. Adams and R. M. Adams (eds) *The Problem of Evil,* Oxford, Oxford University Press: 83–109.

—— (1993) *Warrant and Proper Function,* New York: Oxford University Press.

Plantinga, A. and Wolterstorff, N. (eds) (1983) *Faith and Rationality. Reason and Belief in God,* Notre Dame, University of Notre Dame Press.

Plato (1970) *The Laws of Plato,* tr. T. J. Saunders, Harmondsworth, Penguin.

—— (1977) *Timaeus and Critias,* tr. D. Lee, Harmondsworth, Penguin.

Pojman, L. P. (ed.) (1987) *Philosophy of Religion. An Anthology,* Belmont, Wadsworth.

Prevost, R. (1990) *Probability and Theistic Explanation,* Oxford, Clarendon Press.

Priest, G. (1981) 'The argument from design', *Australasian Journal of Philosophy* vol. 59: 422–31.

Rawls, J. (1972) *Theory of Justice,* Oxford, Oxford University Press.

Rolston, H. (1987) *Science and Religion. A Critical Survey,* Philadelphia, Temple University Press.

—— (1988) *Environmental Ethics. Duties to and Values in the Natural World,* Philadelphia, Temple University Press.

—— (1989) *Philosophy Gone Wild,* Buffalo, Prometheus Books.

—— (1994a) *Conserving Natural Value,* New York, Columbia University Press.

—— (1994b) 'Does nature need to be redeemed?', *Zygon: Journal of Religion and Science* vol. 29: 205–29.

—— (1995) 'Disvalues in nature', in A. Brennan (ed.) *The Ethics of the Environment,* Aldershot, Dartmouth.

Rowe, W. (1990a) 'The problem of evil and some varieties of atheism', reproduced in M. M. Adams and R. M. Adams (eds) *The Problem of Evil,* Oxford, Oxford University Press: 126–37.

—— (1990b) 'Evil and the theistic hypothesis: a response to Wykstra', reproduced in M. M. Adams and R. M. Adams (eds) *The Problem of Evil,* Oxford, Oxford University Press: 161–7.

Sarot, M. (1992) *God, Passibility and Corporeality,* Kampen, Kok Pharos.

Sartre, J.-P. (1969) *Being and Nothingness. An Essay in Phenomenological Ontology,* tr. H. Barnes, London, Methuen.

Schama, S. (1996) *Landscape and Memory,* London, Fontana.

Schellenberg, J. (1993) *Divine Hiddenness and Human Reason,* Ithaca, Cornell University Press.

Schlecht, L. (1997) 'Re-reading "The will to believe"', *Religious Studies* vol. 33: 217–25.

Schlesinger, G. (1988) *New Perspectives on Old-Time Religion,* Oxford, Clarendon Press.

Schweitzer, A. (1933) *My Life and Thought. An Autobiography,* tr. C. T. Campion, London, George Allen and Unwin.

Sherry, P. (1992) *Spirit and Beauty. An Introduction to Theological Aesthetics,* Oxford, Clarendon Press.

Smart, N. (1972) *The Concept of Worship,* London, Macmillan.

Smart, J. J. C. and Haldane, J. (1996) *Atheism and Theism,* Oxford, Blackwell.

Soper, K. (1995) *What is Nature?,* Oxford, Blackwell.

Spencer-Smith, R. (1995) 'Reductionism and emergent properties', *Proceedings of the Aristotelian Society* vol. xcv: 113–29.

Swinburne, R. (1982) *Faith and Reason,* Oxford, Clarendon Press.

—— (1983) 'Mackie, induction, and God', *Religious Studies* vol. 19: 385–91.

—— (1991) *The Existence of God,* Oxford, Clarendon Press, revised edition.

—— (1993) *The Coherence of Theism,* Oxford, Clarendon Press, revised edition.

—— (1994) *The Christian God,* Oxford, Clarendon Press.

—— (1996) *Is there a God?,* Oxford, Clarendon Press.

Taylor, C. (1989) *Sources of the Self. The Making of Modern Identity,* Cambridge, Cambridge University Press.

Teilhard de Chardin, P. (1959) *The Phenomenon of Man,* tr. B. Wall *et al.*, London, Collins.

Tennant, F. R. (1930) *Philosophical Theology,* vols i and ii, Cambridge, Cambridge University Press.

Tuan, Y. -F. (1993) 'Desert and ice: ambivalent aesthetics', in S. Kemal and I. Gaskell (eds) *Landscape, Natural Beauty and the Arts,* Cambridge, Cambridge University Press: 139–57.

Turner, H. (1977) 'The primal religions of the world and their study', in V. C. Hayes (ed.) *Australian Essays in World Religions,* Bedford Park, Australian Association for the Study of Religions: 27–37.

Ulrich, R. (1993) 'Biophilia, biophobia, and natural landscapes', in S. Kellert and E. O. Wilson (eds) *The Biophilia Hypothesis,* Washington D.C., Island Press: 73–137.

Van Inwagen, P. (1995) *God, Knowledge and Mystery. Essays in Philosophical Theology,* Ithaca, Cornell University Press.

Walker, K. (1978) *Kant,* London, Routledge.

Ward, K. (1994) *Religion and Revelation. A Theology of Revelation in the World's Religions,* Oxford, Clarendon Press.

Wilson, E. O. (1978) *On Human Nature,* Cambridge, Mass., Harvard University Press.

—— (1984) *Biophilia,* Cambridge, Mass., Harvard University Press.

—— (1993) 'Biophilia and the conservation ethic', in S. Kellert and E. O. Wilson (eds) *The Biophilia Hypothesis,* Washington D.C., Island Press: 31–41.

Wisdom, J. (1953) 'Gods', reproduced in *Philosophy and Psycho-Analysis,* Oxford, Blackwell: 149–68.

Wittgenstein, L. (1966) *Lectures and Conversations on Aesthetics, Psychology and Religious Belief,* ed. C. Barrett, Oxford, Blackwell.

Wykstra, S. (1989) 'Toward a sensible evidentialism: on the notion of "needing evidence"', in W. Rowe and W. Wainwright (eds) *Philosophy of Religion. Selected Readings,* second edition, San Diego, Harcourt Brace Jovanovich: 426–37.

—— (1990) 'The Humean obstacle to evidential arguments from suffering: on avoiding the evils of "appearance"', reproduced in M. M. Adams and R. M. Adams (eds) *The Problem of Evil,* Oxford, Oxford University Press: 138–60.

Wynn, M. (1993) 'Some reflections on Richard Swinburne's argument from design', *Religious Studies* vol. 19: 325–35.

—— (1996a) 'A priori judgments and the argument from design', *International Journal for Philosophy of Religion* vol. 39: 169–85.

—— (1996b) 'From world to God: resemblance and complementarity', *Religious Studies* vol. 32: 379–94.

—— (1996c) 'Evil and opportunity cost', *Heythrop Journal* vol. xxxvi: 139–54.

—— (1997a) 'Simplicity, personhood and divinity', *International Journal for Philosophy of Religion* vol. 41: 91–103.

—— (1997b) 'Primal religions and the sacred significance of nature', *Sophia* vol. 36: 88–110.

—— (1997c) 'Beauty, providence and the biophilia hypothesis', *Heythrop Journal* vol. xxxviii: 283–99.

—— (1997d) 'Trust-relationships and the moral case for religious belief', *International Philosophical Quarterly* vol. 37: 179–88.

—— (1998) 'Design arguments', in B. Davies (ed.) *Philosophy of Religion. A Guide to the Subject,* London, Cassell: 59–64.

—— (1999a) 'Emergent phenomena and theistic explanation', *International Philosophical Quarterly* vol. 39: 141–55.

—— (1999b) 'Natural theology in an ecological mode', *Faith and Philosophy* vol. 16: 27–42.

Yandell, K. (1993) *The Epistemology of Religious Experience,* Cambridge, Cambridge University Press.

—— (1994) 'Tragedy and evil', *International Journal for Philosophy of Religion* vol. 36: 1–26.

Index